Above: Mares and foals, Kladruby Stud, Czechoslovakia.

AN ILLUSTRATED INTERNATIONAL ENCYCLOPEDIA OF

HORSE
BREEDS & BREEDING
Jane Kidd

Exmoor Ponies

Caspian Pony

Above: A Shire mare and foal.

AN ILLUSTRATED INTERNATIONAL ENCYCLOPEDIA OF

HORSE
BREEDS & BREEDING
Jane Kidd

Above: Dülmen Ponies

CRESCENT BOOKS
New York

A Salamander Book

This 1989 edition published by Crescent Books,
distributed by Crown Publishers, Inc.,
225 Park Avenue South,
New York, New York 10003.

Printed and bound in Italy

ISBN 0-517-67691-5

h g f e d c b a

Credits

Editor: Jonathan Elphick
Designer: Roger Hyde
Color Reproductions: Rodney Howe Ltd,
London, England
Filmset: Modern Text Typesetting Ltd,
Essex, England

Copyright © Salamander Books Ltd.,
52, Bedford Row, London WC1

Author's Acknowledgments

Writing this book has involved collecting vast amounts of information.
Various breed societies the world over have been extremely helpful.
Those of many countries have provided detailed literature on all the
native breeds, while for other countries I have had to rely on individuals
—in particular, I should like to thank Professor E Sasimowski from
Poland, and Vivienne Burdon in England, who provided invaluable
advice and authentication for the Russian breeds and who wrote the
entry on the USSR in the Guide to International Breeds. I am also
indebted to the veterinarian Russell Christie who checked my manuscript of the section on Horse Breeding. Finally, I should like to thank
the illustrator, John Francis, for his painstaking artwork, and the chief
photographer, Kit Houghton, who has shown great flair and enterprise
in obtaining so many superb pictures for this beautifully illustrated
book; thanks are also due to the picture agencies and individual
photographers who have supplied the rest of the photographs.

Above: A pure-bred Arab.

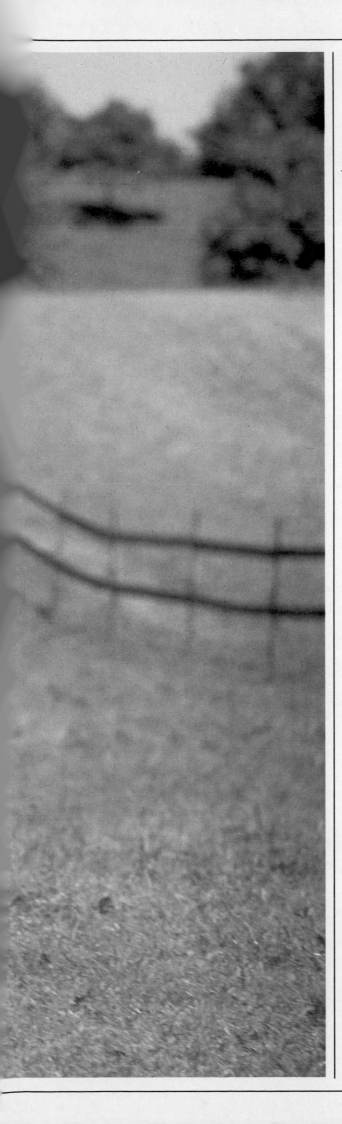

Contents

THE EVOLUTION OF THE HORSE

The numerous breeds of horses and ponies, from the 7-hand-high Falabella pony to the 18-hand Shire, are all members of the same species, *Equus caballus*. There are other species within the larger biological group (or genus) *Equus: Equus przewalski* (Asian Wild Horse or Przewalski's Horse) is the only other living horse (see page 42). There are 4 species of wild ass, all rare today: *Equus hemionus* (Mongolian or Asiatic Wild Ass), *Equus kiang* (Tibetan Wild Ass), *Equus onager* (Persian Wild Ass) and *Equus asinus* (African Wild Ass, the ancestor of the donkey).

Three species of zebra exist in Africa today. These are *Equus zebra* (Mountain or Cape Colony Zebra), *Equus grevyi* (Grévy's or Somaliland Zebra) and *Equus burchelli* (Common Zebra of East Africa).

All these species can be traced back to the Eocene epoch, more than 50 million years ago. Their common ancestor is *Eohippus,* the Dawn Horse (also known as *Hyracotherium,* a name derived from the Greek word for hog). Although "Dawn Horse" is a more romantic title, *Hyracotherium* was more apt. The originator of the horses was rather ugly and bore little resemblance to today's handsome creatures. There was so little resemblance that when horse fossils were first discovered they were not considered to be those of horses. It was not until much later that the evolution of *Equus caballus* was pieced together.

Eohippus had four-toed forefeet, three-toed hindfeet, an arched back and higher hindquarters than forehand. It took over 50 million years for this 10-inch (25cm)-high creature to gradually evolve, through many intermediate forms, into the horse Man first began to use around 1,750 BC.

It was a classic evolution—a gradual adaption to the changing environment. Those species that did not adjust died out. *Eohippus'* habitat was the forests and swamps. It was a browser, reaching for lush vegetation that it broke off with its small sharp teeth. It hid, rather than fled, from its enemies and probably had a striped coat that camouflaged it in the dappled light of the forests.

In the Miocene epoch (beginning about 26 million years ago and ending about 7 million years ago), the habitat began to change. The climate became drier, and the rain forests and swamps gradually changed into prairies. The horse's ancestors survived over millions of years by adapting to these changes. There were many species that did not make successful

adaptions and died out, but some of the family Eohippae evolved into Mesohippae, then Merychippae, and eventually Pliohippae, gradually changing from forest dwellers into prairie dwellers.

An early adaptation of the primitive horses was to eat the grass instead of tearing off vegetation, so the sharp teeth became large flat molars that provided the grinding power needed for chewing. The muzzle lengthened to accommodate these teeth, as did the neck, allowing the animals to reach food on the ground as the species grew larger.

Another need was to run fast enough to flee from predators across the open grasslands where there was no place to hide. The horses grew larger, which enabled them to take longer strides. Their feet became streamlined, and lost all but the middle toe, which ended in a special nail, called the hoof. The limbs became stronger because of their greater length and the need to absorb the shock created by the small area of the hoof landing on the ground. Ligaments and tendons developed. Although these gave more strength, they also prevented the original lateral movement of the foot.

Another important change was to the senses. From being rather sluggish swamp dwellers, horses gradually became more alert to danger through improvements in hearing and vision. The eyes moved farther apart to give a wider range of vision, which in the modern horse spans about 215°.

The result was that *Pliohippus* of the Pliocene epoch (2 to 7 million years ago) developed into *Equus* by the time Man had evolved into *Homo sapiens.* The new *Equus* horses evolved into a variety of different forms. It seems likely these variations arose largely according to the habitat, depending on whether the animals were adapted to survive in the damp heat of swamps, the dry heat of scrubland or semi desert or the tough, cold conditions of high mountains.

Fossil remains of the original swamp-dwelling Dawn Horse are confined to North America, so this was probably its original home. Extraordinarily, the lack of fossils in America from about 6,000 BC indicates the horse became extinct in its original homelands. Primitive horses migrated from America across the Bering Straits land bridge to Europe, Asia and Africa. This occurred over millions of years, beginning in the Pliocene epoch and ending with the last Ice Age, during the Pleistocene epoch. The period of the migration and

Above: Przewalski's Horse is now extinct in its native Mongolia, but over 600 have been bred in zoos.

Below: This fossil of a primitive 50-million-year-old horse, called

Propalaeotherium, *was found in 1982 in a disused oil-shale mine at Darmstadt, West Germany. It is so well preserved, the ear and tail hair and undigested food in the stomach are visible.*

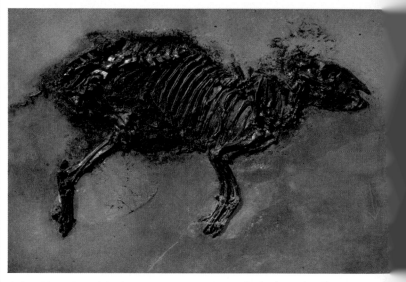

Below: Evolution of the horse through its most important genera (zoological groups), from the tiny Eohippus *to today's* Equus. *Larger scale drawings of the forefeet of each group show the development of the hoof. Along the bottom*

are the geological epochs. Time is shown in millions of years before present-day (m).

Right: Götland Ponies are among the oldest members of the horse group. They live today in Sweden.

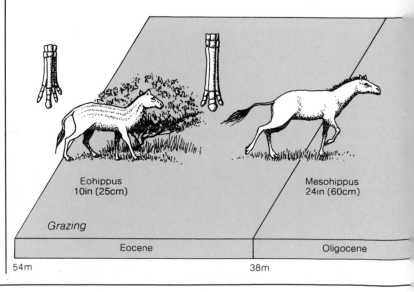

Eohippus
10in (25cm)

Mesohippus
24in (60cm)

Grazing

Eocene

Oligocene

54m

38m

Merychippus
40in (1m)

Pliohippus
50in (1·25m)

Equus
Height varies

Browsing

| Miocene | Pliocene | Pleistocene |

26m

7m

2m

the climatic conditions of the time were probably the two major influences on the evolution of *Equus* into different species. It seems likely that the earliest migrants, arriving when the climate was still warm and tropical, were the most primitive members of the group, which became the species of zebras and asses.

The next group of migrants were the leggy Pliohippae. They adapted to the warmer climate in America and survived the Ice Age in Eurasia by moving south, where they became the Southern Group of horses.

Of these, one subgroup, the Steppe Horses, roamed a vast area, from the Atlas mountains and Spanish sierras in the west to Turkmenistan in the east. In the arid conditions of this environment, the Steppe Horses had to be tough, lean and fast. They tended to be rangy types with large long heads (the greater surface of mucus membrane in the elongated mouth and nostrils aided breathing in very dry air) and with big ears for acute hearing. Their coats were thin and fine. They appeared to have a capacity to grow tall; some Steppe types have been found that reached as high as 18 hands.

Some experts believe the Steppe Horse is the only Southern Group Horse. But Michael Schafer, a German veterinarian, has put forward a plausible theory that there was also a Proto-Arab sub-group. It is believed these horses migrated from America about the same time as the Steppe Horse but roamed into hill country with a subtropical climate that lay between East Asia and North Africa. With easy grazing, their teeth remained small, and research has proved intelligence is in inverse proportion to the size of teeth. Today's Arabs have a tapering jaw and small teeth and are noted for their intelligence.

At the end of the Ice Age, the

Above: A Common Zebra grazing in Kenya. Three species of zebra live in Africa today.

Below: One of several species of ass, the African Wild Ass was the ancestor of the domestic donkey.

Proto-Arabs lost their lush habitat, as about 10,000 years ago their homelands gradually turned into deserts. Too short a time has passed for any noticeable further evolution.

Biologists believe the other main group of what was to become *Equus caballus,* the modern horse, migrated much later than the Southern Group, when conditions in America were becoming tougher and colder, and the horses had evolved accordingly. They tended to stay farther north when they reached Asia and Europe, and became the Northern Group. The first subgroup of Northern Group horses are the Primeval Ponies, which spread over a larger area—all over Europe and Asia—than the other three subgroups.

The Primeval Pony seemed able to adapt to many conditions. It could acclimatize to high rainfall, growing a two-layered coat and a long, thick mane. It could also adapt to hotter, dry weather, when its mane remained upright, because it was no longer needed to protect the head and neck from rain. An important feature of these ponies

Below: The Persian Wild Ass, or Onager. The asses and zebras are, like the horses, members of the genus (group) Equus.

Above: Mustangs are America's wild horses. They roam the same plains as did their distant ancestors before the latter migrated to Europe.

Right: Welsh Mountain Ponies, of ancient ancestry, are tough enough to survive harsh conditions on their native hillsides.

was their short legs and cannon bones, together with a rather restricted action. They did not have the long strides of the Steppe Horses but took short steps instead. They quickened, instead of lengthened, their strides to move faster.

The less mobile subgroup of Northern horses, called the Tundra Horses, is the ancestor of the modern cold-bloods. Some cold-bloods grew very tall. Unlike the Primeval Ponies, which had been quick to migrate seasonally, and to avoid the permanent arctic conditions of the Ice Age, the Tundra Horse was more sluggish, and less agile. Instead of moving, it adapted to life in the subarctic tundra, in marshlands and in the Siberian swamps. At times, it may even have managed to survive on the fringes of the ice-free zone during the last Ice Age. Giant forms of the Tundra Horse (about 18hh) have been excavated in Greece and close to Vienna, although the average size was about 13·2hh (54in). Growing to a large size meant the body surface was smaller in relation to its bulk. It radiated less heat and helped the animal better survive the cold. The Tundra Horse usually had an extra lumbar vertebra in its lower backbone, which allowed the digestive organs more room to accommodate fodder. It also had a big, coarse head with a Roman nose, which must have made breathing in the cold air easier. The feet were very broad, reducing the risk of sinking into the marsh, and the action had a pulling effect from the forehand rather than a pushing from the quarters, which helped the horses move across boggy terrain.

The existence of these four wild types of *Equus;* the Primeval Pony, the Tundra Horse, the Steppe Horse and the Proto-Arab, helps explain the different types of modern horse. Our knowledge of their evolution is based on examination of fossils, cave drawings and evidence from modern horses, but early information is scanty. Zoologists have put forward a number of theories. None can be authenticated because the horse has been domesticated, while the original types died out or were crossbred. Only one wild horse still exists today: *Equus przewalski Poliakoff* (see page 42). Some experts claim all modern breeds come from this single wild form, but with the great variety of domestic horses, the multi-origin school of thought seems more convincing.

The breeds in this book are largely the result of human adaptations of the species for industry, war and pleasure. The natural evolution that took place over 55 million years has been

Above: The Arab has had an enormous influence on the development of modern horse breeds.

largely replaced by selective breeding methods. Few of today's breeds have evolved naturally. Most are the result of arranged cross-breeding and improvement of the animal's environment to make the horse faster, taller, stronger, more refined, more athletic, better tempered or a combination of any of these characters.

The breeds do fall into cagetories that are best explained by the theory suggesting the existence of four forms of wild horse. The first group is the ponies—the smallest equines—that also tend to have most primitive features and breed truest to type. Their size has limited their use to human beings, which means there has been less reason to crossbreed and destroy old breeds. However, ponies have

been used for crossbreeding with larger stock and have contributed to the development of other groups.

The second group is the work horses—or cold-bloods—whose ancestors were probably the Tundra Horse, although the Steppe Horse, with its capacity to grow taller, may have played a part. Work horses are the slow, powerful horses that have made a major contribution to the economies of countries for centuries. The name "cold-blood" refers to these horses' placid nature, not to any peculiarity of their circulatory system.

The third group is the largest today. With mechanization, the demand for work horses has fallen. Instead, the horses bred for leisure and sport have become very popular. The progenitor of most of these horses is the Arab, but the Steppe Horse has also made a contribution. The majority of sports horses, however, have had quite a mixture of ancestors, including

Right: Shires were once renowned as outstanding work horses. They continue to flourish as show animals, although there is little work for them.

Below: The Thoroughbred is the finest example of man's development of a breed to suit his purposes, in this case racing.

Below: Norwegian Fjords are an ancient breed of pony. They have probably survived for so long because they are versatile and tough.

ponies and work horses. Some breeds of sports horses are very old; others have only been developed over the last decade. All over the world there has been a great increase in the number of breeds of sports horses to supply the growing number of riders and drivers.

Sports horses are divided into two major groups, the hot-bloods (Arab and Thoroughbred) and the warm-bloods (all other sports horses). As with the cold-bloods, the name refers to the animals' temperaments.

Over the last 3,500 years, the human race has been influencing the form and other characteristics of the horse. The results have led many people to become fascinated by the breeding of horses, whether homely Shetland Ponies or valuable racehorses. Breeders can have an effect—they can improve the chances of breeding a talented horse or one that is more true to type to a particular breed. But this influence must be kept in proportion. Evolution has led to much more dramatic changes, over a period of 50 million years.

In the following pages 220 breeds are described. Most of these breeds have been created through crossbreeding to suit our demands. Breeds, such as some ponies and work horses, are always dying out because they are no longer needed, while others, such as the various national Warm-bloods, are created to meet new demands. The breeds that are described in this book reproduce their own distinct form and characteristics with a certain degree of consistency.

PONIES

The official definition of a pony is an animal that is under 14·2hh (58in). However, height is not the only criterion for the definition of a pony. Most have other features that distinguish them from their larger relatives. It's possible for a very small pony, such as a Shetland, to be bred with a very large horse, such as a Shire, because they are all members of the species *Equus caballus*. But most ponies are not considered miniature horses. There are exceptions to this, such as the Caspian (pages 18-19) and Falabella (page 27), which do have horse features. But the majority of breeds described on the following pages are distinguishable from horses.

At birth a pony has the same proportions as the adult. It is not a long-legged animal with higher hindquarters than forehand, as are the foals of horses. Ponies tend to be stronger than horses relative to their size, and can pull greater weights in proportion to their height. They usually have shorter legs in proportion to their bodies, particularly short cannon bones. Their strides are usually shorter and less free than those of horses.

Equestrian experts often use the phrase "pony cunning." This refers to the fact that ponies seem to have great powers of survival and are quick thinkers.

The original members of the equine race would all conform to the official definition of a pony—under 14·2hh. Horses have been developed from ponies, increasing their size largely through selective breeding and favorable environmental conditions. Consequently, pony breeds are much closer to the original equines than are horses. Many of today's breeds, such as Exmoor, Norwegian Fjord, and Mongolian, resemble ancient types.

The extensive range of ponies, from the tiny, fragile Falabella to the strong, broad, muscular Norwegian Fjord, is living proof that ponies have long been used for many purposes. While the Falabella can never be much more than an unusual pet, the Fjord and the many other tough, native breeds have been economically important, working the fields, pulling carts and carrying packs and people. However, the demand for working ponies has diminished, as with the Cold-bloods, while that for children's riding ponies is increasing. The trainable, athletic breeds, created mainly by crossing older, sturdier pony breeds with small Arabs and Thoroughbreds, are multiplying most rapidly.

Right: Dartmoor Ponies grazing wild on their native moorland.
Below: A Hackney Pony trained to be driven.

AUSTRALIAN PONY

Country of origin
  Australia.
Height
  12-14hh (48-56in).
Color
  Any.
Features
  Based on Arab and Welsh blood, this is a particularly elegant pony. It has great presence, quality and character which makes it very popular with children.

Like many other countries, Australia discovered that most purebred ponies are rarely ideal for children. Crossbreeding is needed to refine them and make them faster and more athletic.

The most important foundation stock for the elegant Australian Pony has been Arab and Welsh, and in particular the Welsh Mountain Pony stallion Grey Light, which was imported in 1911. Infusions of blood have also come from Timors (one of these ponies was known to have been imported as early as 1803), Shetlands, Exmoors and Thoroughbreds. In the 1920s the Australian Pony began to emerge as a definite type, and in 1929 The Australian Pony Stud Book was formed.

The Australian Pony has a fine, Arab-like head, large dark eyes, a long crested neck, good sloping shoulders, a deep body, short back and powerful hindquarters.

Below: A fine example of an Australian Pony—a relatively new breed, developed this century.

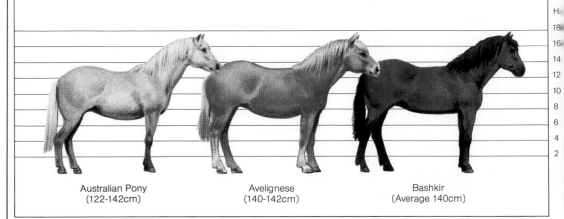

Australian Pony
(122-142cm)

Avelignese
(140-142cm)

Bashkir
(Average 140cm)

Above: The Avelignese is the Italian version of the Austrian breed called the Haflinger. It has the same flaxen mane and tail, but is a stockier and somewhat heavier animal.

AVELIGNESE

Country of origin
  Northern Italy.
Height
  13·3-14hh (55-56in).
Color
  Chestnut, with flaxen mane and tail, and white markings.
Features
  This stocky pony, with its short thickset neck, long back and short legs, is powerful for its size. It is also renowned for its tractable temperament and longevity, features that have made it an extremely popular breed both for draft and pack work.

In Italy today, one of the most numerous and oldest breeds is the Avelignese Pony. There are about 3,000 mares registered with the breed society. The original territory of the Avelignese was the mountainous area in the province of Bolzano, and it is still bred there, as well as in Tuscany and around Venice. Although there were no official documents for the breed until 1874, its close connections with the Haflinger make it of ancient lineage. Both breeds allegedly descended from the old Roman breed of Avelinum-Haflinger, but the Avelignese is a stockier pony than its Austrian relative. It is capable of carrying heavy weights through rough mountain terrain. Because it is exceptionally sure-footed, it has been an extremely popular pack horse in the Alps and Apennines. Its toughness and strength have also made it useful as a farm horse, particularly on mountain farms where larger horses would have difficulty working.

The Avelignese has an elegant head, which is probably due to its partly Oriental ancestry. The body, however, is powerful, compact, broad and deep through the girth. The cannons are short and there is little feather on the legs. The hooves are largish and very hard, enabling the ponies to pick their way along the stony mountain tracks without becoming footsore.

Above: The head of a Bashkir (or Bashkirsky) Pony, a breed that originated in the USSR, where it is still widely bred. It also has representatives in the USA.

BASHKIR

Country of origin
Urals, USSR.

Height
Around 13·3hh (53in).

Color
Bay, chestnut and light brown are most common.

Features
This tractable, strong pony has been a reliable all-rounder, invaluable to the Bashkiri people. It has a wide range of functions, from serving as a riding horse or a draft animal to pulling sleighs and providing meat, milk and clothing. Recently, the original native pony has been upgraded by adding Budyonny, Don and Orlov Trotter blood.

This ancient breed has lived for centuries in the Ural Mountains where it has been reared by the Bashkiri people. Bashkir Ponies have provided their owners with an important means of livelihood, because they are strong and sensible enough for pack and agricultural work. They can be ridden and when old, they can be used for meat.

The most unusual feature of this breed is that younger mares are milked. They produce such large quantities of milk—as much as 3-6 gals (14-27 litres) each day—that they are often kept in milking herds. The milk is used for cream and butter or drunk. It is also fermented into a medicinal (though intoxicating!) drink called *kumiss* by the Bashkiris.

The Bashkir has the ability to survive freezing temperatures as low as −40°F (−40°C) is based on a thick coat, which may be noticeably curly and up to 6in (15cm) long in winter, so their hides are used for clothing.

Although the Bashkir's homelands are in the USSR, the breed was also discovered living in the United States, in Nevada, at the end of the 19th century. They may have been brought by the Russians to Alaska or by the Mongols via the Bering Straits. However they arrived, they bear a striking resemblance to the Russian breed. The distinctive feature of the American version is a curly coat with a kinky, fine mane and tail that is shed each summer. A register for the American Bashkir Curly was started in 1971.

The Bashkir is a thickset pony with a big head, a short dumpy neck and a straight back with well-rounded hindquarters. The legs are short with good bone. The mane and tail of this breed are long and extremely thick.

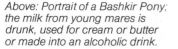

Above: Portrait of a Bashkir Pony; the milk from young mares is drunk, used for cream or butter or made into an alcoholic drink.

BASQUE
(Pottock)

Country of origin
Southwest France.
Height
11·2-13hh (46-52in).
Color
Most.
Features
The tough, small Basque has roamed wild for centuries in France. But it has shown a remarkable ability to adapt to a domestic life and be a good riding pony.

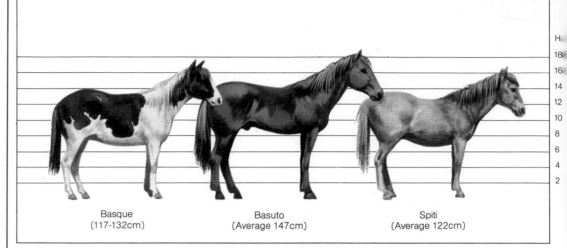

Basque
(117-132cm)

Basuto
(Average 147cm)

Spiti
(Average 122cm)

This ancient breed, which exhibits a number of primitive features, still roams free in the mountains of the Pyrenees and Atlantic cantons of France. Basque Ponies have owners, and they are rounded up periodically, traditionally on the last Wednesday in January, to be branded and released again or sold at the local markets.

To live in these hilly, spartan regions, Basque Ponies must be tough. Survival of foals is aided by rapid growth to maturity: they reach their adult size when only 1 to 2 years old.

Earlier this century, these small ponies were used in French and British mines as pit ponies. Today, they are in demand as children's ponies because they adapt well to domestication. To improve them for this latter purpose, some have had Arab and Welsh blood added. But the French are taking steps to safeguard the continued purity of this ancient breed, which now numbers between about 2,500 and 3,000 purebred Basque Ponies.

The Basque Pony has a small body and a large head, which has a basically rectangular profile with a slight depression at the level of the eyes. The ears are short, and the eyes small and lively. The neck is short, with a thick mane. The back is long. The legs are strong and the feet are small and hard.

Left: The Basque Pony, or Pottock, breeds in the wild, high in the Pyrenees Mountains between France and Spain. Basque Ponies are rounded up periodically and branded, then set free or taken to fairs such as this one to be sold.

Below: Although bred in the wild, Basque Ponies have owners, Here a stallion is being led over the steep terrain typical of their breeding areas.

BASUTO

Country of origin
Basutoland, South Africa.
Height
About 14·2hh (58in).
Color
Chestnut, brown, bay and gray.
Features
This is one of the strongest ponies, and it has great powers of endurance. It gained fame during the Boer Wars when the British bought as many as 32,000 Basutos. This increased the mobility of British forces and helped turn the tables in the war on the Boers who had their own pony—the Boerperd.

The Basuto Pony is named after the area where it is found in South Africa, but it is not indigenous to that region. It developed in the 19th century from the Cape Horses, which were brought to Basutoland after raids and left to fend for themselves in this tough country.

The Cape Horse in its turn had been developed in the southern province of South Africa from imported stock. Importing began in the 17th century with ponies from Java, and they were later upgraded by using Arabs, mainly from Persia. After 1770 a trade developed with India, when the tough, intelligent Cape Horses were sold in large numbers as remounts to the British Army. This success encouraged additional improvements to the breed, and 40 Thoroughbred stallions were imported to help the Cape Horse develop into a military horse of world renown.

In 1828, the Sotha (Basuto) Chief, Moshesh, raided the Cape, captured some of its Cape Horses and took them home. After a few generations of unfavorable climate, bad grazing, overexertion and inbreeding, they became smaller and tougher. Those that survived became known as Basuto Ponies, and proved to be exceptionally strong and brave.

Basutos have been used for military purposes, and also for racing and polo. They are extremely tough, with great powers of endurance, and can carry a rider for many miles each day. Not surprisingly, they are very popular for trekking.

The head usually shows the elegance of its Arab and Thoroughbred forebears. The neck is long and thin and often ewe-shaped The shoulder can be rather upright, while the back is long, the legs short and the feet very hard.

Basuto Ponies are also frequently used in various parts of South Africa for general riding.

Above: Spiti Ponies very heavily laden near Manali, India.

BHUTIA AND SPITI

Country of origin
India (the Himalayas).
Height
12-13·2hh (48-54in).
Color
Gray.
Features
Their strength and sure-footedness has enabled them to carry humans or packs around the mountainous regions of the Himalayas.

The Bhutia is a larger version of the Spiti. These two breeds are found in the Himalayas of India and have similar origins to the Tibetan (Nanfan). Both derive from the Mongolian Pony.

The smaller, less stocky Spiti (which averages 12 hands high, as compared to the Bhutia's average height of 13·1 hands) is bred in the high mountains by a tribe of high-caste Hindus called Kanyats. They have practised in-breeding on the Spiti in order to keep it small in size.

The Spiti's homelands are the mountainous regions of the Kangra District. There and in surrounding regions they are in demand as pack ponies. Their small size and sure-footedness enables them to carry loads with safety along the narrow, precipitous mountainous tracks.

In both breeds, the head is intelligent with alert ears, the neck is short and thick, the shoulders rather straight, the back strong and short and the quarters muscular. The limbs are short with good bone and the feet are hard and round.

BOER PONY
(Boerperd)

Country of origin
South Africa.
Height
13·3-15·3hh (55-63in).
Color
Black, brown, bay, chestnut, gray, roan, dun and palomino.
Features
This calm, tough pony is often capable of five gaits: walk, trot, canter, slow gait and rack. It is a slightly larger animal and has more quality than its close relative the Basuto Pony.

Boer Pony
(140-160cm)

Bosnian
(130-152cm)

Caspian
(100-122cm)

This pony has similar origins to the Basuto Pony (page 17). It developed from the Cape Horse in the 19th century. During that time, however, it was influenced by imported stock, such as Flemish, Hackney and Cleveland. The Boers looked after their breed better than did the developers of the Basuto, and it did not have to survive such rough conditions. Consequently, the Boer Pony has become a better-developed animal.

In the Boer Wars, its great mobility and toughness helped the Boers move around and hold out against the British Empire for three years.

Various attempts were made to form a Boerperd Society, and in 1973 the Boerperd Society of South Africa was formed. Today, Boerperds are found in isolated herds in the south-east Transvaal, northern Natal, eastern Free State and north-eastern Cape. They are used as utility horses on farms and for the increasingly popular sport of endurance riding.

BOSNIAN

Country of origin
Yugoslavia.
Height
12·3-15hh (51-60in).
Color
Bay-brown and black are most common, but they are sometimes a light yellowish brown or chestnut.
Features
This mountain breed's intelligence, strength, sure-footedness and powers of endurance mean that even in modern times it is used in large numbers by farmers and transporters in the Balkans.

These ponies are bred in large numbers all over the Balkans, but their homelands are the hilly, mountainous regions of Bosnia and Herzegovina in Yugoslavia. They are selectively bred by the Yugoslavian government because the Bosnian is useful to the economy, both on the farms and in transportation, particularly in the mountains. There are more than 130,000 in Yugoslavia.

In appearance, this breed is similar to the Huçul, the mountain pony of Poland. Both are descendants of the wild breed of Tarpan and have been upgraded with a good deal of Arab stock. With selective breeding at the Borike stud, the Bosnian's size is being increased from that of a small pony to a small horse.

It is a compact, broad pony with a long, slightly sloping croup and very thick long mane and tail. It has great powers of endurance, great strength and all the assets of a mountain breed, and is frequently used in pack trains over the mountains.

Below: Stocky and powerful, the Yugoslav-bred Bosnian is highly valued as a working pony over the whole of the Balkan region.

CASPIAN

Country of origin
Iran.
Height
10-12hh (40-48in).
Color
Bay, gray, chestnut and occasionally black and cream. Some white markings may be found.
Features
This kind, intelligent, narrow pony has been used as a work pony in Iran for centuries but these features also make it ideal as a children's pony. It has a natural floating action, great powers of acceleration and athletic ability over fences. It is also a good harness pony and has been used as such over the past 1,000 years or so.

In 1965 a few lean, scraggy ponies were found on the northern shores of Iran, that border the Caspian

Below: The Caspian is a miniature horse with a very ancient history.

Sea. The importance of this discovery was that they did not have the features of ponies, but looked like miniature Arabs with the same big, bold eyes, prominent jaws, dished face and high-set tail. They were miniature horses that bore a striking resemblance to the equines carved on the ruins of a staircase of the ancient Persian city of Persepolis in the late sixth or early fifth century BC. Some authorities believe the Caspians' forebears could be Iran's native wild horses which were used by the Mesopotamians in the third millenium BC. They were probably the forerunners of most breeds of hot-bloods, including the ancient Arab.

There had been no records of this breed of miniature horse for about a thousand years until 1965, but their authenticity has now been confirmed by scientific research, following archaeological digs on ancient remains in Iran. Identification is helped by the Caspian's unique features, such as its blood hemoglobin construction, the skeletal structure of its small skull, with a broad forehead, and the well-developed parietal and frontal bones of its spine, which make it a much narrower shape than any other pony.

For the missing 1,000 years, these ponies were bred in a very small area and were known locally as Monleki or Ponseki. They never ventured farther from the Caspian shores than the northern slopes of the Elburz mountains, but it meant that this ancient breed was

preserved and not crossbred into oblivion. Since 1965, the importance of the breed has been realized. The Shah of Iran was one of the first to help their promotion. Despite the subsequent political upheavals in Iran, enough Caspians have been exported to Britain, America and Australia to ensure their survival.

The Caspian does not look like any other pony. Its tapering head has a forehead that is wide and vaulted, the cheek bones are deep, and the muzzle is small. The eyes are large and often prominent. The nostrils are low-set and large. The ears are short and set wide apart and often turned in at the tips. The body is narrow with a longish neck, a long sloping shoulder and a deep girth.

Above: For centuries, Caspian Ponies have been pulling carts on the shores of the Caspian Sea. Today they are used for competition driving in Western countries.

The limbs are particularly fine and strong, and the hooves strong and oval.

Below: A portrait of the Caspian Pony shows its unique features.

CONNEMARA

Country of origin
Western Ireland.

Height
13-14·2hh (52-58in).

Color
Gray, black, bay, brown and dun. Occasionally roan and chestnut. More than 50% of the registered ponies are gray. The dun and palomino were once common but are now becoming rare.

Features
This ancient inhabitant of the British Isles is one of the best breeds of children's ponies. It is also strong enough to carry an adult and sensible enough to work well in harness. It is a high-class utility breed.

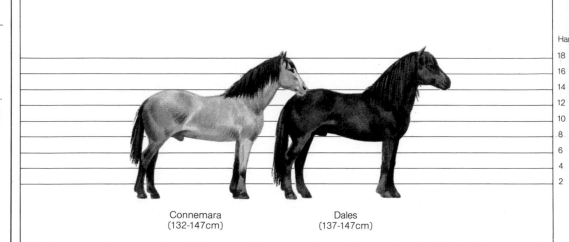

Connemara
(132-147cm)

Dales
(137-147cm)

The Connemara is the first of the British Mountain and Moorland ponies to be described in this book. All nine (Connemara, Dales, Dartmoor, Exmoor, Fell, Highland, New Forest, Shetland and Welsh) are named after the regions where they have bred and run wild for centuries. The Connemara is indigenous to the west of Ireland in the area of Connaught, a small part of which is known as Connemara, bounded on the west by the Atlantic and on the south by Galway Bay. This bleak area consists mainly of mountains and bogs. There is only rough grass for food, and the Connemara has had to be tough to survive. It has lived there in a wild state for centuries and is thought to be one of the oldest equine residents of the British Isles.

There is no authentic evidence as to its origins, but it is certainly a primitive type. Some say it is based on the same stock as the Highland, Shetland, Icelandic and Norwegian Fjord. Certainly, the Connemara has a touch of class, an oriental influence. The typical Connemara is more beautiful and athletic than an ordinary mountain pony. One legend claims it derived from horses shipwrecked in the Spanish Armada of 1588, but it is more likely that Galway merchants, who traded with Spain during the 16th and 17th centuries, imported some good Oriental horses. Some of these must have managed to break free and bred with the native pony stock in and around Connemara.

This combination of primitive toughness plus Oriental beauty and athleticism has produced a pony that is popular today all over the world.

The Irish Government has taken steps to preserve its ancient lineage, and a society was formed with its assistance in 1928 to preserve and improve the Connemara Pony. Crossbreeding was restricted, and foundation stock established. The stud book is now closed to all but full-pedigreed parents, and the result is a more uniform type than was found at the beginning of the 20th century.

There is great temptation to crossbreed with the Connemara. When it is put in a better environment than its bleak homeland, and kept warm and fed well, it usually

grows larger. This tendency to grow larger is greater in the Connemara than in other native British breeds. Consequently when crossbred with a horse, it tends to produce sizable competition horses.

As purebreds, Connemaras are one of the most popular children's ponies and are capable of all forms of equitation from dressage to hunting. They are also excellent in harness and are becoming very popular for the sport of competition driving. They are agile, fast and athletic, having great stamina and commonsense typical of primitive breeds. They also thrive on poor keep, having had to survive for centuries on rough lands. These qualities have made them reliable utility ponies for the Irish. Today, they also include high class competition ponies for children.

The typical Connemara has a harmonious head and neck with a compact deep body and short legs. The bone is hard and flat and measures about 7-8in below the knee. The great substance this bone gives enables the Connemara to carry adults as well as children. The Connemara is an athletic pony, and its action is free, fluent and true.

Below left: Connemara Ponies have bred in the wild for centuries, in Galway in western Eire.

Below: The Irish have traditionally used the Connemaras as work ponies for pulling heavily laden carts.

Above: This is Tulira Blue Hawaii, who won the ridden Connemara class at the Bath & West Show, England.

DALES

Country of origin
Britain (eastern Pennines).
Height
13·2-14·2hh (54-58in).
Color
Black and brown are most common, but some are gray and bay. The only permissible white markings are a star or snip on the head.
Features
This strong, energetic and intelligent pony has been a major aid for transportation and agriculture in the past. Today it is popular for harness work and trekking, and as an all-around utility pony capable of jumping, endurance racing and general riding.

The Dales Pony is bred on the eastern hills of the Pennines. Its close relative, the Fell, is bred on the west of these hills. The Dales has long been bred as a pack pony, because the moors were famous sources of lead. This heavy metal had to be transported across rough land to the ports on the coast. Pack ponies, until 100 years ago, were the best means of moving it. The ponies worked in groups, with one mounted man herding the loose, heavily laden ▶

▶ ponies. The Dales fulfilled this important function.

Foundation stock for these load carriers was the Scottish Galloway, which in its turn had some Friesian blood (see Fell, page 28). The Galloway was a fast, sturdy pony and was Britain's original racehorse. It was also used as foundation stock for the Thoroughbred, the Norfolk Trotter and the Clydesdale. The Scottish Galloways, which became extinct by the early 19th century, were bred to the native Fells that roamed wild on the moors. Only the tough survived, and only the biggest and most powerful of the offspring were used as pack ponies and for further breeding. It was a rough form of selective breeding.

The Dale Galloway, as it became known, soon earned fame for its strength, intelligence and agility over rough country. Farmers began to use them because they could pull more than a ton in weight. They were ridden, also, and their ability to trot fast led to further crossbreeding. In the 18th and 19th centuries, there were some outside influences. One of these was probably the Clydesdale and the other the Norfolk and Yorkshire Roadsters. The latter were becoming famous as fast trotters. Pulling light vehicles in harness provided a speedy means of transport. Some stallions of these Roadster breeds, notably Merry Driver, Shales Merrylegs, Sir George and Sir Harry, were bred to speed up the Dales.

Another influence was Comet, a

trotting cob believed to be an early Welsh Cob that came to Westmoreland in the 1850s and sired many good Dales. In the 20th century, two steps were taken to preserve and promote the breed. In 1916, the Dales Pony Improvement Society was formed and a stud book opened. Sadly, World War II led to terrible disruptions, so that by 1955 only four ponies were registered. The formation of The Dales Pony Society in 1963 has led to

distinct improvements in quality and quantity and an increasing interest in this tough and adaptable breed of pony.

The Dales Pony should have a neat, ponylike head, with bright alert eyes set well apart. The ears should curve inwards slightly. The neck should be long and strong, the shoulders sloping and the withers fine. The body should be compact and deep, and hind-quarters deep, lengthy and powerful. The limbs should be short

with good bone, measuring about 9in, and set square. The feet are renowned for their strength and are open, large and round in shape — many ponies never need shoeing. There should be a little silky feather on the heels and an abundance of hair in the mane and tail.

The action of the Dales is distinguished, with great flexion of the joints to produce a high knee and hock action. They have tremendous energy, and are cour-ageous, intelligent and kind.

Above: The Dales Pony is a fast
and spectacular trotter in harness.

Left: One of the many uses of the
tough Dales Pony is for shepherding.

Left: The Dales Pony breeds free
on the east side of the Pennine
Hills in northern England.

Above: Portrait of a Dales Pony.

DARTMOOR

Country of origin
Britain (Dartmoor).

Height
A maximum of 12·2hh (50in).

Color
Bay, brown, black and gray are most common. Occasionally chestnuts and roans are found, but piebalds and skewbalds are not allowed. White markings are permissible but not in large areas.

Features
This sturdy pony has particularly good conformation and a kind temperament, which makes it an excellent child's pony and good foundation stock for larger riding ponies. Its ability to survive in its rugged homeland enables it to thrive in most climates.

Dartmoor
(Maximum 127cm)

Dülmen
(Average 130cm)

The Dartmoor Pony is another of Britain's Mountain and Moorland ponies. Its homelands of Dartmoor are the most southern of any of these nine breeds. Ponies have roamed these austere moors, which stand over 1,000 feet above sea level, for centuries. The earliest reference to this pony is in 1012 in the will of a Saxon bishop named Aelfwold of Crediton. It is also known these ponies were well used in the era of tin, when they carried the metal from the mines on the moor to the Stannary Towns. When the tin mining ended, they were once again let free to roam and breed on the Devonshire moors.

It was at the end of the last century, in 1898, that the first attempts were made to officially define and register the breed. By 1902, the Dartmoor Committee laid down that ponies with more

Below: Dartmoor Ponies breed wild on the moors in Devon, South-west England, after which they are named.

than 25% alien blood could not be entered in the stud book. This rule was ignored a few years later, when in 1920 a stallion named The Leat, which looked like a Dartmoor but was sired by a desert-bred Arab, was allowed to stand. He proved to be a very successful sire, and most of today's Dartmoors trace back to him.

In 1957, the stud book was finally closed to entry by inspection. Soon after there was a great upsurge in interest in the Dartmoor, and many of the ponies were exported.

The Dartmoor has proved to be an excellent first pony for children. It is economical to keep, has a quiet, kind reliable temperament and is a good size for young children. It is a particularly versatile breed, and has the ability to hunt, jump and be driven.

The Dartmoor has a small, elegant head with small, alert ears. The neck is strong but not too heavy, too long or too short. The shoulders are well set back to give the rider a 'good front.' The back is of medium length; the loins and hindquarters are strong and muscular. The tail is full and

Above: A typical Dartmoor head: intelligent, with small ears.

Right: Standing square, a Dartmoor Pony shows off its conformation.

set high on the hindquarters. The limbs have a medium amount of bone. The feet are well-shaped and strong. The Dartmoor moves with free, low strides that make it a particularly comfortable ride.

DÜLMEN

Country of origin
Germany (Westfalia).
Height
Around 12·3hh (51in).
Color
Black, brown and dun are most common.
Features
The Dülmen, together with the Senner (now nearly extinct), are Germany's native wild ponies. The Dülmen is said to have played a part in the development of the Hanoverian breed.

The Dülmen is a German breed of wild pony. Its homeland is the reserve of Mierfelder Bruch on the Duke of Croy's estate in the state of Westfalia. It was mentioned as being there as long ago as 1316, but today relatively few are left.

There has been some out-crossing with ponies from Britain and Koniks from Poland, and the resulting animals do not breed particularly true to type.

The Dülmen does not have very good conformation. It has rather weak hindquarters. The head is small with a straight face. The ears are small; the neck and back are short and the shoulders are rather upright.

Crossed with Arabs, Dülmens have sometimes been used to produce children's riding ponies.

Right: The Dülmen Pony from Germany is becoming quite rare.

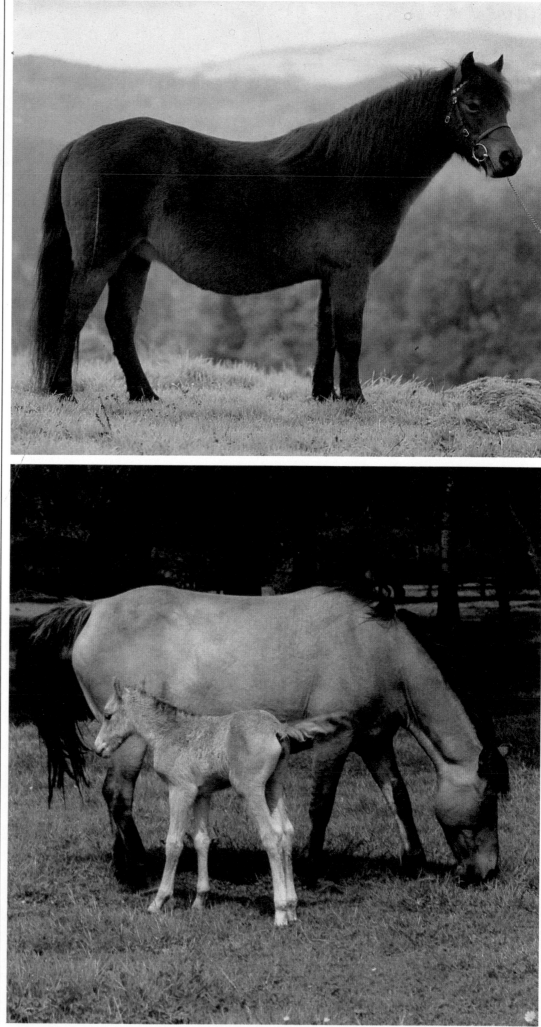

EXMOOR

Country of origin
Britain (Exmoor).

Height
Mares not exceeding 12·2hh (50in) Stallions and geldings not over 12·3hh (51in).

Color
Bay, brown or dun, with mealy markings on the muzzle, round the eyes and inside the flanks. No white markings anywhere.

Features
This is the oldest breed in Britain, and is thought to be the Celtic pony that pulled the chariots of the Celts. It has unusual features like the "toad" eye and mealy muzzle.

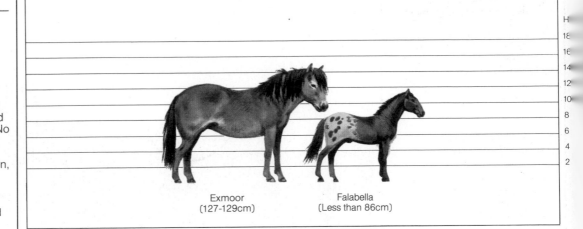

Exmoor
(127-129cm)

Falabella
(Less than 86cm)

The Exmoor is claimed to be the oldest of Britain's native ponies and is likely to have roamed Exmoor in Somerset since the Bronze Age. Roman carvings of chariots, found in the West Country, are pulled by ponies looking much like today's Exmoor.

The other exciting bit of evidence about their antiquity is that fossils of ponies found in Alaska have the same jaw formation and the same indications of a seventh molar tooth as the Exmoor. It seems the Exmoor has changed little from the time when its ancestors crossed the land bridge of the Bering Straits from the horse's original home in America and spread through Europe.

The Exmoors that remained in the West Country have been isolated and have not been subjected to out-crossing. They are remarkably purebred.

Research into the Exmoor's history has been carried out by Britain's Royal School of Veterinary Studies. This confirms that the Exmoor can be considered England's indigenous pony, and was probably foundation stock for Britain's other breeds.

Records of Exmoor Ponies roaming the moors date back to the Doomsday Book of 1085. Today, they still run wild in herds, but these are privately owned and are registered in a stud book. The earliest pedigree records can be traced to 1820, but a breed society was not formed until 1921. Registration today depends on inspection and pedigree. This happens in autumn, when the ponies are "gathered" and driven down to the farms. If they are accepted as good specimens of the breed, they are branded with an individual number on the near flank together with the Society's star and their herd number on the near shoulder.

Exmoor Ponies have a native cunning that helps them take care of themselves and their riders. They have long been used as pack animals and for herding sheep by the farmers. Some taken straight off the moor appear wild but if well-trained, they make high class children's and harness ponies.

The Exmoor has also been good foundation stock in the past and is still used as such. The Grand National winners, The Colonel and Zeodene, had Exmoor blood in their veins.

The Exmoor is typically "pony" in appearance. The particular features of its head are the short thick ears, the wide forehead and prominent "toad" eyes. The muzzle is an unusual mealy color. The neck is long enough to give a good length of rein. The shoulders are well laid back, the chest is deep and wide, and the back is broad and level as far as the loins. The legs are short and well apart. The hindlegs are nearly perpen-

Below: Probably the oldest native British pony, the Exmoor is likely to have roamed the West Country since Bronze Age times.

dicular from the hock to the fetlock, with the point of the hock in line with the pelvic bone. There is a wide curve from the flank to the hock joint.

The coat is close, hard and springy, which helps insulation. It is hard and bright in the summer but has no shine in the winter.

The Exmoor's action is straight and quite low to the ground.

FALABELLA

Country of origin
Argentina.
Height
Less than 8·2hh (34in).
Color
Any.
Features
Falabellas have the appearance of scaled-down horses rather than that of ponies. They are very rare but are bred in Argentina at Señor Falabella's ranch and in England at the Kilverstone Stud at Thetford, Norfolk.

The Falabella is a miniature horse that stands no higher than 34in (86cm). This extraordinary breed is produced at Señor Falabella's ranch in Argentina and has been since his grandfather's time. During the 19th century, an Irishman named Newton, the maternal grandfather of the present Señor Falabella, settled in Argentina, where he encountered the Indians

living in the region. The Indians watered their horses in a river that ran through Newton's land. One day, a small stallion appeared, which was said to have "the dwarf sickness". Newton was fascinated. He kept it and bred small horses from it for his daughter.

No-one knows anything more

Above: Falabella Ponies were developed in Argentina. They are so small and fragile that they are rarely strong enough to be ridden; they are usually kept as pets.

Below: A portrait of the Falabella Pony.

about this unique stallion, but when put to other stock, it was found his genes for small size were dominant. Mares bred with him produced much smaller foals than themselves, and the result was the gradual development of the breed of Falabellas.

Many breeds have been used to produce Falabellas, in many different colors. Today on the ranch, different-sized ponies can be seen, for it takes a few generations to "shrink" them down to the average Falabella height of less than 34 inches (86cm).

Falabellas have been exported all over the world, and the genes that produce small horses remain dominant.

The Falabella is not a small pony but a miniature horse. It is proportioned like a horse, with fine bone and small feet. It cannot be ridden and cannot be compared with that other small breed, the Shetland, which has a deep girth and short legs and is extraordinarily strong.

Falabellas are delicate and must be looked after like Thoroughbreds. They need to be blanketed when it is cold and fed concentrates, such as oats.

An unusual feature of the Falabella is the gestation period is two months longer than for most horses and ponies—close to 13 months. The foals are tiny—just 16-17in (41-43cm)—but they grow very quickly in their first year.

Falabellas also have two fewer ribs and vertebrae than the normal horse or pony.

These ponies are not strong enough to be ridden, but are used in harness. For their size, they are great jumpers but this can only be seen when they are loose.

FELL

Country of origin
Britain (West Pennines).
Height
13·1-14hh (53-56in)
Color
Black, brown, bay or gray. A small amount of white markings is permissible.
Features
Breeds remarkably true to type, which proves its ancient lineage. It is a tough, hardy, eye-catching pony with great energy and strength.

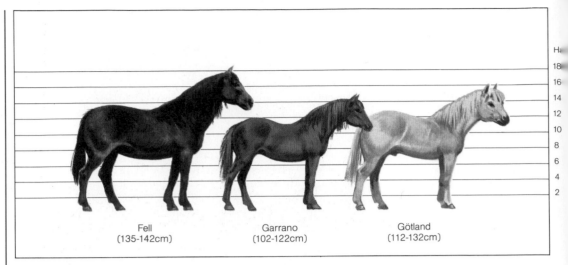

Fell
(135-142cm)

Garrano
(102-122cm)

Götland
(112-132cm)

The Fell Pony is a close relative of its neighbor, The Dales. It lives on the opposite (western) side of the Pennine Hills in northern England. Although it has roamed wild through Cumbria, Northumberland, and even south Lancashire and north to the Scottish borders, most have been found on the moorland surrounding the Lake District, around Ullswater, Windermere and Derwentwater.

The foundation stock was believed to have been strong alert ponies of less than 13 hands. They were agile enough to move quickly around the moorlands to seek their forage. The first known influence on them was the Friesian Horse. Friesians were brought to the area after the Roman Emperor Hadrian decreed in AD 120 that a huge wall be built across Britain to shut out the warring Picts.

The Romans hired labor from Friesland (now part of Holland and Germany). The Frieslanders brought with them some handsome black horses that stood close to 15 hands. When the Romans left Britain they did not take the horses, which allegedly amounted to about 1,000 Friesian stallions. These were probably foundation stock not only for the Fell and Dales but also for the Shire, and for the extinct Galloway Pony from Scotland.

The Friesian blood, mixed with the local native mares in the Pennines, resulted in a pony very similar to today's Fell. Few other influences reached the Pennines, and the result is a pony that breeds truer to type and is more easily recognizable than any of

Britain's native ponies, except the Exmoor (see page 26).

There was probably some mixing with the Scottish Galloway Pony, but it had similar foundation stock. More importantly, with the industrial revolution and the demand for larger, stronger horses, most of the northern and Scottish horses were bred to the bigger Clydesdale. This had some effect on the Dales, which became a heavier, larger pony, but the fact that the Fell stayed about the same proves that little Clydesdale blood was mixed with it.

Some good trotting blood has been added. The Fells are naturally fast trotters, and with the vogue for racing and using such horses in harness in the late 18th and 19th centuries, this aspect was

developed. Some Norfolk and Yorkshire Roadster stallions were used, and in the 1850s the Welsh Cob stallion, Comet, was stood at stud in the Orton district and put to Fell and Dales mares.

Through the ages this agile, strong, energetic, yet thrifty, pony has been well used. It is perhaps most famous, like the Dales, as a pack pony. From the 13th century, Fells were used in pack-pony droves with one ridden pony guiding groups of heavily laden free ponies. They used to be driven as far as London, but the advent

Below: Fell Ponies have similar origins to those of the Dales and breed close to them on the west of the Pennine Hills in England.

Right: A Fell mare grazes content-edly with her foal by her side. She has bred in captivity.

of railways reduced the demand for their use in transportation. They have also been used extensively by farmers for herding sheep and for general work, as well as between shafts as a speedy means of transport.

As with other British Mountain and Moorland ponies, the first official attempts to organize the breed were made at the end of the 19th century by the National Pony Society.

The Fell Pony Society was formed in 1912, and it has helped to ensure the continuance of this breed. Fells are used extensively for riding, particularly trekking, but it is with the growth of driving that the breed has found a real outlet. They breed so true to type that it is easy to find a matched pair or team. They have tremendous energy but lack the speed needed to excel in top class Combined Driving.

The Fell stands up to 14 hands. The head is ponylike, with a longish neck and well-laid-back shoulders. The quarters are muscular and strong. The hocks are well let-down. The limbs are strong, with good bone, and the hooves are blue, round and open. The feather should be silky on the legs and the mane and tail are long and thick.

The Fells are renowned for their energetic action, which is also free and straight.

GARRANO

(Minho)

Country of origin
North Portugal.
Height
10-12hh (40-48in).
Color
Usually chestnut.
Features
Work pony of ancient lineage.

In northern Portugal, in the provinces of Garrano de Minho and Traz do Montes, the Garrano has been bred for centuries on mountain pastures. It is believed to come from ancient stock, having changed little for thousands of years, although some upgrading has been carried out recently by introducing Arab blood.

It is a small pony, never more than 12hh (48in), yet is strong enough to be used by the army and local people as pack ponies and timber haulers.

In the past, the Garrano was used in trotting races, but these are rarely held today.

This pony has a small, attractive head with large eyes and small ears. The body is light but compact and deep. The legs are quite short. There is an abundance of hair in the mane and tail.

GOTLAND
(Russ)

Country of origin
Sweden (Island of Gotland).
Height
11-13hh (44-52in).
Color
Although bay and black are most common, other colors are found, including dun and palomino. A dorsal stripe along the back is usual.
Features
This ancient breed has changed little since the Stone Age, yet it is still useful in modern times as a child's pony and competitor in trotting races.

The Gotland has been bred since the Stone Age on the Swedish island after which it was named It is also known locally as the Russ. Its island life has left it relatively free from alien blood, although some Arab has been added over the last 100 years.

The Gotland ancestor is believed to be the Tarpan, and such primitive features as a dorsal stripe are found on many ponies.

Today, the Gotland still runs wild in the forests of Lojsta on Gotland, but many are now found on the mainland. The Gotland has proved to be a good children's pony and also such a fast trotter that it was used for races. It was also invaluable to the farmers until mechanization reduced the need for horsepower.

Continuance of this ancient breed is now aided by the government-supported Swedish Pony Association.

Above: The Gotland Pony has bred in the wild on the island of Gotland, Sweden, for centuries, probably since the Stone Age. Most are now bred on the mainland. A few have this eye-catching palomino color, although most are bay or black.

This is a light, elegant pony. The head has a straight face, broad forehead, small alert ears and big eyes. The neck is short and strong, with a long sloping shoulder. The back is long, but the quarters are round and short. The pony does not have great substance; the bone is light, yet strong. The hooves are small, hard and well-shaped.

The movement of the Gotland Pony is good at walk and trot but not in the canter and gallop.

GREEK PONIES

(Skyros, Pindos, Peneia)

SKYROS

Country of origin
Greece (island of Skyros).
Height
9.1-11hh (37-44in).
Color
Usually gray but also bay, brown or dun.
Features
The smallest Greek pony.

Greece once had many native breeds of ponies that proved invaluable for transportation and agriculture. With mechanization, the demand for them has decreased, and most of the breeds have died out. The most popular today is the Skyros, which is the smallest of the Greek ponies. It is named after the island on which it originated.

Skyros ponies run wild in the mountains most of the year, but at harvest time some are rounded up and chased over the corn as a primitive, but effective, method of threshing it.

The Skyros has a small, pretty head with small ears, and a short neck. Its body is narrow and its quarters are not very muscular. The limbs are relatively long and there is a tendency to have cow hocks (see Glossary, page 198).

Below: The Skyros is both the best known and the smallest of the Greek ponies. This stallion has the smallish head and small ears typical of the breed, as also are the thick mane and tail.

Skyros (94-112cm)   Pindos (122-132cm)   Peneia (102-142cm)   Hackney Pony (Less than 142cm)

PINDOS

Country of origin
Greece (Thessaly and Epirus).
Height
12-13hh (48-52in).
Color
Usually gray but also bay or brown.
Features
This eye-catching pony is used for all types of work; the mares are sometimes used for breeding mules.

The Pindos comes from the mountains of northern Greece, from the regions called Thessaly and Epirus. It is a larger, more elegant pony than the Skyros, and is said to have Oriental origins.

Like the Skyros, it is used for pack work and farmwork, but because of its mountainous origin, it is particularly surefooted and agile.

The Pindos is lightframed, with little muscle on the neck and quarters. The limbs are relatively long and the feet are narrow and boxy. The tail is set high.

PENEIA

Country of origin
Greece (Peloponnese).
Height
10-14hh (43-56in).
Color
Most colors but usually brown, bay, chestnut or gray.
Features
Stallions are sometimes crossed with female donkeys to breed hinnies (mules).

The Peneia is less well-known than the other surviving Greek pony breeds. It is named after its homelands in the Peloponnese. Like the Pindos, it shows signs of Oriental ancestry. It varies in size more than the other Greek breeds and can grow as high as 14 hands (56 inches).

Like its close relatives, it is a tough and willing worker and is used for transport and farmwork.

HACKNEY PONY

Country of origin
England.
Height
Under 14hh (56in).
Color
Bay, brown and black are most common.
Features
Its spectacular action makes this an ideal show pony. Spectators love to watch it, but its high spirits mean it needs careful handling. It is rarely a good children's pony.

The Hackney Pony is the small version of the Hackney Horse (see pages 106-107) and shares much of its history. Both are based on Norfolk and Yorkshire Roadsters, breeds that were developed in the 18th century as fast trotters to pull light carriages and provide a speedy means of travel. The Yorkshire version was based on Thoroughbred and Coach Horse crossbreds and the Norfolk one on Trotters, Galloways and Thoroughbreds.

The Norfolk foundation Thoroughbred sire was Shales the Original (foaled in 1755), an offspring of Flying Childers, the son of Darley Arabian. Shales produced such good lines that Yorkshire breeders used some of the Norfolk stock, and this led to the development of the Hackney.

The pony version was started by Christopher Wilson of Westmorland. He used a Roadster stallion, with Yorkshire and Norfolk blood, named Sir George (foaled in 1866). He was put to the very best Fell mares. In the 1870s, Wilson started breeding ponies for use in many activities, including racing. He was so successful that they became known as "Wilson ponies".

Ponies that were from Sir George started a new breed, which became known as the Hackney Pony. Sir George was 14 hands (56in), but most of the Fell mares were only about 13 hands (52in). Wilson kept the height of his new ponies down by turning them out on the moors. This also kept them

tough, so only sound individuals survived. Sir George's assets were his "high class" (Flying Childers was in his pedigree), speed and elegance. The Fell mares' qualities were their high knee action, power and substance. The result was the spectacular, high-stepping Hackney Pony that became so popular that one filly sold for $1,000 (£900) in 1896.

Hackney Ponies were exported the world over; they were, and still are, exhibited at shows and used to deliver goods. They are tough, energetic workers and also great "show-offs", with their flashy appearance and extraordinary movement.

The Hackney Pony should look like a genuine pony with a small, intelligent head. The neck should be long, the shoulders powerful, the body compact and the limbs strong.

The most important aspect of the Hackney is its brilliant action. This should be fluent and spectacular, with the knee raised as high as possible and the feet flung forward in a rounded movement. The hocks should come well under the body and lift so high they nearly touch it.

Above: The Hackney Pony has a spirited nature and is most popular as a harness pony. It is rarely ridden, but is often driven in classes where it is judged for its conformation, action and manners.

Below: The spectacular action of the Hackney Pony makes it a feature item at many major shows.

HAFLINGER

Country of origin
  Austria (Southern Tyrol).
Height
  13·1-14·2hh (53-58in).
Color
  Palomino or chestnut, with a
  flaxen mane and tail.
Features
  This Austrian breed has proved
  to be one of the best workers in
  the high mountains. Today, this
  quality makes them popular as
  mounts for tourists. In the past,
  before mechanization, these
  attractive ponies were a major aid
  for transport and agriculture.

Haflinger
(135-147cm)

Highland
(132-147cm)

The Haflinger developed high
in the mountains of the South
Tyrol, in areas between 5,000
and 6,600ft (1,500-2,000m).
Isolated from other influences and
subject to a rigorous climate, it
developed into a robust animal
that bred true to type.

Its history cannot be proved, but
the main center of breeding was
in the valley of Sarn around the
village of Hafling. Its inhabitants
are believed to be descendants
of the Ostrogoths, who settled
there after they had been driven
out of Italy in the mid-6th century.
They brought with them small
Arab horses that had been used
in the war, and crossed them with

the mountain ponies to produce
the native foundation stock for
the Haflinger.

The first written evidence of the
breed was in 1868, when the stallion
El Bedavi XXII was described
as being used to upgrade the
local stock. He was the son of an
Arab stallion, from the famous
Hungarian stud at Babolna, and
an Arab mare. El Bedavi XXII was
bred to local stock, and it is to
him that today's Haflingers can be
traced. His son, 249 Folie, became
the foundation sire. Folie had the
typical chestnut coat, white mane
and white tail. With a considerable
amount of inbreeding in the late
19th century, these traits proved

to be 99% inherited.

With its sturdy constitution,
sure-footedness, docility and
strength, the Haflinger has been
a valuable aid to the Austrian
hill farmers. It was used also
for pack work in peace and war.
Just before World War II, the
Germans promoted the breeding of
Haflingers because they wanted
to use them for transportation
in the mountains.

Today, the Austrian government
supports their breeding. The
emblem with which they are
branded is an "H", combined
with Austria's national flower,
the eidelweiss.

The Haflinger's head is small

and has the same elegance as
the Arab's. The eyes are large,
and the ears are small and alert.
The neck is strong and the shoulder
long and sloping. The back is
straight and broad; the quarters
are muscular and rounded. The
legs are quite short with good
bone. There is a little feather on the
legs and an abundance of hair
in the mane and tail.

---

*Right: The Haflingers are the work
ponies of their native country of
Austria. Strong and sensible, they
are ideal for harness work.*

*Right: A portrait of the
Haflinger Pony.*

HIGHLAND

Country of origin
Scotland.

Height
13-14·2hh (52-58in).

Color
Various shades of dun, gray, brown or black are most common. Bay and liver chestnut, with silver mane and tail, are occasionally found. Most have a dorsal eel stripe, and many have zebra markings inside the forelegs. White markings, apart from a small star, are disliked.

Features
This intelligent, strong, docile, sure-footed pony is one of the most versatile of Britain's native breeds.

The Highland Pony has been part of Scotland's history for centuries. It has provided its main form of transport for a long time. Although it is one of the oldest breeds of the region, its origins are obscure. It was not isolated, as were the Exmoor and the Fell, and in recent times there have been a number of outside influences. These have included Arab stallions introduced by the MacNeills of Barra and high-class French stallions sent to James IV of Scotland by Louis XII of France.

In the past, the ponies varied from area to area, according to local needs and climate. Those on the islands (known as Western Isles) tended to be smaller and faster than those on the mainland (known

as Garrons). Crossbreeding has caused these distinctions to disappear.

For hundreds of years, Highland Ponies have been valued by the Scottish people. In addition to providing transport, they have been used as pack animals, and by sportsmen for hunting and carrying game. In the forests, they are still used for pulling felled trees and are used on farms for carting and sheep herding.

Today, other uses have been found for these versatile ponies.

They carry tourists across Scotland. They are also used for driving competitions, for general riding and as foundation stock for breeding Hunters and Eventers.

Highland ponies are particularly hardy and have an unusual winter coat that consists of a layer of strong, badger-like hair over a soft, dense undercoat. This enables them to live outside all year, even in the worst weather.

The Highland's head is broad in width and short in length, but the muzzle is not pinched. The

Above: The Highland Pony has served Scottish farmers for centuries; today, it is used mainly for general riding and showing.

neck is strong and arched with a clean throat. The shoulder is well-laid-back with a pronounced wither. The back is compact and deep and the quarters are powerful. The legs are short, with well-shaped hard, dark hooves. The bone is flat and hard. There is a little silky feather on the legs.

HUÇUL
(Hutsul)

Country of origin
  Poland (Carpathian mountains).
Height
  13-13·2hh (52-54in).
Color
  Bay, black, mouse-gray or occasionally chestnut.
Features
  This mountain pony is still used as a work pony in Poland.

The Huçul is a primitive-type pony, which evolved in Poland in the eastern Carpathians. It is known locally as the Hutsul after the Ukrainian mountains which are also called the Hutsuls.

Its origins are fairly directly connected to ancient wild horses. It is believed to be a cross between Tarpan derivatives and Mongolian breeds derived from Przewalski's Horse. Later there have been infusions of lighter horses, notably the Arab.

The small robust Huçul has great powers of endurance and that highly-developed instinct of mountain horses. It has worked in the mountains for centuries where it has been a pack pony and a harness pony, especially for the carting of wood, and it has been used for riding, especially in the very hilly regions. Today it is also used by children.

The ponies are selectively bred at the state stud of Siary. Their breeding is aided by the government as they are still used as work ponies in many parts of Poland and help the economy of the country.

The Huçul resembles Poland's other pony, the Konik, but its legs are shorter.

It also looks like the Tarpan, with its rather long, broad head. The body is compact and strong but there is a tendency for the limbs to be cow hocked.

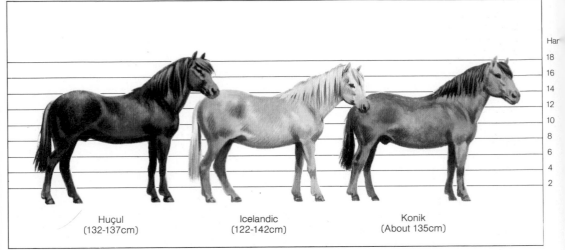

Huçul	Icelandic	Konik
(132-137cm)	(122-142cm)	(About 135cm)

Below: The Huçul is a native of Poland and is descended from the Polish Wild Pony, or Tarpan. Both horses share many of the same primitive features, such as the long broad head.

Above: The Icelandic Pony has been a mainstay of the economy of its country, helping with transportation and farmwork for centuries. It is found in many colors, including this pinto type.

ICELANDIC

Country of origin
  Iceland.
Height
  12-14hh (48-56in).
Color
  Most colors are found, but the most popular ones are the various shades of dun and chestnut, including liver chestnut with a flaxen mane and tail.
Features
  The tough, docile Icelandic has provided its country's residents with an important aid to the economy. Indeed, it was their sole means of transport for over 1,000 years. Many are now exported, and until recently large numbers were used as pit ponies in British coal mines.

The forbears of the Icelandic Pony were brought to Iceland by settlers in the late 8th and early 9th centuries. The settlers came from Norway, from Scotland and the islands of Orkney and Shetland, and the ponies they brought with them were from their homelands. There must have been some ponies of the Celtic type, because ponies found in south-west Iceland look very like the Exmoor

The foundation stock never completely blended into one breed, and even after hundreds of years of isolated breeding, there is still variety between the ponies found in Iceland, although all are agile and sure-footed. Their traits are not dominant, because if an Icelandic is put to another breed, very few are transmitted.

These ponies are greatly valued as working animals by the Icelandic people, and there are still large numbers of them. They once carried soldiers into battle. They are still bred for their meat, because beef cattle are not tough enough to survive the northern winter. Icelandic farmers have also relied on them to plow, transport goods and to shepherd flocks. They were the main form of transportation, and still remain so today because there are few roads. They are used as pack ponies, as draft animals for pulling carts, and for riding. They are also used for sport, and race meets are held for them

throughout the summer.

An unusual feature of these ponies is their homing instinct; it is customary to turn them loose after a long trip, when they will find their own way home. Most provide very comfortable, fast rides. In addition to the usual trot, canter and gallop, they have the gaits of pace and running walk. Although docile by nature, Icelandic Ponies are not particularly tractable. They have a highly independent nature, and shouted commands seem to be the best means of control.

Icelandics are stocky ponies with large heads, intelligent eyes and short, muscular necks, with a thick mane. The body is compact and deep. The quarters are sloping, the limbs short and strong, and the feet well-shaped and strong.

KONIK

Country of origin
Poland.
Height
About 13·1hh (53in).
Color
Mouse gray or dun with a black dorsal stripe and transverse stripes on the forearms and second thighs.
Features
This primitive-type pony is directly descended from the Wild Tarpans.

Below: A portrait of the Icelandic Pony, which has a mixed origin, and sometimes does not breed true outside it own blood.

These primitive-type ponies are supposed to have developed directly from the Wild Horse, or Tarpan. The name means "small horse" and it was the addition of some Oriental blood that helped to make it horselike. Koniks have been bred throughout Poland for centuries, but today their breeding is concentrated in the northern part of Rzeszow province.

The Koniks are bred and allowed to roam free at the Experimental Stud of the Polish Academy of Science at Popielno in Mazury, at the Racot State Stud and at the Roztocze National Park.

This pony has influenced a large number of other breeds. It was used as foundation stock for regional Polish breeds (most of which are now extinct) and also neighbouring countries' breeds, such as the Viatka from Russia.

Koniks have very good temperaments, and they are strong. They are also frugal feeders. This has made them popular with farmers for draft work and with children for riding.

They are similar to the Huçul in appearance and temperament.

Above: The Konik is similar to Poland's other native pony, the Huçul, shown at the foot of the opposite page. It is used extensively in Poland as a work and riding pony.

They have the same large, rectangularly-shaped head. The body is well proportioned, but the limbs are not always well-set and they tend to have "cow hocks". Although used for riding, they have a very short stride. They have a long life-span but take a long time to reach maturity.

LANDAIS
(Barthais)

Country of origin
France.
Height
Not more than 13·1hh (53in).
Color
Bay, brown, black or chestnut.
Features
A pony with Arab-like features and character that have made it an excellent children's riding pony.

This French pony has ancient origins, but over a period of time it has been strongly influenced by the Arab. The first Arab addition was from the horses left behind after the French victory over the Muslim horsemen at Poitiers in AD 871. Finally, in 1913, an Arab stallion was used on the Landais mares. These additions explain the Arab-like features of the pony, but it is a little more robust than its Oriental ancestors, because it has been subjected to wetter and colder conditions.

The Landais has run wild on the Barthes plains and Landais marshes along the Ardour river for centuries. It is still found there today. This hard life has made it a tough and cunning pony.

During this century, its numbers have dwindled, and the French now use occasional Arab or Welsh Section B stallions to help maintain the breed.

The Landais is used as a

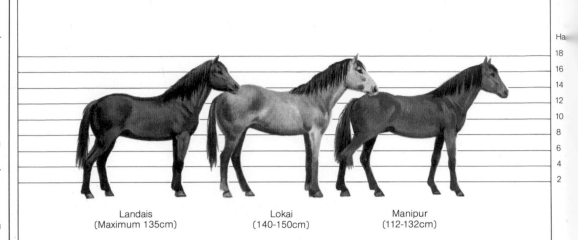

Landais
(Maximum 135cm)

Lokai
(140-150cm)

Manipur
(112-132cm)

children's pony, and for harness work, and it is an excellent trotter.

This breed is not particularly homogenous, but all Landais are fine, elegant, intelligent, robust ponies. They usually have an Arab-like head with the Arab's concave face, large eyes and small pointed ears. The neck is long and the shoulder sloping. The back is short and straight, with the tail set high. The limbs have bone of about 6·5-7in (17-18cm). The coat of the Landais is fine.

Below: The Lokai has long been used as a pack and riding horse by the tribesmen in the USSR after whom it was named.

LOKAI

Country of origin
USSR (Uzbekistan).
Height
13·3-14·3hh (55-59in).
Color
Most are bay, gray, chestnut or black. Occasionally they are dun and sometimes they have a golden sheen to the coat.
Features
Its agility and sure-footedness make the Lokai a good worker in its native mountains.

The Lokai is a tall pony from Southern Tadzhikstan in the USSR. Originally a mountain pony, it

evolved from Steppe horses and those from Central Asia. It is used by the Lokai tribe of Uzbekistan: hence its name. It has been crossbred with other breeds, including the Iomud, Karabair, Akhal Teke and Arab, to improve its 'class' and increase its height.

It is a sure-footed pony that is still used for work in the mountains, where it can be ridden or used as a pack pony. In the sporting world, it is most famous as the mount of the Tadzhik riders in the game of *kopar,* in which a mounted man carries a goat that others try to take from him by chasing after him.

The Lokai is a light-framed pony. The head has a straight face and sometimes even a Roman

Above: A Lokai being ridden by one of the Lokai tribesmen at Dushanbe, Tadzhikstan, near Afghanistan.

nose. The neck is muscular and set low on the shoulder. The withers are long and not prominent. The body is deep and the loins are straight, but the croup slopes. The forearm is long, but the cannons are short. The feet are hard and strong.

MANIPUR

Country of origin
India (Manipur).
Height
11-13hh (44-52in).
Color
Most.
Features
This tough, maneuverable pony is famous both as a polo pony and as a cavalry mount, but it has also been used extensively as a work pony.

The Manipur has been bred for centuries in the state in India after which it is named. It has gained fame as being one of the earliest breeds to be used as a polo pony. There is a manuscript dating back to the 7th century discussing the introduction of polo to the state and the use of the ponies bred there in the game. Manipurs were certainly the ponies being used to play polo in India when the British discovered the game during the last century. This pony has also been used in wartime. The Manipur cavalry was always noted as being particularly well mounted.

The Manipur is similar to the Burmese (Shan) Pony and is likely to have been derived from the same origins—a basis of the Mongolian Pony, with a little Arab blood to provide speed and a more refined conformation.

This thick-set pony has a fairly long head with a broad muzzle and well dilated nostrils. The body is broad and deep. The tail is set quite high.

Right: The Manipur was the original polo pony, and is so strong that it can carry heavy men or packs for many miles without tiring.

MONGOLIAN

Country of origin
 Mongolia.
Height
 12·2-14·2hh (50-58in).
Color
 Black, bay and dun are most
 common.
Features
 This ancient type of pony is very
 tough, frugal and fast. It is a
 working pony in Mongolia and
 can be used for many other
 activities, including racing.

Mongolian
(127-147cm)

New Forest
(Maximum 142cm)

Norwegian Fjord
(132-147cm)

Large numbers of this heterogeneous pony are found in vast
areas of the Far East, where it
breeds and is used as a general
work pony. It is found all over
Outer Mongolia, Tibet and China,
and it has close relatives in the
surrounding countries.

The Mongolian is an ancient
type. Its foundation stock was
Przewalski's Horse (or Mongolian
Wild Horse, page 42). It was
thought to be the domesticated
version of the Wild Horse, but it is
now known that there has been
crossbreeding with other horses
and ponies. Today there are many
types of Mongolian because of
differences in ancestors, climate

and feeding. These include the
Wuchumutsin Heiling Kiang,
Hailar, Sanho, Sanpeitze and Ili.
The Ili is larger because it has
been crossed with Russian breeds.

Mongolian Ponies are traditionally
bred in large herds by the Mongol
tribes. In the past, these tribes
conquered foreign territory, which
led to the spread of the pony
to many parts of the world. It has
been important foundation stock
for breeds such as the Turkoman,
the Spiti, the Bhutia, the Manipur
the Tibetan and the China Pony.

In its home territory this fast,
frugal pony is used by the
Mongols for pack work, herding
and the few agricultural activities
that take place. The mares are
often milked; the milk is used
for cheese or fermented to make
a form of alcohol called *kumiss*.

The Mongolian has a heavy head
with small eyes and short, thick
ears. Its neck is short and thick, with
a full mane. Its shoulders are
heavy, its chest deep, its back short
and strong and its tail set high,
with thick hair at the roots. The legs

are strong with good bone, and
the feet are hard and round. This is
a description of a typical pony,
but Mongolians do not breed true
to type, and they vary greatly,
particularly between regions.

*Below: The Mongolian Pony is
the work pony of its vast, bleak
homeland in northern Asia. It
is remarkably strong and fast-
moving. Together with a derivative,
the China Pony, it is used for
racing and for playing polo.*

NEW FOREST

Country of origin
Britain (New Forest, Hants.).

Height
Maximum 14hh (56in); although there is no lower limit few are under 12hh (48in).

Color
Bay and brown is most usual, but all colors are acceptable, except piebald, skewbald or blue-eyed cream. White markings on head and legs are permitted.

Features
This breed combines the strength, agility and intelligence of native British ponies with a narrower frame, speed and a tractable temperament. The New Forest is an ideal pony for the entire family. It has been used in most equestrian sports, including driving, and has even been raced. There has been some cross-breeding with Thoroughbreds and Arabs to produce small riding horses.

The New Forest Pony is the second largest of Britain's Mountain and Moorland ponies. It is also the most heterogeneous, showing a large range of types. This is because it has occupied a territory—the 60,000 acres of the New Forest, in Hampshire—that is not as wild or remote as the habitats of Britain's other ponies.

Through the centuries, many different types and breeds of pony were free to roam the area, and at times this has been deliberate policy. In 1852, for example, Queen Victoria allowed an Arab stallion called Zorah to be let loose in the forest for eight years to "improve" the breed. Thoroughbreds have also been used and, during the 20th century, stallions from other native breeds.

The origins of the breed are obscure. The first known fact is that in the 11th century, during the reign of King Canute, there are records of horses running free in the New Forest. The first systematic efforts to improve the breed began at the end of the 19th century.

In 1891, the Society for the Improvement of New Forest Ponies was founded and it offered premiums for quality stallions to run in the forest. This was followed in 1905 by the formation of the Burley and District New Forest Pony and Cattle Breeding Society, which started registering mares and their young stock. In 1938, these two societies merged, and during this period it was laid down that no further outside blood could be used. ▶

Above: This chestnut New Forest Pony foal has a small star on its head. It was born in the open in England's New Forest region.

Below: A group of New Forest Ponies photographed in their natural habitat, which consists mainly of heather and grass.

▶ Like the other native ponies, the New Forest is no longer confined to its natural home but is bred all over the world. It is the closest in conformation and action to a riding pony and is used for riding and driving. This riding type of pony has substance. The head should be ponylike, well set on, with a long sloping shoulder. It should have a good deep body, powerful quarters, good bone, straight legs and hard, round feet. Narrower than other native ponies, the New Forest is a good ride for children. All but the smallest ponies, nevertheless, are stong enough to be ridden by adults. Its movement is free, active and straight but not exaggerated.

NORWEGIAN FJORD

Country of origin
Norway.
Height
13-14·2hh (52-58in); about 14hh (56in) is standard.
Color
Various shades of dun (usually cream or yellow) with a dorsal stripe from tail to forelock. The legs are dark and usually have zebra markings on them. The tail is dark. The mane is dark in the center, with silver hairs on either side.
Features
For centuries, the coarse mane of the Fjord has been clipped in a curve to give the neck a distinctive shape and to allow the dark hairs to be seen just above the silver. These ponies are depicted in Viking runestones. The Fjord's kind nature, sturdy constitution and great strength have made it useful to man for centuries. Once indispensable on farms and in the mountains, today it is used in driving competitions, as a children's pony and for the popular European activity of vaulting.

The Norwegian Fjord, with its pale dun color and dark, clear-cut eel stripe bordered on the mane by lighter hairs, bears the distinct features of the primeval pony. The hairs in the mane are bristly, which makes them stand upright for a few inches. This is similar to the manes of ancient types that did not have to contend with a rainy environment; a mane falling over protects against the wet. The mane does eventually fall over in the Norwegian if it grows very long.

Some theorists claim that all domestic horses are descended from the primeval pony, of which Przewalski's Horse (page 42) is the wild example. The Norwegian Fjord, despite centuries of domestication and use by man, bears a close resemblance to it. This shows there has been little crossbreeding for thousands of years. This remarkable pony breeds very true to type and produces its primitive features generation after generation.

Above: This closeup of a Norwegian Fjord pony shows its concave head and the unusual mane.

Below: A Norwegian Fjord mare and foal. The foals are very tough; they are often born in northern Scandinavia.

Right: The Norwegian Fjord is a strong pony, with endless stamina and a kind, even temperament. This has made it a high-class work pony. It is popular throughout Scandinavia and in Germany. This one is pulling an extremely large cart.

The Norwegian Fjord is still very similar to the pony on which the Vikings waged war and had their playful fights on horseback. It must have been the pony they took to Iceland in AD 871 and acted as foundation stock for the Icelandic Pony. The Vikings' ponies were not used solely for warlike activities because the Vikings were the first people to use the horse to pull the plow. It was through their invasions of other lands that horse plowing became widespread. The ancestors of the Norwegian Fjord probably were the original plow-pullers on the mountainous farmlands of Scandinavia. The breed has since been used in the mountains for pack work, on the farms and as a weight-carrying pony. Its strength, tractable nature and ability to live on relatively little food has made it popular as an all-around work pony both in its homeland and in those countries without a native work pony (all over Scandinavia and in Germany).

This sturdy pony has a small head, with a broad, flat forehead and large eyes set well-apart. The head is refined and the face tends toward being concave rather than convex. The ears are small and well apart. The mane is coarse and stands upright for a few inches. The neck is short and thick and merges into the body without a clear division. The withers are rounded and not distinct. The back is of medium length but muscular and rounded. The hindquarters are strong, the limbs are short and sturdy, with good bone, and there is a little feather on the heels.

Below: A pair of Norwegian Fjord foals. They are usually born with fluffier, lighter-color coats than when they are mature. Their manes tend to become stiffer as they grow older.

PONY OF THE AMERICAS

Country of origin
United States (Iowa).
Height
11·2-13·2hh (46-54in).
Color
Appaloosa coloring.
Features
This miniature spotted horse is eye-catching and well-made, which makes it popular for riding and in the showring.

This new multi-colored breed was created in the 1950s by Leslie Boomhower of Mason City, Iowa. The foundation stock was a Shetland pony stallion and an Appaloosa mare. These spectacularly colored ponies have multiplied and are popular for riding and showing with both children and adults alike.

A Pony of the Americas has the appearance, in miniature, of a cross between a Quarter Horse and an Arab. The head is often slightly concave, with large eyes and pointed ears. The neck is slightly arched. The shoulders slope, and the withers are prominent. The body is well-rounded, short and muscular. The croup is long, level and muscular. The movement is free and easy; the pony takes long, straight strides. In the trot, there is good hock action.

Pony of the Americas
(117-137cm)

Przewalski's Horse
(122-132cm)

Sable Island
(142-152cm)

The chief distinguishing feature of these ponies is their coloring. They should have Appaloosa coloring, including a mottled skin and exposed sclera of the eye (the white circles round the eyes, as in our own). They should be white over the loin and hips with dark, round or egg-shaped spots, and have mud-colored shading around the mouth and nostrils. The hooves are often striped.

Below: The Pony of the Americas is an eye-catching new breed. All have appaloosa coloring, like this multi-spotted pony, and also white sclera (circles round the eyes).

PRZEWALSKI'S HORSE

Country of origin
Western Mongolia.
Height
12-13hh (48-52in).
Color
Yellowish dun with a mealy muzzle and dark mane and tail. There is a dorsal stripe down the back and zebra markings on the legs.
Features
This is the only true wild horse. It is a different species from the domestic horse.

Przewalski's horse, *Equus przewalski poliakoff,* is the only true wild horse. It is unlike other 'wild horses' that have escaped from domestication. It is the only horse that has survived since prehistoric times. It it believed to be a distinct species, different from *Equus caballus* (the domestic horse), although closely related, because *Equus przewalski* and *Equus caballus* can be crossed, and the hybrids are fertile.

This wild horse is believed by some to be the foundation stock for all domestic horses. It *was* probably the foundation stock for the Mongolian and Burmese ponies, ponies from India and some from the USSR, but it seems probable that there were as many as four basic types of wild horse (see page 10). Przewalski's Horse is most likely to be a member of the first subgroup of the Northern Group Horses, known as the Primeval Ponies.

Przewalski's Horse was discovered by the Russian explorer Colonel Przewalski in 1881 in the northwest part of Mongolia. He found a small herd in the Tachin Schara Nuru Mountains, on the edge of the Gobi Desert. The breed was named after him. In an effort to preserve these rare animals, the Chinese and Russians have now forbidden hunting. For centuries, various nomadic tribes killed them for meat.

Although it is planned to re-establish herds of Przewalski's Horse in the wild in western Mongolia, most representatives of the breed are captive. They are kept in zoos all over the world, where they breed and can be studied and observed to help scientific research on equine evolution.

Przewalski's Horse is very wild and timid around humans. It has a massive head with small ears and eyes, a big jaw and very big teeth. The body is broad and short coupled. The neck is short, and the shoulder is straight. The hindquarters are not very strong and lack muscle. The legs are fine-boned, and the cannon bones are rather short. The mane is short and upright, but it can fall over on the neck, particularly in winter when the hair grows. The tail is distinctly tufted at the end.

SABLE ISLAND

Country of origin
Canada (Sable Island).
Height
14-15hh (56-60in).
Color
Mostly chestnut, but some are bay, brown, black or gray.
Features
These are tough ponies that have to survive rigorous conditions in their natural habitat.

This pony is named after the small island where it still runs wild today. It has to survive bleak conditions; Sable Island lies in the Atlantic 100 hundred miles offshore from Nova Scotia.

Although legends claim that ponies have been on the island since the 16th century, evidence points to their being taken there in the early 18th century. They were believed to be of New England stock.

Sable Island ponies have multiplied in numbers, and today there are 40 or 50 herds on the island. Some of the ponies are caught and used both in harness and under saddle.

They have largish heads with a straight face and large ears. The body is finely built and rather short. The limbs are short and there is some feather on the heels.

Above: A Sable Island mare and foal. They breed in the wild on Sable Island, to the west of Novia Scotia, Canada.

Right: A portrait of Przewalski's Horse, with a foal.

SHETLAND

Country of origin
  Britain (Shetland Isles).
Height
  Not more than 10·2hh (42in).
Color
  Black is the foundation color but ponies may be bay, brown, chestnut, gray or part-colors.
Features
  This tiny pony is the strongest horse in the world relative to its size. This power has enabled it to help the inhabitants of its homelands for centuries. Today it is popular for harness work, as a children's pony or simply as a pet.

Shetland
(Maximum 107cm)

Sorraia
(122-132cm)

The Shetland is the smallest British Mountain and Moorland pony. Its diminutive size is not due to the bitter weather in its northerly homelands of the Shetland Isles, off Scotland: if it is bred in warmer climates, it is still small in size. It is believed to trace back to a dwarf variety of the "Exmoor type" brought to England by some of the first people to cross the seas to Britain. Drawings that date from the Stone Age in caves along the Bay of Biscay in France and Spain show ponies with Shetland features. No existing breeds, other than the Shetland, show these features today—the Shetland is unique.

Isolated in its bleak islands for nearly 2,000 years, this tough pony was not subject to any outside influences until it began to be taken to the mainland during the 19th century. For hundreds of years, it has helped the people of Shetland; its main work has been to cart peat for fuel (there were no trees), to carry fresh seaweed (used as manure) or burned seaweed (used as fertilizer) to the fields. As a pack pony, it is very strong, and is able to carry more weight in proportion to its size than any other horse or pony in the world.

Right: A Shetland Pony. This famous breed is very tough and capable of surviving in the snow.

Below: A Shetland Pony mare and her foal. Although small, the breed is extremely strong.

In the 19th century the value of this pony was realized, particularly for work in the mines. Many Shetlands were taken from their homelands to be used as pit ponies. They were bred for quantity, and there was a deterioration in quality. Then, in 1870, the Marquess of Londonderry established studs in Bressay and Noss, and through selective breeding, he helped to establish a good type of Shetland. Most of today's best Shetlands can be traced back to Londonderry stock and in particular the stallion Jack.

The Shetland was the first British native pony to have its own society. It was started in 1890 and a stud book was opened. At times, this was open to inspected stock, but in 1969 it was finally closed to all but the progeny of registered parents.

The Shetland has been extensively exported, and many countries now have their own stud book.

The Shetland's head is broad in the forehead, with a fairly straight face. The neck is slightly crested (more so in stallions) and a good length. The shoulder is sloping, and the body is thick-set and deep. The back and loins are short, with strong quarters. The limbs are strong and well-placed. The feet are strong, round and of a good shape. There is an abundance of hair in the mane and tail and some feather on the legs. The action is straight and free with good hock and knee flexion.

An unusual feature of the Shetland is its coat; although smooth in the summer, it grows two layers in the winter.

The American Shetland is a more slender and refined version. It is shown in hand or in harness with high front and rear action.

SORRAIA

Countries of origin
Portugal and Spain (near the Sorraia River).
Height
12-13hh (48-52in).
Color
Usually dun or gray with a dorsal stripe and zebra markings on the legs.
Features
A tough primitive pony that has lived on the Iberian peninsula for centuries.

The Sorraia is similar to its neighbor, the Garrano. Its homelands are along the Sorraia River and between its tributaries, the Sor and the Raia. It is found in western Spain and Portugal and it has lived there from ancient times. Some authorities believe it was one of the first horse breeds to be domesticated. The Sorraia is a primitive pony, bearing certain similarities to Przewalski's Horse and the Tarpan, from which it must have been descended.

It is very tough and able to survive heat and cold, as well as a lack of food. It was formerly used for rounding up cattle and other farm-work. Today, the Sorraia runs wild and one purebred herd has been kept in its natural state by the d'Andrade family.

Below: The Sorraia Pony breeds in Portugal and Spain along the river valley after which it is named.

Above: A Sorraia Pony of the typical dun coloring. The dorsal stripe on the back is also visible.

The head is large but varies in shape. In some individuals it resembles the Tarpan. The ears are long, with black tips. The neck is long, with upright shoulders. The quarters are rather weak. The legs are slender and long.

TARPAN

Countries of origin
Poland and Russia.

Height
Average 13hh (52in).

Color
Ranges from mouse to brown dun with a dorsal stripe. There are zebra markings on the legs, and the mane and tail are dark.

Features
This ancient strain was hunted for its meat. Domestic versions were used as work ponies, but today the Tarpans run wild in reserves, where they are studied by scientists.

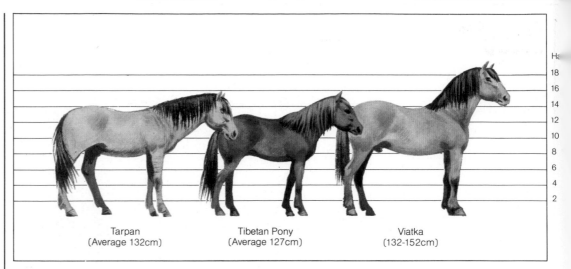

Tarpan
(Average 132cm)

Tibetan Pony
(Average 127cm)

Viatka
(132-152cm)

Tarpan is the Russian word for "wild horse." Some claim that this animal, together with Przewalski's Horse, is one of the original species of wild horses. It has been given the species name *Equus przewalskii gmelini antonus.* But evidence now seems to point instead to the Tarpan being a hybrid of the Proto-Arab group of the Southern Horses and the pony group of Northern Horses. The fact domestic descendants of the Tarpan—the Konik, Huçul and others—are all resistant to extremes of temperature helps support this theory.

The Tarpan of today is an artificially "restored" breed. It was recreated largely by Professor T. Vetulani in the 1930s. All genuine specimens of this wild horse had become extinct. Today, Tarpans live the life of wild horses in the forests of the state reserve at Popiellno, in Poland.

Many original Tarpans ran wild across the steppes of Russia, south of the Ural mountains. Another type, the Forest Tarpan, roamed the forests of central and eastern Europe. These animals were foundation stock for many of the European and Eastern breeds of horses and ponies, but they were hunted for meat. By the end of the 18th century they were close to extinction.

Some Tarpans were gathered into reserves like those of Count Zamoyskii of Poland. But most of the ponies escaped, died out or were captured and domesticated by peasants. However, some claim it was the remnants of this Zamoyski stock, together with some from another reserve in the Bialystock forests, that were used to re-create the Tarpan in captivity. Even if today's animals are not purebred Tarpans, careful selective breeding has meant they bear the distinctive features of this ancient breed.

The head is long and broad. The face has a straight or even convex profile. The ears are long. The neck is short and thick, and the shoulder sloping. The back is long, the hindquarters weak and the tail set high. The limbs are long and fine.

Below: The Tarpan Pony became extinct last century, but the breed has been "reconstructed" by Polish scientists.

TIBETAN PONY
(Nanfan)

Country of origin
Tibet (Himalayas).
Height
12·2hh (50in).
Color
A white coat with an unpigmented skin is most common.
Features
Sure-footed, strong pony ideal for mountain packwork.

The Tibetan comes from the Himalayas. It is similar to the Spiti and Bhutia from India. Like them, it is derived from the Mongolian.

This pony is sure-footed and able to carry heavy packs along steep mountain trails. On flat ground it is a fast walker. However, it is most suited to the colder climate of the mountains and can withstand rugged, freezing conditions better than the heat.

It is a strong, compact pony. The legs are short, with plenty of bone. The mane and tail are very thick.

Right: The Tibetan is a tough mountain pony, used for centuries as a sturdy, hard-working pack horse in the Himalayas.

VIATKA

Country of origin
USSR (Kirov and Udmurt).
Height
13-15hh (52-60in).
Color
Dun and light brown are most common. The mane and tail are black. There is often a dorsal stripe.
Features
Energetic, tractable and frugal, with great stamina, these are useful work ponies in harness or under saddle.

The Viatka is a primitive type pony. It seems likely to have evolved mainly from the Tarpan. However, there has also been some influence from the strong cobby types (not a breed) of working ponies from Estonia in the USSR. These are called *Kleppers* (the local word for 'nag'). They have practically died out because most were used for the upgrading needed to establish the Toric. The Viatka is bred in the Baltic states of the USSR in Kirov Province and the Udmurt Republic. Its original home was along the River Viatka.

The Viatka has a fast trot and was used in the past for pulling the troika sled (three horses pulling one sleigh). Today, they are used in harness and under saddle, for farm work and general transport. They have inherited many of the primitive features of their ancestors. They possess strength, frugality

and stamina. They also grow an unusually thick coat which, together with a special subcutaneous layer of fat, enables them to survive very cold weather.

They have the plain, long head typical of Tarpan stock. However, there is a tendency for the face to be a little more concave than their ancestors. The neck is medium length, very muscular and crested. The withers are broad. The chest is deep and strong. The back is broad, straight and long. The quarters are rounded. There is a tendency to have cow hocks.

Above: The Viatka Pony is bred in the Baltic states of the USSR.

The mane and tail are very thick. The action of the Viatka is energetic, but the strides tend to be short and quick.

WELSH MOUNTAIN PONY

(Section A)

Country of origin
  Britain (Wales).
Height
  Not to exceed 12·2hh (50in).
Color
  Any solid color.
Features
  Beauty, strength and an ancient lineage have made this good foundation stock, as well as a good children's pony.

Welsh Mountain Pony
Section A
(Maximum 127cm)

Welsh Pony
Section B
(Maximum 137cm)

Welsh Pony
Section C
(Maximum 137cm)

The Welsh ponies are the last of Britain's Mountain and Moorland ponies to be described. They cover a wide range of types. Because of this, the stud book is divided into four sections. The first (Section A) is for the most beautiful of the native ponies—the Welsh Mountain, not to exceed 12·2hh (50in); the second (Section B) is for the slightly larger riding type—the Welsh pony, not to exceed 13·2hh (54in),

the third (Section C) is for the stockier Welsh pony of Cob type, (not to exceed 13·2hh (54in) and the fourth (Section D) is a horse type. It is covered in the Sports Horse Section of this book; see pages 142-143. Also called the Welsh Cob, it stands over 13·2hh (54in) and has similar features to the Section C pony.

The oldest of these four types is the smallest, the Welsh Mountain.

Some believe it is derived from the Celtic pony and was in the Welsh hills for over 1,000 years. Its beauty, with its elegant head and well-proportioned body, probably comes from infusions of Arab blood (probably in Roman times) and Thoroughbred blood. It is certain the Welsh Mountain Pony itself has been foundation stock for breeds such as the Hackney, Welsh Pony and Cob, as

well as possibly the Thoroughbred. It has also been used for cross-breeding to produce types such as the Polo Pony, the Riding Pony, the Hack and the Hunter.

The Welsh Mountain Pony is not only beautiful but, because it has lived wild for centuries in the Welsh hills, it is also courageous, sound, tough and intelligent.

These assets have been confirmed in today's breed through

Right: The Section A Welsh Mountain Pony. This is one of the prettiest of the native British ponies.

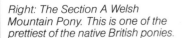

WELSH PONY
(Section B)

Country of origin
Britain (Wales).
Height
Not to exceed 13·2hh (54in).
Color
Any solid colors; not piebald or skewbald.
Features
An eye-catching type of riding pony that is very tough and intelligent.

The Welsh Pony is a larger, more modern version of the Welsh Mountain Pony. It is based on the smaller pony and is similar to it but with a little more substance and greater emphasis on riding qualities.

Welsh Ponies were originally bred by Welsh hill farmers. They provided them with transport and a means of herding their livestock in the mountainous pastures. To do this work they were good tempered, fast, strong, hardy, balanced and agile. These are qualities that stand them in good stead today as children's riding ponies.

At times, the stud book for Welsh Ponies (Section B) has been opened to part-bred Welsh stock but it has always been at least 50% Welsh. The Welsh part-bred stock tends to be lighter and taller than pure Welsh Mountain. The most influential in the 1920s were Craven Cyrus and Tanybwlch and in the 1950s Solway Master Bronze.

Conformation and action are similar to those of the Welsh Mountain.

This is the most common breed in the United States.

careful selective breeding. The Welsh Pony and Cob Society was founded in 1901, and its products have been the most numerous exports of any British pony. They have been sent all over the world, and for good prices, making it worthwhile for breeders to take trouble with breeding.

The Welsh Mountain Pony is an athlete, a good jumper and a good show pony. Consequently it has been in great demand

as a children's pony as well as foundation stock for other breeds and types.

The head should be small, with neat pointed ears, big bold eyes and a broad forehead. The jaw is clean-cut and tapers to a small muzzle. The silhouette of the face is concave or 'dished,' never convex or too straight. The neck is a good length and well carried, with shoulders sloping back to a clearly-defined wither. The limbs

Above: The Section B Welsh Pony is larger than the Welsh Mountain and more of a riding pony.

are set square, with good, flat bone and round, dense hooves. The tail is set high and carried gaily.

The action is straight, quick and free. The hocks and knees flex distinctly.

WELSH PONY
(Section C)

Country of origin
Britain (Wales).
Height
Not to exceed 13·2hh (54in).
Color
Any color except piebald or skewbald.
Features
This is a smaller version of the Welsh Cob and shares its action and conformation. This makes it a highly versatile animal, capable of trekking, riding, jumping, hunting, working and competing in harness.

This Cob-type pony is based on Welsh Mountain blood but with Andalusian and Cob blood added. This has made it into a stocky pony; it is active, strong and sure-footed. It is as versatile as its larger relative, the Welsh Cob, and shares the latter's history, conformation and action. The Welsh Cob is described on pages 142-143.

Left: This is the cobbier Section C Welsh Mountain pony.

WORK HORSES

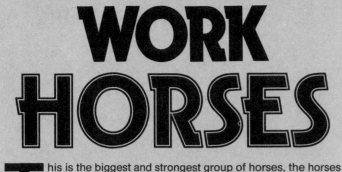

This is the biggest and strongest group of horses, the horses on which the world once depended for transport and power in agriculture and industry. For centuries, and especially since the improvement of roads and the beginning of the Industrial Revolution, they were a vital part of the economy. However, with the development of the internal combustion engine, demand for them has declined dramatically. As a result, horse populations all over the world have dropped considerably, because work horses (or "heavy horses") made up the largest proportion of the total number.

Today, heavy horses are still used in countries with non-industrialized economies and on farms where mechanization is difficult. They are used in draft work, especially by breweries that benefit from the publicity generated by magnificent teams of horses delivering their beer. The major use today for heavy horses is in demonstrations and shows. Horse lovers do not want to see this vital part of our heritage die out, so various breed societies have been promoted. Each organizes regular events where the general public can admire their particular breed.

A more technical name for the work horses is the cold-bloods. This doesn't mean their body temperatures are lower than those of the hot-bloods and warm-bloods, which are described in the next section. The term 'cold-blood' is derived from the German 'Kaltblütigkeit', which means calmness and stolidness. Because of their overall size and large muscles, work horses tend to be sluggish and slow to react.

There has been a great deal of disagreement about the evolution of the cold-bloods, but it seems probable that they were developed from the Tundra Horse and the Steppe Horse; both had the tendency to grow larger. These horses tended to increase in size in an environment of marshy lands with good sources of vegetation and a temperate to cold climate. It is an advantage to be bigger in cold weather because larger horses have a relatively smaller surface area from which heat is lost by radiation.

Right: Shires in action at the Royal Show in England.
Below: Ardennes heavy horses ploughing.

ARDENNES
(Ardennais)

Countries of origin
Belgium and France (Ardennes),
but a version is also bred in
Sweden.
Height
15·1-16·1hh (61-65in).
Color
Bay or roan, although some are
dark or liver chestnut.
Features
This ancient breed is a willing,
powerful worker, used greatly in
the past. Today, with mechan-
ization, its numbers are dwindling.

Ardennes
(155-165cm)

Boulonnais
(165-170cm)

The Ardennes breeds take their
name from the mountains from
which they come. These mountains
lie between France and Belgium.
This has led to a distinction being
made between the French and
Belgian Ardennes Horse. To
complicate matters still further,
there is also a Swedish Ardennes,
established when Ardennes were
imported in Sweden and crossed
with the North Swedish Horse.
The Swedish versions are similar
to their foundation stock from
the mountains, but they are a
little smaller and more agile.

The ancestors of this sober,
robust horse have allegedly been
bred on the plateaus of the
Ardennes for more than 2,000

years. The climate and vegetation
suited the raising of heavy horses
that were particularly well-built
and energetic. It is believed they are
some of the earliest specimens of
cold-bloods. They were mentioned
and used by Caesar, who talked
about the horses of Gaul (Northern
France). Nero was also supposed
to have favored them.

It is believed that in the 8th
century they were refined into more
handsome, agile horses through
the introduction of Arab blood.
More recently, the other Belgian
Heavy Horse—the Brabant—has
been crossbred to the Ardennes
to increase its size and strength.

In the early 19th century Napoleon
valued highly the strength and
endurance of the Ardennes, and he
used the smaller versions for
his armies.

Napoleon was not alone in
exploiting the hardworking
Ardennes for military purposes. The
Dutch Army made extensive use of
them in World War I, especially as
artillery wheelers.

This breed is renowned for
its toughness, its ability to withstand
all types of climate, its eagerness
to work and its frugal feeding. It is
still used for draft work in France,
Sweden and Belgium. In Belgium
farmers claim it is "the ideal tractor

on hilly and forested land."

The head of the Ardennes is
distinctive; small with a straight
face, prominent eye sockets and
pricked ears. It is also thick
through the jowl. The body is
stocky, broad, deep and compact.
The legs are relatively short, so it
stands close to the ground. There
is a little feather on the limbs.

*Below: A pair of handsome
Ardennes cold-bloods being driven
in their working harness.*

BOULONNAIS

Country of origin
France (Boulogne).
Height
Small: 15·1-15·3hh (61-63in).
Large: 15·3-16·3hh (63-67in).
Color
All shades of gray. Sometimes bay, chestnut, roan or black.
Features
This is the most elegant of the heavy horses, but it is sadly facing a falling demand. At present, its major use in France is as meat.

The Boulonnais is bred in northern France in the region of Calais. It is alleged its ancestors were Caesar's horses, which were stationed for some time in this area waiting to cross to England. It is said they brought to the Boulonnais some Oriental influence.

Through the centuries, Arabs continued to be crossed with the Boulonnais, which helps to explain why many consider this to be the most distinguished of the cold-bloods. The breed has been used to upgrade other cold-blood breeds, as the Thoroughbred is used to improve sports horses.

Additional use of the Arab was made by French crusaders who brought back horses from the Levant. Later, infusions of Andalusian blood were another

Above: A Boulonnais demonstrates how agile a heavy work horse can be. This breed is one of the most elegant of the cold-bloods.

Below: A fine Boulonnais cold-blood stands square to show off its well-proportioned body and handsome appearance.

important element in the mixture.

In the 17th century the breed was named Boulonnais, from the town of Boulogne. Two varieties were, and still are, recognized— one large (the Dunkirk), and the other small (the Mareyeur). The breed was not confined to Boulogne because it was also popular in Picardy, Artois, Haute Normandie and certain areas of Flanders.

The smaller version is particularly agile for a heavy horse. It has good action and stamina, and was used to pull coaches, providing a fast connection between the coast and Paris. It was called the Mareyeur, from the French word for 'fresh fish' because the most important goods carried on the coaches were oysters and other seafood.

Its fame as a speedy, strong horse spread far beyond France, and the Boulonnais was exported to many countries to be used for transportation and breeding to upgrade local stock.

Boulonnais mature quickly. This factor, together with their elegance, means they are still used on farms and for draft work. However, they are now mainly bred for meat in France.

The head of the Boulonnais is short and broad with a straight face, wide flat forehead, large alert eyes, small erect ears and a small mouth. The neck is short, often crested, with a long, thick mane. The back is straight and broad, the body deep and wide, the flanks short and the quarters rounded. The limbs are strong and muscular, the cannon bones are short, and the bone is big and strong. There is no feather. The coat of the Boulonnais is beautifully silky.

BRABANT
(Belgian Draft Horse)

Country of origin
Belgium.
Height
15·3-16·3hh (63-67in).
Color
Most are red roans with black points.
Features
This calm, docile horse is one of the strongest of the heavy horses. In Belgium, it is said to be "the most powerful living tractor in the world." It is still bred in large numbers; 700 foals are entered in the Belgian stud book annually.

Brabant
(160-170cm)

Breton
(152-165cm)

The center for the development of this breed was the fertile plain of the low-lying Brabant region in the middle of Belgium. Belgium has long been famous for her heavy horses. Much has been written about the Flanders Horse as the mount of knights in armor in medieval times. Some Flanders Horses were supposed to have been imported to Britain, where they were used as foundation stock for that country's horses.

The Brabants are direct descendants of the Flanders Horses. There are three slight variations within the Belgian breed, which were recognized as separate breeds until the beginning of the 20th century. They are the Big Horse of the Dendre, the Gray Horse of Nivelles and the colossal horses of Mehaignc. Today they vary little in conformation or color. The distinction was based mainly on different areas and bloodlines.

Belgian farmers have been proud breeders for centuries, using selective methods and—with few exceptions—shunning any outside blood. The result is that the Belgian Draft breeds true to type.

Its strength, good temperament and willingness to work has made it popular all over the world. Many have been exported, particularly

Below: The Belgian Draft Horse, or Brabant, is large, very heavy and extremely powerful.

Above: Belgian Draft Horses at work, bringing in the harvest. This sight is rarely seen today

because mechanized harvesters have replaced horses in Belgium on all but a few farms.

Below: The Breton is one of the most energetic of all breeds of heavy horses.

to the United States. It has also been used to improve or found breeds: the Rhineland or Rhenish-German Cold-Blood from Germany was based on it. The Ardennes' size has been increased through breeding with Brabants.

The head of the Brabant is light and expressive. It is square in shape. The neck is short, thick and crested. The shoulders and quarters are massive. The body is short and deep. The limbs are strong, lean and sound, and carry some feather.

BRETON

Country of origin
France (Brittany).
Height
15-16·1hh (60-65in).
Color
Chestnut, bay roan, strawberry roan, gray and black.
Features
The Breton is a strong, energetic worker that is used to this day in France and other countries for farmwork and, sometimes, for pulling coaches.

For centuries, Brittany has bred her own types of heavy horses to suit the local climate and demands of the people. In the Middle Ages, we know there were the Sommier, a robust horse used for agricultural work, light draft and pack transportation, and the Roussin, a lighter version of the Sommier used for riding. The Roussin was well-known for its fourth gait—the 'amble,' a comfortable and fast pace for getting across country.

The Roussin was particularly popular in southern and central Brittany. More recently, Arab and Thoroughbred blood was added to

the Roussin to create the Corlay, a Breton used for riding and racing. Today, this breed is almost extinct.

In northern Brittany, a heavier horse was needed for draft work. Outcrosses with the Percheron and Boulonnais were made. Another popular mixture, particularly in mountainous regions, was with the Ardennes. These heavier Bretons were known as the Draft Breton.

Another important subdivision of the Breton was created in the 19th century, when Norfolk Trotters and Hackneys were imported and used for breeding. This mixture created the Postier Breton, a fine horse with active paces.

Today, the last two divisions to the Breton are still recognized— the heavier stronger Draft Breton and the more active, lighter Postier Breton. These horses are registered in a stud book. Two separate books were started in 1909, but they were soon joined together and maintained with two divisions. Since 1920, the use of outside blood has not been allowed, and since 1951 the Breton stud book has been closed.

The Breton has a great ability to adapt to different climates and conditions; it is energetic and robust. It is still in demand as a work horse, particularly in under-

developed countries and in the vineyards of the Midi.

The Breton is also quick to mature, a quality that has made it a good animal for the French meat market.

The Postier Breton is popular with farmers in Brittany, and it is also used for coaching.

The head is relatively square, with a straight face, bright eyes and small ears. The neck is strong, slightly crested and a little short. The shoulder slopes but is not very long. The back is short, muscular and broad, with powerful hind-quarters. Limbs are short and muscular with a little feather.

CLYDESDALE

Country of origin
Scotland.
Height
16·3-18hh (67-72in).
Color
Preferably bay or brown, with a white stripe on the face and white stockings on the limbs up to, and over, the knees and hocks.
Features
This close relation of the Shire is one of the world's most popular work horses.

Clydesdale
(170-183cm)

Comtois
(150-160cm)

Døle
(147-157cm)

The Clydesdale was developed in Scotland to meet the demands of the Industrial Revolution. Improved roads meant pack transport could be replaced by more efficient horsedrawn vehicles. A strong animal was needed for hauling, to turn machines and to work the lowland farms.

The first development of Clydesdales was in the late 18th century when local native mares were crossed with larger, stronger imported Flemish stallions. Some believe one of the best of these was named Clyde, and he gave the breed its name. But the concentration of breeding in the area of Clydesdale is the more probable reason.

The major development came in the mid-19 century, particularly in Lanarkshire, when large numbers of Black Horses (later to become Shires) were brought north from the Midlands. Scottish breeders bought some of the very best English stock to establish the Clydesdale. Although local mares were used in this development, the Clydesdale became very similar to the Shire.

The Clydesdale was the first of the British Heavy Horses to have its own society. It was started in 1877 and helped encourage the best possible breeding. The Clydesdale Society was able to promote one of the most successful systems of breeding: stallion hiring. This was started in the 1830s and helped develop successful breeding of carthorses.

Owners of about 100 mares in one neighborhood got together to hire the best stallion available. One hundredth of the fee was an affordable amount for each individual; also the district could change stallions as advisable and ensure the next one chosen was a good mate for the daughters of his predecessor. This system helped establish this excellent breed, which became so much in demand that at a public auction in 1919 the stallion Baron of Buchlyrie was sold for £9,500 (about half a million dollars today).

Today Clydesdales still bring high prices for export, mainly to the United States. The valuable animals are used chiefly for showing and breeding. Poorer quality ones are used for work in the Scottish woodlands. Unlike tractors, they can avoid damaging the remaining trees. They are also used for British deliveries where they are

economically competitive with motorized transport. Another use for the Clydesdale is for crossbreeding. The first cross with a Thoroughbred is a useful, heavy-weight type. The second generation (quarter Clydesdale) has often proved a high-class competition horse.

The Clydesdale's head looks intelligent and is carried high. The forehead and muzzle are broad, and the profile of the face is straight. The eyes are alert

and the ears large. The neck is arched and long, springing out of an oblique shoulder with high withers. The back is short and strong, with well-sprung ribs. The quarters are long and muscular, with the tail set quite high. The limbs are long, with an abundance of fine silky feather.

The forelegs are planted well under the shoulder. The hindlegs are set close together, with the hocks turned inward. The second thigh and cannon bones are long.

The feet are large, round and strong.

The Clydesdale moves with great energy. The feet are lifted clear of the ground.

The general appearance of the Clydesdale is of strength, power and activity. These are all valuable assets for a work horse.

Below: A pair of Clydesdales competing in a plowing contest.

COMTOIS

Country of origin
France (in the Jura mountains).
Height
14·3-15·3hh (59-63in).
Color
Bay or chestnut.
Features
This is a light draft animal is still used extensively in France. It is second only to the Breton in numbers.

This mountain work horse has been bred in France's Jura mountains for centuries, but today it is also found in the Massif Central. It was used as far back as 1544 to improve the horses of Bourgogne, but became most famous as an army horse. Louis XIV used Comtois for his cavalry and artillery, and they were taken to Russia in Napoleon's campaign.
The Comtois has not remained pure from the 19th century. Percheron, Anglo-Norman and Boulonnais were used for cross breeding but without good results. At the beginning of this century, breeders found that using the small mountain Ardennes gave a better mix and provided a stronger horse.

This active, robust, long-lived horse is easy to train. It is used for work in the forests or in the vineyards, as well as for pulling sleighs at ski resorts. The Comtois is appreciated also outside France and has been exported to North Africa. Like other French breeds of heavy horses it is also kept for meat production.
Typically the head is square, with lively eyes. The ears are small and mobile. The neck is straight and muscular. The wither is prominent and the body deep and broad. The back is strong, and the hindquarters round and broad. The limbs are strong, with good bone. The feet are strong, and there is a little feather.

DØLE
(Gudbransdal)

Country of origin
Norway (Gudbransdal Valley).
Height
14·2-15·2hh (58-62in).
Color
Usually black, brown or bay.
Features
This small cold-blood is tough, active and has great stamina. It is a high-class, all-round animal.

Above: A Clydesdale shows off the white socks and face that are typical of this breed.

Below: A Døle mare. This Norwegian breed is one of the smallest cold bloods.

For centuries this small heavy horse has inhabited the Norwegian Gudbransdal Valley, which connects the Oslo region with the North Sea coast. The Gudbransdal was a major overland route. The Døle is similar in appearance to the Friesian, Dale and Fell. It is questionable whether this is because they were all derived from the same prehistoric stock or because of an interchange of blood lines. The latter theory seems more likely, in view of the fact that during the period AD 400-800 Friesian merchants traded extensively between Norway, Britain and the Rhine Delta. It is highly likely that they took their black Friesian horses to both Norway and Britain.
This breed has an attractive trot and great pulling power. It is used as an all-round general purpose horse.
The Døle varies in size and type. Some are light due to Thoroughbred influence, while others are heavy draft horses. This variety means individuals can be found for many different tasks. The Døle is the most influential, widespread Norwegian breed.
Despite their variability, Døles have important features in common. They all have a small pony head, with a straight face and good width between the eyes. The neck is usually slightly crested. The shoulder tends to be a little upright. The body is strong and deep. The back is long and the quarters muscular and rounded. The limbs are short. There is an abundance of feather on the heavy types.
The Døle is a particularly active heavy horse with a very good trot.

DUTCH DRAFT

Country of origin
  Holland.
Height
  Up to 16·3hh (67in).
Color
  Chestnut, bay, gray or black.
Features
  This massive animal is docile, willing and active. It matures quickly and lives to a great age. These qualities make it a popular heavy draft animal.

Dutch Draft
(Maximum 170cm)

Finnhorse Draft
(145-180cm)

The Dutch Draft is a modern development and was established as a breed in the Netherlands this century. Most foundation stock came from the neighboring country, Belgium, in particular the Ardennes.

These introductions were crossed with native Netherlands stock, and the result is one of the most massive, muscular breeds of heavy horses.

The Royal Dutch Draft Horse Society was founded in 1914. Since 1924 its stud book has been confined to horses with known pedigrees, which has helped to establish the breed. There is also a Preferential Stud Book for breeding stock that has passed conformation tests.

Today, breeding stock is selected on the basis of easy movement, fertility and low cost to keep. The Dutch Draft's major use is as a show horse and for draft work in cities as an aid to advertizing for companies.

The Dutch Draft is a massive horse that is strong and solid. The head has a straight profile and short, lively ears. The neck is short and it has a strong-muscled front. It has good withers, heavily-muscled broad loins and quarters with a sharply sloping croup. The legs are good and well-muscled, with good feet. The movement is free and easy.

Below: The Dutch Draft Horse was developed in the 20th century from Ardennes stock. The similarity can be seen by comparing this picture with that of the Ardennes on page 52. The Dutch Draft is one of the largest cold-bloods.

FINNHORSE DRAFT

Country of origin
  Finland.
Height
  Usually around 15·2hh (62in) but can vary from 14.1-17.3hh (57-71in).
Color
  Most.
Features
  Agile, sure-footed, strong, small cold-blood that is still used extensively in the forests of Finland.

Finnhorses, which have lived for a long time in Finland, are descendants of the North European domestic horse. The basic stock has always been tough enough to withstand the cold climate, but variations have been larger or smaller, heavier or finer, according to the demands of the day. Today there are three types of the Finnhorse—the draft, trotter and riding horse. These vary in the degree of substance and sturdiness of frame, but all are quite similar in conformation. They are muscular, robust, well-proportioned horses. The neck is short and the back long, with a rounded or sloping croup. The limbs are strong. There is an abundance of hair in the mane and tail and light feather on the limbs.

Finnhorses are calm and easily trainable but lively and intelligent. They make particularly good

trotters, because selective breeding has produced a specialized type of Finnhorse racing trotters, which are much finer and faster than the Draft Horse.

Since 1907, when the stud book was first established, the principle of pure breeding has been strictly adhered to. About 50 years ago, performance tests were introduced for breeding stock, and the draft test allows only the best workers to breed for this Finnhorse section. Trotting ability is an important performance test for all sections, which ensures the Finnhorse is an all-round performer.

As a draft horse, the Finnhorse is unusually agile and able to move easily over difficult terrain. This is an especially useful asset for its major function of thinning forests. Tree pulling is still better done by horses than tractors because they are less likely to damage remaining trees.

Right: The Finnhorse often pulls sleighs rather than carts.

Below: A portrait of a typical Finnhorse Draft.

FREIBERGER
(Franches Montagne)

Country of origin
Switzerland (Juras).
Height
14·3-15·2hh (59-62in).
Color
Most.
Features
An agile, sure-footed, light draft horse specifically bred to help the Swiss Army and the farmers in the mountains.

Freiberger
(150-157cm)

Irish Draft
(152-173cm)

Italian Heavy Draft
(152-163cm)

The Freiberger originated in the Jura mountains in western Switzerland. It has a mixture of ancestors—some Norman, Thoroughbred and Anglo-Norman, some British Thoroughbred and Draft breeds, and some Belgian draft horses. More recently, outside influences have been restricted to Anglo-Norman and Arab blood. Today all Freiberger breeding stock is controlled and tested by the Swiss National Stud at Avenches. The Swiss are aware of the importance of this light draft breed to their country and take extensive measures to ensure the production of the best animals possible.

The Freiberger's importance relates to the mountainous nature of its native country. The Swiss Army cannot rely on mechanized transport for patrols and carrying artillery—horses are still vital. They are also still used by farmers who live in the high mountains and cannot use tractors on their steeply sloping fields. The Swiss are aware of the increasing costs of energy production and the harmful effects of pollution; they are keen to maintain a good stock of horses as an alternative source of power. For all these reasons, the Freiberger

remains an important national asset, and the government promotes its breeding financially and administratively.

The variety of breeds used in the past means there has been a range of types within the Freiberger breed. Today, the breed is becoming more uniform because of the controls exercised by the National Stud and the extensive tests used for breeding stock. Nevertheless, as the breeding program is directed more toward producing soundness, character and ability, conformation still varies.

The Freiberger is a compact, sturdy horse with a small head, a harmonious muscular body, strong limbs and little feather. It is energetic, but docile, easily trained, agile and sure-footed for its work in the mountains.

Below: The Freiberger is a Swiss cold-blood used both for farmwork and for transporting army personnel and equipment.

IRISH DRAFT

Country of origin
Ireland.
Height
15-17hh (60-68in).
Color
Bay, brown, chestnut or gray are most common.
Features
This light draft breed is a utility horse capable of working on farms, transporting goods and hunting. Today its major purpose is for crossbreeding with Thoroughbreds to produce hunters and competition horses.

The Irish Draft is almost light and fast enough to be classified as a warm-blood. The aim of breeders was to produce a multi-purpose animal, and it is certainly one of the most versatile of all the cold-bloods. The Irish farmers wanted an animal that could

pull their plows, transport their goods and families in carriages and take them hunting. The Irish Draft has been doing this for centuries, although its size, conformation and type have changed according to the demands of the time.

The original Irish horses were ponies. Some early outside blood was Spanish or Arabian, but the first confirmed history of the Irish Draft was the use of Thoroughbred sires on native Irish mares in the 18th and early 19th centuries.

The Irish Draft flourished until the agricultural recession of 1879 led to a marked decline in their numbers. When the situation improved for farmers, there was a great shortage of horses. Clydesdales and Shires were imported from Britain, but this led to coarser animals and the increase of feather on the legs.

This century, the Irish government has become increasingly aware of the importance of these horses and has taken steps to promote breeding. In 1907, registration plans were introduced for stallions. In 1911, plans were made for mares, and then inspections were started.

In World War I, the Irish Draft made an important contribution. To ensure their continuing production, an Irish Draft Stud Book was started in 1917.

Since World War I, there has been a declining demand for work horses. However, the Irish Draft was found to be an excellent cross with the Thoroughbred in the production of hunters and competition horses. Ireland became an exporter of partbred Irish Drafts but the foundation purebred stock began to disappear. The formation of the Irish Horse Board in the 1970s marked a major attempt to halt this decline, and today there is an effective Irish Draft Society preserving this breed.

The Irish Draft has an intelligent head with a straight face. The neck is short, thick and usually slightly crested. The body is long, and the hindquarters slope sharply but are very powerful. The limbs are strong, with good flat bone and very little feather. The forelegs tend to be straight. and the feet are large and round.

The Irish Draft is an active

horse, and its powerful hindquarters make this handsome breed a good jumper.

ITALIAN HEAVY DRAFT

Country of origin
  Italy.
Height
  15-16hh (60-64in).
Color
  Liver chestnut, with flaxen mane and tail is most common, but some are roan and chestnut.
Features
  The Italian Heavy Draft is one of the fastest of the large work horses.

These heavy horses are called *TPR's,* an abbreviation for *Tiro Pesante Rapido,* or quick draft horses, in Italy. The breed originates from the mid-19th century, when Arab, Thoroughbred and Hackney blood was used to breed speedier mares. In the 20th century the most important blood has been from the Breton, to which the Italian Heavy Draft now bears great similarity.

The main breeding areas were in the plains and hills around Verona, Padova, Vicenza, Venice, Treviso and Udine. The Italian Heavy Draft was an important breed for Italian farmers because it is large, docile, strong and fast. But today, the tractor has almost replaced it. The declining numbers of the breed (currently about 1,000 brood mares) are kept mainly for meat.

The head is relatively long but fine and elegant. The neck is short and crested, the body is broad and deep, and the hindquarters are rounded and muscular. The limbs are muscular, the feet are a little boxy and there is some feather.

Below: The Italian Heavy Draft is a breed based on the Breton.

Right: A close-up shows the Italian Heavy Draft's handsome head.

Above: The champion Irish Draft mare Baultic Rossi. This versatile breed is almost a warm-blood.

JUTLAND

Country of origin
Denmark (Jutland).
Height
15·1-16hh (61-64in).
Color
Usually chestnut, but it can be sorrel or roan.
Features
This strong, kind-tempered breed of draft horse has very early origins and has acted as important foundation stock.

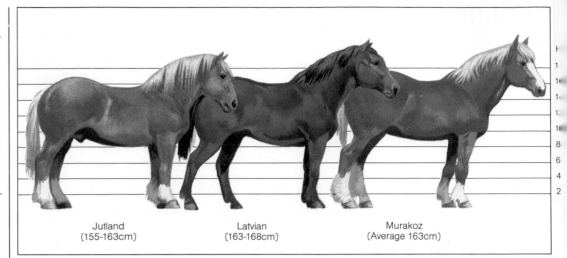

Jutland
(155-163cm)

Latvian
(163-168cm)

Murakoz
(Average 163cm)

This famous Danish breed comes from Jutland, the region after which it was named. It is believed to be very ancient, and types similar to it were taken to Britain by the Vikings in the 9th and 10th centuries. The British breed, the Suffolk Punch, is very similar, indicating joint origins.

In the Middle Ages Denmark's heavy horses became famous as war horses. Many were exported because their agility and strength made them popular mounts for the heavily-armored knights.

The modern Jutland was strongly influenced by British breeds. Yorkshire Coach horses and Cleveland Bays were imported to lighten it, but most influential of all was a stallion named Oppenheim LXII, who was imported to Denmark in 1860. He is claimed by some to be a Shire and by others to be a Suffolk; most modern authorities believe he was a cross between the two breeds. He is the ancestor of all important Jutland stock, including Aldrup Munkedal (born in 1893) who set the type for today's Jutlands. There are now two important lines — both traceable to Oppenheim — the Fjandø line and the Dux line.

Danish farmers have a long tradition of horse breeding. They use selective methods, and the result is a high-class breed of draft horse that has been used to improve other countries' cold-bloods and to act as foundation stock.

The Jutland has tremendous substance for its size. The head is plain, the ears are long and the neck short and thick. The body is broad and deep, and the quarters are round and muscular. The limbs are short, with tremendous bone and an abundance of soft, smooth feather.

This kind-tempered, strong, medium-sized draft animal is still used on some Danish farms and for transport.

Below: A pair of Jutlands, a Danish heavy horse breed, in harness.

LATVIAN

Country of origin
USSR (Latvia).
Height
16-16·2hh (64-66in).
Color
Normally black, but bay, brown and chestnut are found.
Features
Latvian Horses vary in type to suit different demands, from draft work to competitions.

In Latvia, a Baltic state of the USSR, a local cold-blood has been bred for centuries. In the past, it was used on farms and as transportation. More recently, with the declining demand for work horses, the Latvian has been lightened. Some draft types remain, but two further divisions have developed. One, the Harness Horse, arose originally through introduction of Norfolk Roadster and Anglo-Norman blood, and later with the introduction of Oldenburg and Hanoverian breeds.

Then, even more recently, some of the Harness types have been crossed with Arab, Thoroughbred and Hanoverian stallions. This has produced riding horses that are talented in jumping and eventing.

Latvians vary considerably in type and are the USSR's multi-purpose breed. According to their type and the areas where they are bred, the Latvians do draft work, harness work or are used for riding. They are popular with farmers and riders because they have great powers of endurance, and are very strong.

The substance, amount of bone, frame and height varies but most have large heads with a straight Roman-nosed face and big eyes. The neck is slightly crested and long (longer in the riding type).

The body is thickset, deep and broad. The quarters are round and muscular. The legs are long and have a little feather. The mane and tail have plenty of hair.

MURAKOZ
(Murakozer)

Country of origin
Hungary (South).
Height
Around 16hh (64in).
Color
Usually chestnut with flaxen mane and tail.
Features
A medium-sized draft horse with a kind temperament, strength and a willingness to work.

The Murakoz, Hungary's heavy draft horse, was developed as a breed at the end of the 19th century and the beginning of the 20th on the farms around the Mura River. The foundation stock

was native Hungarian mares (known as Mur-Insulan), Ardennes, Percherons, Norikers (from Austria) and some Hungarian half-bred stallions.

The Murakoz was very popular with farmers and was used extensively by the army in both world wars. Today, it is still used on the land, although its numbers have dwindled.

The Murakoz is a small draft horse, active and strong. It has a large head, and the face tends to be convex. The eyes have a generous outlook, and the ears are large. The neck is short and slightly crested. The withers are barely noticeable. The body is broad but has a pronounced dip to the back. The quarters are rounded and the croup slopes. The legs are short with a little feather and round feet.

Above: The Latvian varies in type from a heavy work horse to a riding horse. This is one of the riding types, but it still shows plenty of strength.

Below: A Murakoz from Hungary. This breed of cold-bloods was very popular as a work horse, but with mechanization, its numbers are dwindling.

NORIKER
(Pinzgauer)

Country of origin
Austria.

Height
16-17hh (64-68in).

Color
Chestnut, bay, black, grey, dun, sometimes spotted with small patches like a Dalmatian dog.

Features
This breed, which has ancient origins, is still used extensively by the Austrian farmers and army, particularly in mountainous areas.

Noriker
(163-173cm)

North Swedish Horse
(155-160cm)

Percheron
(157-168cm)

This cold-blood is of ancient origins. It is named after the Roman province of Noricum, which included most of modern Austria. The horses the Romans bred in this area were well-known to contemporary observers, and were allegedly brought by them from Thessalonika, northern Greece.

The Noriker proved an invaluable worker in mountainous areas, with its good temperament, adaptability and sure-footedness. It was used extensively in agriculture, transport and by the Army. Different strains have developed. The best-known of these is found around Salzburg, which became known as Pinzgauer Norikers. Another well-known strain are those in Bavaria, which were called South German Cold-Bloods (see page 71).

The Pinzgauer Noriker got its name from the Pinzgau district of Austria. This line became renowned as a spotted horse. It was supposed to have developed around the time of the Renaissance, when Andalusian and Neapolitan blood was introduced. Today, spotted horses are rarer, but the Noriker has retained all the assets that make it a high-class, all-round mountain worker. Large numbers are still bred in Austria.

The Noriker has a plain, large head and a straight face. The neck is short and thick. The body is broad and deep, the back is long and the legs are short and have a little feather. The feet are strong and round.

Right: Norikers are often used in the mountains of Austria for pulling logs.

Below: The Pinzgauer Noriker, with its distinctive spotted coat, is rare today.

Above: North Swedish Horses are
small work horses that have been
used for centuries by Swedish
farmers, foresters and the Army.

NORTH SWEDISH HORSE

Country of origin
Sweden.
Height
15·1-15·3hh (61-63in).
Color
Any solid color.
Features
Active, tough horse that trots
well and is similar to its near
relative, the Døle. It is still used
extensively by the Army and
for forestry work.

The North Swedish Horse has
ancient origins, that are closely
connected with those of its
neighbor, the Døle from Norway.
There has been a lot of crossbreeding, and it was only after
a breed society was established
at the end of the 19th century
that a more uniform type was
produced. Døle stallions from
Norway were used, and at the ▶

Right: A portrait of a Noriker,
an adaptable, sure-footed,
all-around Austrian work horse.

▶ beginning of the 20th century stringent performance tests for breeding stock were introduced.

The North Swedish horse is tractable, robust, economical to feed and very active. Like the Døle, it is a good trotter. It is still used for log-pulling by farmers and by the Swedish Army.

The North Swedish Horse is dumpy, with a big head and long ears. The neck is short and thick. The shoulders are sloping, the body is deep and the back long. The quarters are rounded, with a sloping croup. The limbs are short, with substantial bone. There is an abundance of hair in the mane and tail.

PERCHERON

Country of origin
France (La Perche).
Height
15·2-16.2hh (62-66in).
Color
Gray or black with a fine coat.
Features
This clean-limbed, powerful, free-moving, docile-natured, good-looking horse is one of the most popular cold-blood breeds in the world.

The Percheron is one of the oldest and handsomest breeds of cold-blood. It originated in north-west France, in an area called La Perche. The soil and climate in the area are conducive to breeding good, large horses. The foundation stock were the Oriental horses, left by the Moors after their defeat in 732 AD, and the heavy Flemish horses.

Additional infusions of Arab blood were made when Oriental stock was brought back by the French Crusaders and when the

Above: Percherons are particularly handsome cold-bloods and are often used to pull carriages.

Below: Cold-bloods, like these Percherons, have gentle temperaments and get along well together.

government stud at La Pin used two Arab stallions, Godolphin and Gallipoly, on selected Percheron mares early in the 19th century. This Arab blood has helped make the Percheron an active, elegant draft horse.

The Percheron first earned fame as a war horse, but with the passing of the heavily armored knights it was used for transport and agriculture. The Percheron's heyday was from 1880 to 1920. Today, although its numbers are much smaller, it is used for agricultural work, draft work in cities and for showing all over the world. The breed is very popular in the United States, Argentina, Britain and France.

In its homelands, the Percheron is divided into two types — the Heavy Draft and the Postier. The Postier was developed at the end of the 19th century as a horse to pull the omnibuses in Paris. The Heavy Drafts are the most numerous and are in demand for export. There have been other divisions (such as Draft Maine and Draft Bourbonnais), according to the area bred, but they are all now covered by one stud book. Like

Above: Percherons in a row of stalls. This form of stabling makes it easier to look after large numbers of horses.

Below: The Percheron is a very good-looking heavy horse. Its Arab ancestors have given it more elegance than most work horses.

other breeds of heavy horse in France, the Percheron is in demand by the meat trade.

The head is intelligent, short in length, with a straight face, a deep curved cheek, good breadth between the eyes and erect, medium-sized ears. The neck is slightly crested (well-crested in stallions), muscular and a good length. The chest is wide, and the shoulders well laid back. The back is strong and short. The ribs are wide and deep, and the quarters are wide and long from the hips to the tail. The limbs are strong and muscular. The knees are big, and the hocks are broad. The cannons are short and the feet are a strong, black horn. There should be as little feather as possible—an unusual feature in a heavy horse. It makes the Percheron less likely to develop skin problems in the legs.

The Percheron is a straight, free mover, taking longer, less choppy strides than most heavy horses. The hocks flex well and move close together. Despite its docile nature, it is not sluggish. This action makes it a very showy animal, highly suitable for demonstrations and advertising.

POLISH DRAFT

Country of origin
Poland.

Height
15-16·3hh (60-67in).

Color
Most.

Features
Poland's draft breeds have been developed to suit local demands and environments. They still play an important role on farms.

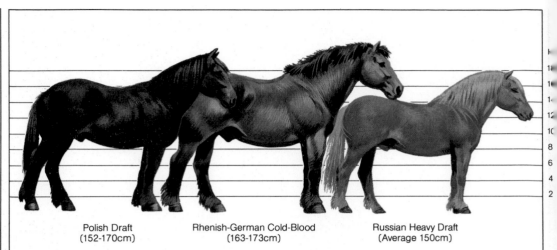

Polish Draft
(152-170cm)

Rhenish-German Cold-Blood
(163-173cm)

Russian Heavy Draft
(Average 150cm)

In Poland, there are five regional breeds of heavy draft horses. These vary according to their environment and foundation stock. The most massive is the Sztum, which originated from local stock crossed with Belgian, Rhenish, Jutland, Ardennes and Døle stock. It is usually chestnut but can be bay or roan.

The Løwicz is similar to the Sztum but a little lighter. Its main foundation stock is Ardennes and Belgian stallions. Løwicz are the same colors as the Sztum.

The Sokølka was also founded on Ardennes stock, but there is also some Breton and Døle, which give the breed its good free movement. Sokølkas are frugal feeders. The most common color is chestnut, but there are occasional bays and roans.

The Garvolin is similar to the Sokølka, except that Boulonnais blood was added. This has led to some members of this breed being gray.

A smaller Polish draft horse is the Lidzbark, derived from Oszmian horses. These were primitive horses of West European cold-blood stock and the North Swedish breed.

The smallest of the Polish horses is the Kopczyk Podlaski, whose foundation sire was Kopczyk 20, a stallion born in Podlaska in 1921. He was of unknown origin and was crossed with local mares to produce offspring that are small, stout, active, economical feeders and usually bay or chestnut.

Below: A Rhenish-German Cold-Blood standing loose in a field.

RHENISH-GERMAN COLD-BLOOD

Country of origin
Germany.
Height
16-17hh (64-68in).
Color
Chestnut, red roan with flaxen mane and tail, red roan with black points.
Features
This cold-blood was very popular in its heyday at the beginning of the 20th century, but now there is little use for it.

The Rhenish was developed as a breed in the Rhineland less than 100 years ago. Local heavy horses from Rhineland, Westphalia and Saxony were used, but the main foundation stock came from Belgium. The Belgian Heavy Draft was imported in large numbers to establish what was to become Germany's most numerous breed of heavy horses. Some Ardennes blood was also used.

The heavy horses of Germany now make up only 2% of its equine population. The Rhenish is one of four German heavy horse breeds (the others are the Black Forest, Schleswig and South German), and its numbers today are very small.

The Rhenish is similar to the Belgian, with a huge muscular body. Its head is plain, and the neck is short and strong. The body is compact, broad and deep, and the hindquarters are very muscular. The limbs are strong and short and have feather.

RUSSIAN HEAVY DRAFT

Country of origin
USSR (Ukraine).
Height
14·3hh (59in).
Color
Chestnut, bay and roan are most common.
Features
This is one of the smallest of the cold-bloods. It is a popular horse and is agile, active and strong.

This clean-legged, small draft horse was developed in the Ukraine about 100 years ago. Originally it was called the Russian Ardennes, because it was based on the

Above: A Russian Heavy Draft cold-blood. During the 20th century the Russians have developed this breed by crossing native with imported stock.

Belgian imports that were crossed with local cart mares. Together with many other Russian breeds, it was reorganized and renamed in the 1950s.

These active, small draft horses have great longevity. They are used for log pulling and agricultural work in western Russia.

This is a very short-coupled, broad and deep horse. The head is medium-sized, and the neck is short and thick. The withers are flat, the back dipped and the croup sloping. The hindquarters are strong and the legs are short, with a little feather. The action is free and light.

SCHLESWIG HOLSTEIN

Country of origin
West Germany (western area of the province of Schleswig).

Height
15·1-16hh (61-64in).

Color
Almost all are chestnut with a flaxen mane and tail, but a few are grey or bay.

Features
This dumpy cold-blood has a tractable character yet it is strong and energetic and a good mover. This makes an excellent worker.

Schleswig Holstein
(155-163cm)

Shire
(163-183cm)

South German Cold-Blood
(163-168cm)

The Schleswig-Holstein is at the opposite end of the spectrum of cold-blood to the Shire. Compared to the Shire, the Schleswig Holstein is small and dumpy: it stands no more than about 16 hands (64 inches). Indeed, some consider it to be a cob. However, it is derived from distinctive cold-blood ancestors; its neighbor, the Jutland, and its close relation, the Suffolk Punch, have been the strongest influences on the breed. In 1860, the Suffolk Punch Oppenheim LXII was imported from England to become what was probably the most important foundation sire of the breed. His son Munkedal 445 and inbred descendants, Prins of Jylland 1000 and Høvding 1055, were also very important. However, some authorities believe Oppenheim LXII was not a Shire. Because this stallion lived before stud books were introduced, his breed is not absolutely certain.

The Schleswig-Holstein was developed as the breed we know today to meet the demand for horsepower in the 19th century. The Schleswig Breeders' Association was formed at the end of the 19th century to regulate and promote its breeding. A stud book was started in 1891, but it was not until 1938 that the use of the major foundation blood—the Jutland—officially ceased. Other breeds that played a smaller part in its development were the Breton, the Boulonnais, the Thoroughbred and the Yorkshire Coach Horse. These breeds were introduced chiefly to counteract faults such as a too-long back and soft feet. These other breeds also served to lighten the Schleswig Holstein and give it more energy than its cold-blooded ancestors. This enabled it to be useful as an artillery horse and as an animal suitable for heavier draft work on farms and in industry.

The heavy, cob-type Schleswig-Holstein stands low to the ground on short, muscular legs with a little feather. The head is large and plain, with a tendency toward a convex face. The neck is crested, short and thick and merges into the back because there is no distinctive wither. The girth is deep and the front broad, although the body is long and flat.

SHIRE

Country of origin
Britain (Midlands and Fens).

Height
Mares can be 16hh (64in) but males should be at least 16·2hh (66in) and the standard height is above 17hh (68in).

Color
Black is very common. Brown, bay and gray are less common. There should be no large splashes of white.

Features
This massive horse has a docile nature. It is very strong, and is usually able to pull a load of 5 tons. It is quick to mature and is often worked at 3 years old. Because of these qualities, demand for it was heavy in industry, agriculture and transportation. Today, its practical assets, together with its commanding appearance, make it a popular show horse and draft worker for displays and brewery firms.

Right: Shire mare and foal.

The Shire is the tallest, heaviest breed among the cold-bloods. Stallions and geldings are usually over 17 hands (68in) and are often as high as 18 hands (72in). Weight is between 17 and 22cwt (860-1,120kg).

There is much argument about the history of these massive horses. Some say they are descended from the horses William the Conqueror brought to England. More certainly, they are probably descended from the Great Horses and Old English Black Horses of the Middle Ages on which knights rode into battle. Influential continental ancestors must have been the horses of Flanders and the smaller, black Friesians.

The Shire's history becomes clearer in the 18th century, when the Old Black English Cart Horse was popular for draft work. In the 19th century, the Black Horses of the Midlands and the Fens were well-known as some of the most popular cart horses. They were in great demand as transport in fast-industrializing Britain. Some authorities believe Thoroughbred blood was introduced to these types, which could account for the size of the Shire. There was indiscriminate breeding after Waterloo (1815) to meet this demand, and in 1878, a Society was formed (originally named the Cart-Horse Society but later changed to the Shire Society) to try to raise standards and to breed for quality, not just quantity. The breed flourished until well into the 20th century, when mechanization drastically reduced demand.

In recent years, there has been a revival of the Shire. Today, an increasing number of enthusiasts produce these horses for the show ring and for displays. Since shortly before the Shire Society's centenary in 1978, the breed's numbers and quality have improved considerably.

These magnificent horses have

a long, lean head with a slightly Roman nose. The eyes are large and docile in expression; wall eyes are unacceptable. The ears are long and lean, and the neck is long,

Above: A team of Shires at a show. It is rare to drive them four abreast because they are unwieldy, but they do provide a magnificent spectacle.

slightly arched and well-set. The shoulders should slope well. The Shire is deep and broad in the girth, 6-8ft (2-2·5m) for stallions. The back is short, strong and muscular, and the loins are clearly shaped and not flat. The hindquarters are long, wide, well-muscled and let down toward the thighs. The forelegs should be straight, to the pastern. The hindlegs should be well-apart and set below the hindquarters. Sickle hocks are not of value. There should be some fine feather on all the limbs, but the fashion for very hairy animals (defects of the limbs could thereby be covered up) is past. The bone should be flat and strong and should measure 11in (28cm), although 12½in (31·75cm) has been recorded. The feet are wide, with a large circumference around the coronet. The action should be powerful and straight. Mares usually have shorter legs and cannons than stallions and geldings.

SOUTH GERMAN COLD-BLOOD

Country of origin
Germany (Bavaria).
Height
16-16·2hh (64-66in).
Color
Most.
Features
This is the lighter German version of the Noriker.

This is the German branch of the Austrian draft horse, the Noriker (page 64). It has been bred in the Bavarian Mountains for a long time, but during the 19th century, Norman, Cleveland, Holstein, Hungarian, Clydesdale and Oldenburg blood was added to establish this distinctive relative of the Noriker. It is lighter and better adapted to work in the mountains than the Noriker.

Today, the center of breeding is the Marbach State Stud in Württemburg. The Baden State Stud also breeds the South German Cold-Blood together with some Rhenish stock.

The South German Cold-Blood has been the main foundation stock for another German draft breed, the Black Forest Chestnut. This is a smaller version of the South German Cold-Blood with added Rhenish blood. It is used on small farms in the region.

The South German Cold-Blood has been used extensively by the Army for carrying packs and artillery in the mountains. Today, some are still used for this purpose, but usually it is the small mountain farmer who makes use of this breed.

The conformation and action of this breed is similar to the Noriker; it is simply a lighter version.

Below: South German Cold-Bloods being driven at Schwarzwald, which is close to their stud at Marbach.

SOVIET HEAVY DRAFT

Country of origin
USSR.
Height
15·2-15·3hh (62-63in).
Color
Chestnut and roan are most common, but can be bay.
Features
A strong, tractable cold-blood breed, which is found in large numbers in the USSR.

This breed was developed, in western Russia, mainly from Belgian Heavy Horses that were imported from 1850 on. Some other breeds were used in smaller quantities; these included the Percheron, Ardennes and Suffolk, together with some native Russian stock. The result was a lighter, smaller, more-energetic version of the Belgian. It was officially recognized as a breed in 1952.

The Soviet is an early maturer and is used extensively for draft work. The head is of medium size, as is the muscular neck. The body is broad, the back is occasionally weak and the loins are straight, while the croup slopes. The legs are tough but do not have great bone.

SUFFOLK HORSE

Country of origin
Britain (Suffolk)
Height
About 16hh (64in).
Color
Chestnut with no white other than a small star on the face or a few silver hairs on the body. Seven shades of chestnut, from dark to bright, are recognized, but by far the most common is the bright chestnut.
Features
Its great width, in front and behind, and the short legs give the Suffolk Horse a low point of draft and great pulling power. This was recognized early because there is a record of an advertisement for pulling contests (the best of twenty pulls) for Suffolks in 1766. It has long been used on the farms of East Anglia, particularly in Suffolk, but it has also been popular with the Army. The horse has been successfully crossbred.

The Suffolk Horse, also called the Suffolk Punch, is the purest British cold-blood. Its genealogy is traceable into the 18th century. Every member of the breed can be traced to a horse foaled in 1760, and descriptions of his progeny indicate a close resem-

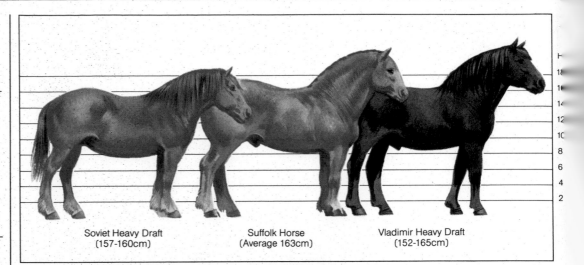

| Soviet Heavy Draft (157-160cm) | Suffolk Horse (Average 163cm) | Vladimir Heavy Draft (152-165cm) |

Above: The Soviet Heavy Draft is one of the largest cold-bloods found today in the USSR.

Below: The Suffolk Horse, also called the Suffolk Punch, comes from East Anglia in England.

blance to the modern Suffolk. Camden's *Britannia* claims that the Suffolk Horse dates back to 1506.

There is evidence that during the 19th century the Suffolk was the best of the British breeds. Representatives won the heavy horse class (when it was open to all breeds) at the Royal Show between 1838 and 1860—14 times out of 23. The Suffolk breed society was formed in 1877, before the Shire's. By the time the Suffolk Society celebrated its centenary in 1977, the Suffolk was less numerous and valuable as a breed.

The Suffolk has tremendous assets: apart from its ability to breed true to color (it is always

Above right: Suffolk Horses are always chestnut and make a good team for demonstrations.

chestnut), it is able to thrive on less food than most horses and has tremendous longevity. It often works well into its 20s and lives until 30. The purity of the breed is proven by the uniformity of color, but there were attempts in the 18th century to introduce a smarter element. Norfolk Trotter, Cob and even a little Thoroughbred were used.

This compact, well-rounded horse stands about 16 hands (64in). The head should is big with a broad forehead. The neck is thick, deep at the shoulders but tapering gracefully toward the head. The shoulders are muscular, long and well-set-back at the withers. The body is broad, deep and rounded, with a graceful outline to the wide level back, the loins and the muscular hind-quarters. The tail is well-set and high. The legs are straight; the second thigh on the hinds is particularly strong. The knees are big, and the hocks long and clean. The particular feature of the breed is its short cannon bones, which have very little feather for a cold-blood. Elbows should not turn in and pasterns should be fairly sloping. The feet are large and round and the horse moves in an active, balanced manner.

Below: The Vladimir Heavy Draft is a modern Soviet work horse. It was first recognized as a true breed in 1946.

VLADIMIR HEAVY DRAFT

Country of origin
USSR (Vladimir).
Height
15-16·1hh (60-65in).
Color
Bay is most common, but some are black and chestnut.
Features
A strong horse that is an all-around draft horse of medium size.

This horse was developed in the province after which it was named at the turn of the 20th century. Today, its breeding is widespread. The imported foundation stock was mainly British, consisting of Suffolk Punch, Clydesdale and Shire. Some Ardennes and Percherons were also used. In 1946, the Vladimir Heavy Draft was found to be breeding sufficiently true to type to consider it a true breed.

This quick-maturing, strong, heavy horse is popular for draft work. It is also used for pulling Vladimir troika sleighs.

The head is large and long, with a Roman nose. The neck is strong and long. The back, although broad, can be weak. The croup is long, with a definite slope. The limbs are long and feathered.

SPORTS HORSES

This century has seen a dramatic change in the use of horses. For over 2,000 years people have depended on them for transport, agriculture, industry and in war. They have provided vital means of power that is now achieved by the internal combustion engine. Today, there is little demand for the horse in its former roles. The total number of horses bred has dropped drastically, though not in all areas. Mechanization has brought us more leisure time. Equestrian sports are becoming more popular, from simple pleasure riding to the highly professional multibillion dollar industry of showjumping and racing.

The governments of many countries sponsor the breeding and use of horses for sport. They do so not simply because it is prestigious, but because riding as a risk sport is a character-building, health-promoting activity.

The number of sports horses is increasing, and many new breeds have been created to meet the demand for horses that have the even temperaments needed to be trained and ridden, and the athletic ability to jump and move well.

Many old breeds, particularly carriage and cavalry horses such as the Hanoverian, have had fresh blood added to make them more suitable for sports and leisure riding.

Sports horses fall into two categories—hot-bloods and warm-bloods. As with the cold-bloods, this term does not refer to a difference in body temperature but to a difference in pedigree and character. Hot-bloods are the breeds with the purest blood in their veins and they have "class" and great spirit. There are only two hot-bloods, the Arab and the Thoroughbred. These famous breeds are the progenitors of most warm-bloods.

The warm-bloods are not so purebred. They were developed through mixtures of hot-bloods, other warm-bloods and sometimes cold-bloods. They are breeds created by crossbreeding and selective breeding to meet current demands. They are not as slow as the cold-bloods nor as high-spirited as the hot-bloods. They have a character that is trainable and suitable for riding and driving.

Right: Monaco, a brilliant event horse, at Badminton, UK.
Below: A Quarter Horse herding cattle.

ARAB

Country of origin
The Arabian peninsula has developed the most famous lines.

Height
14·1-15hh (57-60in).

Color
The originals were chestnut and bay; now can be most strong solid colors. Many are gray. The skin is dark, and the mane and tail are fine and silky.

Features
Stamina, grace, noble shape and outlook, adaptability, intelligence, soundness, longevity, fertility, prepotency and perceptiveness of the senses all make the Arab one of the world's outstanding breeds. Its promoters breed it for beauty and its affectionate nature. They show it, keep it as a pet, ride it and race it. With the Thoroughbred, it is used most often to upgrade and improve other breeds.

Chestnut   Gray   Bay

Arab
(145-152cm)

The Arab is the oldest purebred horse in the world. It is also the most influential. Its blood has been used to improve nearly every other breed. It is the most widespread, with a national breed society found in almost every country. It is easy to understand how with this popularity, a multitude of tales have been told about the past history and origins of the breed.

The "Lady Wentworth school" claims the Arabian peninsula, and in particular the Yemen region in the south, is the true homeland of the Arab. They believe the breed has been there since 5,000 BC. Another claim, made by the German Carl Raswan, is that Nejd, Saudi Arabia, was the main center. The Iranians have always claimed to be the first to domesticate the Arab.

Despite all these rival claims, there is a great deal of evidence the Arab is derived from the proto-Arab type (see page 8), which came from America at a relatively early stage. It spread across the temperate regions from East Asia to North Africa. The belief that the wild ancestor of the Arab occupied this widespread habitat is supported by the discovery of bones similar to the modern Arab in Japan and Western Iran. In both cases bones date back to before the domestication of the horse; this indicates the bones must have belonged to wild horses.

The discovery too of the Caspian (see page 18-19), with its miniature, Arablike features, indicates it was a descendant of a wild horse of Arab type. Later, a prehistoric rock drawing of a horse with Arablike features and a distinctive, concave face was discovered in southern Fezzan in the Libyan Sahara. The picture dates back more than 8,000 years. It seems the wild ancestor was similar to the modern Arab, emphasizing the purity of the breed. It does

Above: The head of this Arab mare shows the finely chiseled features typical of the breed.

not appear to have been a descendant of Przewalski's horse but had its own separate progenitor to that of the ponies and coldbloods. Also, it is unlikely it originated in a small area of desert, and may have wandered over a wide area of the Near, Middle and Far East.

Most of the early stories about the Arab originate from the area around the Arabian peninsula. It was allegedly Noah's great great grandson Baz (3,000 BC) who was the first to capture and tame one of the wild ancestors of today's Arab. Solomon, who ruled Israel from 974 BC to about 973 BC, captured Arabs from Egypt and the Arabian deserts. It is believed he had 1,200 riding horses and 40,000 chariot horses in his stables.

The most famous promoter of the Arab was the Prophet Mohammed in 600 AD. The horse became a foundation stone of his campaign to expand the faith of Islam and the Muslim Empire. The horse played a special part in his religion. Allah was said to have created it, and those who looked after their horses were promised a life in paradise after death. The incentives to breed and care for horses helped build a great Muslim cavalry that

conquered all before it as it moved through Egypt, North Africa, across the Mediterranean into Spain and up into France.

Eventually the Muslims were beaten and pushed back to their homelands, but they left many horses behind. This was the start of the Arab influence on the native breeds of Europe. Almost every modern breed has Arab ancestors.

There are many lines within the Arab breed. The most famous is the desert stock, which is known as the Original or Elite Arab. The major breeders of Original Arabs were the Bedouin —the nomadic tribesmen of Nejd. They needed a horse tough enough to survive a rough, hard life, but beautiful enough to be proud of. Rigorously selective methods of breeding were used

Below: This portrait of an Arab shows the breed's lovely, proud prancing action.

Above: Awtash, a Persian Arab belonging to HRH Princess Anne, gallops free at Windsor, England.

for centuries to achieve this.

The courage and stamina of the mares were tested by using them in battles and for hunting. Stallions were chosen for their beauty, conformation and intelligence. No alien blood was permitted, and tribesmen could quote pedigrees of their stock for many generations. Some in-breeding was practised, which led to the prepotency of the most valued assets—stamina, soundness and beauty.

Some claim it was the Bedouin tribesmen, with their rigorous methods of selective breeding, who developed the Arab breed. But from the evidence discussed above, it seems the modern Arab has changed little from prehistoric times. Man has had little influence on its build or shape.

There are many famous lines spread around the world. The Persian is one of the oldest. The discovery of its bones in western Iran indicates it was indigenous long before domestication. The Persian Arab has been carefully maintained in Iran to the present day and has received only a few injections of desert stock.

The Egyptian type is very old because there is a statue of a ridden horse closely resembling the Arab that dates back to 2,000 BC. This national line is one of the most famous, and its best known promoter was Abbas Pasha, Viceroy of Egypt (1848-1850). The horses he collected are the ancestors of some of the best of

the breed today in the United States, the United Kingdom, and Egypt, where most are kept at the El Zahara National Stud.

Poland has an old and pure line. The early stock arrived with the Turks as war booty in the 16th century but in the 19th century, it became fashionable to collect desert stock. A leader of this trend was Count Rzewuski, who started the Sawran Stud in 1828, with 81 stallions and 33 mares that he collected from the desert. Today, the government promotes their breeding because they have become a valuable export. It runs studs at Janow, Michalow, Kurozweki and Biaka.

The Arab in Hungary has a similar history to that in Poland. Early stock came with the Turkish conquerors in the 16th century, but the main foundation for today's stock came from horses collected from the desert during the 19th century. Babolna Stud became the famous center for Arab breeding, with great sires, such as Shagya and the Bedouin stallion, Kuhaylan Zaid.

The other major European Arab line is in the United Kingdom. The earliest stock came after the Crusades. The horses that came at the end of the 16th and the beginning of the 17th centuries ▶

▶ founded the Thoroughbred. In the sphere of purebred Arab breeding, the stock brought to Britain from Arabia and Egypt at the end of the 19th century was important. The original, highly enterprising collectors were lady Anne and Wilfred Scawen Blunt, who used their imports to begin the famous Crabbet Stud, which was later taken over by their daughter, Lady Wentworth, great Arab authority and promoter.

France has had Arabs for a long time, since the Muslim battles at the end of the 7th century. Two great promoters of the breed were Louis XV, who set up the Pompadeur Stud, and Napoleon, who ordered the import of 221 stallions and 31 Oriental mares.

In Germany, early collectors were the Kings of Württemberg, who founded the Wiel Stud in 1817. Today, the German Central Arab Stud is at Marbach.

Spanish breeds, like the French, were heavily influenced by the Arab and Barb stock left behind by the Muslims in the 7th century. The purebred lines have a more recent origin. Queen Isabella II imported desert stock in the mid-19th century.

In the USSR, too, the Arab has played a vital part in the foundation stock for its breeds. However, purebreds found in Russia can usually be traced back only as far as the 1930s, when Arabs were imported from Babolna, France, the United Kingdom and later as war booty from Poland. After World War II, some Egyptian stallions were added to the purebred stock.

Above: A rider dressed in traditional Bedouin costume poses astride a fine Arab horse.

European countries that bought desert stock today find themselves selling it back to the Middle East. Most of the oil-rich Arab nations are again building up stables of the magnificent Arab horses that were bred for centuries in their deserts.

There is hardly a country in the world that does not have important Arab studs. Those in the United States and Australia are probably developing at the greatest rate. To control the authenticity of pedigrees and to promote the best possible selective breeding, a World Arabian Horse Organization was set up. Today, the Arab is an international breed.

The Arab is often considered the most beautiful of all horses. Its long history of pure breeding is probably responsible for its harmonious proportions and the overall impression of balance.

The head is short, with a prominent forehead, a concave face and a small muzzle. The nostrils are large, and the eyes, set well apart, are large, circular and expressive. The jowl is deep and wide between the branches. The ears are small, alert and curved.

Below: Arabs are popular show horses. This is Prince Mikesha, a winner at The Royal Show at Stoneleigh, UK.

Above: An Arab stallion. The chestnut color with the four white socks is typical. This is one of the original colors of the breed; today, Arabs can be of various solid colors. Below: A handsome gray Arab is shown at the trot in a horse show. Many consider this to be the most beautiful of all horse breeds, with its elegant proportions and free, fast action.

The neck is long and arched. The withers are not too prominent and slope into a strong, level, short back. The shoulder is long and sloping, the chest broad and muscular, and the girth deep. The croup is long and level, the quarters are muscular and the tail is set high.

The limbs have good hard bone and strong, clearly defined tendons. The knees and hocks should also be clearly defined. The pasterns should be relatively long and sloping and the feet hard and round.

With its handsome appearance and action, it is not surprising that this beautiful and aristocratic breed is universally admired and highly valued, both as a purebred and for upgrading other breeds.

The Arab has one less lumbar vertebra in its backbone—five instead of six—than other breeds. It also has one less rib.

This noble breed moves proudly, with its head and tail held high and its ears pricked. In the trot, it takes free, straight strides, but the gallop is its natural pace. It floats across the ground with free, fast strides and has the stamina to maintain speed for exceptionally long periods.

THOROUGHBRED

Country of origin
Britain.

Height
Ranges from 14·2-17·2hh (58-70in), but around 16hh (64in) is average.

Color
Most solid colors.

Features
This is the fastest, most valuable breed in the world. It is used all over the world as a racehorse. Its speed, "class" and elegance are in demand, and the Thoroughbred is used extensively for breeding to upgrade other breeds. It is also crossbred with more substantial, "lower-class" horses to produce "types," such as the hunter, polo pony and hack.

The Thoroughbred is the fastest horse in the world. It is also the most expensive of all breeds and forms the basis of the multi-billion dollar racing industry. Despite many efforts, no one has been able to develop a faster breed. Over the last 100 years no one has been able to improve the Thoroughbred itself—racing times have not become faster, in the same way as those of human athletes.

Records are rarely broken today, yet from the start of the Thoroughbred's development, after the Restoration of Charles II in 1660, until the mid-19th century, records were consistently broken. It took a little less than 200 years to develop this great breed and maximize its potential as a racehorse.

The beginning of this success story must have involved a certain amount of luck when the foundation stock was collected. But British breeders recognized their chance and built on their good fortune, using rigorously selective breeding.

There is little authentic information about the entire range of Thoroughbred foundation stock. We know that prior to the Restoration, Britain's racehorses were a varied group. The original British racehorse—the Galloway Pony—stood a little over 13 hands. Other racehorses included some Oriental stock and halfbreds. But it was Charles II, with his passion for racing, who was responsible for increasing imports of Oriental horses. We also know that in the hundred years following the Restoration, more than 200 Arabs, Barbs and Turks were imported. Of these, about 75% were stallions, and 25% were mares.

From records that exist, it seems few imports were raced. They must have been bought for breeding purposes—to upgrade and establish a type to Britain's heterogenous collection of racehorses.

The records also prove three imported stallions imported

Brown Chestnut Gray

Thoroughbred
(147-178cm; average about 163cm)

Above: The head of Secretariat, an outstanding racehorse in the United States and a successful sire.

produced the offspring on which the breed was based. The Byerley Turk, the Darley Arabian and the Godolphin Arabian are the three sires to whom all Thoroughbreds can be traced.

The first to arrive in Britain was the Byerley Turk, who started life as a charger. He was supposed to have helped his owner, Colonel Byerley, to escape at the Battle of the Boyne (1690). The Colonel then sent him to stand at stud in the north of England. He was used on a large cross-section of mares. It is believed they were British racing mares of Galloway, Spanish, Connemara and perhaps Welsh blood, but the number of Oriental mares was gradually increasing.

At this early stage in the development of the Thoroughbred, there was a good deal of crossbreeding. But by 1704, when the next great sire, the Darley Arabian, arrived in England from Syria, there were mares of the developing breed on which he could be used. He stood in the north of England at the Yorkshire stud belonging to Thomas Darley's brother.

The third great foundation sire, the Godolphin Arabian, was foaled in the Yemen and was bought from the King of France by Edward Coke of Derbyshire. His eventual owner, when he was stood at

the stud from the 1720s, was Lord Godolphin: hence the name. This stallion served mares of a better type. The era of crossbreeding was over, and the Thoroughbred was being consolidated as a breed.

Other imported sires played an important part in the foundation of the Thoroughbred. But because all modern Thoroughbreds can be traced back to one or more of these three, they have become established in the history of Thoroughbred horse breeding as

the foundation sires.

The first "great" British racehorse was a son of Darley Arabian. Named Flying Childers, he was born in 1715; he was never beaten in a race. He passed on his racing ability and it was his great great nephew, Eclipse (born 1764), who became even more famous. He remained unbeaten in 18 races. His progeny, in turn, inherited much of his talent.

Racehorses were becoming faster, but this was no longer due to luck. British breeders rigorously

tested their breeding stock. All except the early imports had to prove themselves on the race-course. Pedigrees became increasingly important. They were kept meticulously, even though they were only private records. Then *An Introduction to a General Stud Book* was published in 1791 and Volume I of the *General Stud Book* in 1808. Any horse entered in these books was entitled to be called a Thoroughbred.

The breeders also changed their aims as they bred faster horses. The original races were over distances ranging from 4 to 12 miles (6·4-19·3km), the weights carried were up to 170 pounds (77kg), and usually finalists had to earn their place by running in a series of heats. To succeed, horses had to be mature and endowed with tremendous courage and stamina. These racehorses were little more than 14·2 hands (58in) and they included the great Eclipse.

At the end of his career, the trend changed. Breeding was becoming big business. Faster returns on investments were needed, and races for younger horses were in demand. With their increasing "class," the developing Thoroughbreds could run faster, but their stamina and weight- ►

Above: Wajima, from the United States, is a magnificent example of the Thoroughbred breed.

Left: A Thoroughbred mare accompanied by her foal.

▶ carrying capacity were sacrificed. Races were shortened so young horses could participate, and speed became the all-important asset.

Speed and early development became the prime criteria for breeders. The horses did not need to be as tough, so they were given more warmth and better food. Gradually they became taller and faster. In the 19th century the normal Thoroughbred's height increased by 6 inches to 16 hands (64in) and speeds on the race-course over the shorter distances improved so rapidly that records were consistently being broken.

By the 1850s, the Thoroughbred had reached its zenith. Between then and the present, there have been few increases in size or speed.

The Thoroughbred was developed as a flat-racehorse, and this remains the main reason for breeding. The largest prices were paid for the horses that had, or appeared to have, the potential to run faster than the others. The most valuable of all are the horses that are at their best as 3-year-olds over 1-1¾ miles. These are called the "classic" distances, and the top races are called "the classics" (such as the Kentucky and British Derby).

Another set of races, the "sprints", cover 5-7 furlongs (1,100-1,590yd, or 1,000-1,450m). The shorter distances suit horses that mature early and have great speed but little stamina. Races that test stamina are for the late-maturing stayers. These are more angular and leggy than the compact sprinters with their powerful quarters. Consequently, there are three categories of flat-race Thoroughbreds: the sprinter, the classic or middle-distance horse and the stayer.

There is a fourth category of Thoroughbred racehorse; those who jump. They race in steeple-chase or hurdle races over longer distances, and the horses must have stamina, toughness and an ability to jump well. Horses are specifically bred for each of these four categories because there are obviously distinct differences in the requirements.

In addition, Thoroughbreds are used for other sports, including hunting, jumping, eventing and dressage. The requirements are different for each event. Substance is needed; so is a good tempera-ment, so the horse can work in harmony with its rider. It's difficult to breed these assets into a Thoroughbred because the major criterion for breeders for nearly

Right: The Thoroughbred breed was created as a racehorse. Here Thoroughbreds are racing at Goodwood Course, England.

Below: A Thoroughbred being trained as a racehorse at Chantilly, northern France.

Below right: Thoroughbreds also race over fences. This is a point-to-point for amateurs.

300 years has been speed and the courage necessary to beat other horses. Consequently, the Thoroughbred is often crossbred with calmer, more robust breeds to produce horses for sports other than racing. This has proved to be another major use for the Thoroughbred—upgrading other breeds, adding "class," elegance and speed to more common horses. Like the Arab, the Thoroughbred has been used to improve other breeds for many years.

Most countries have their own national society that organizes the breeding of their Thoroughbreds. Despite numerous efforts, no other country has been able to develop a faster breed than the British Thoroughbred. Countries all over the world have imported British stock, and now breed their own. Today, the Thoroughbred is even more international than the Arab.

Particular countries have found their soil and climate conducive to breeding top animals. In the United States, breeders started importing Thoroughbreds at the end of the 19th century. Kentucky proved to be the best breeding area. The "blue-grass", combined with huge financial investments in top horses, such as Mahmoud, Blenheim, Nasrullah and Ribot, has led to the current near-supremacy of the American Thoroughbred.

The French Thoroughbred became an official national breed in the 1830s. It has long been a strong competitor to the British Thoroughbred. The French horses are renowned as stayers.

Influential French Thoroughbred sires included Monarque, Le Sancy (a gray), St Simon, Dollar, Brantôme and Galopin.

In 1863, an international race for Thoroughbreds, the Grand Prix de Paris, was started. Two years later, a French horse, Gladiateur, won the British Triple Crown.

Today, French Thoroughbred breeding is carried on mainly around Paris and in Normandy.

Italy's great era was when Frederic Tesio (who died in 1953) bred such fine horses as Nearco, Donatello II and Ribot.

Australia and New Zealand have gradually improved their reputation as Thoroughbred breeders. Other countries all over the world have become major producers of this extraordinary animal.

It is not surprising that with the many categories of Thoroughbreds their conformation varies considerably. However, the best have a refined, intelligent head, an elegant, arched neck, pronounced withers and a sloping shoulder. The back is short, but the body is very deep. The quarters are strong and muscular, and the hock is well let down. The limbs are clean and hard.

The Thoroughbred moves freely, taking long strides with a sweeping, ground-covering action. It can gallop faster than any other horse.

AKHAL-TEKE

Country of origin
USSR (Turkmenistan).

Height
14·3-15.2hh (59-62in).

Color
Pale honey gold, with black points, bay, chestnut, gray and black. Most coats have a metallic bloom.

Features
An ancient breed with endless stamina and an ability to withstand extreme temperatures and lack of food. Originally used as a war horse by the Turkmen warriors, it is now used for racing, competitions and crossbreeding.

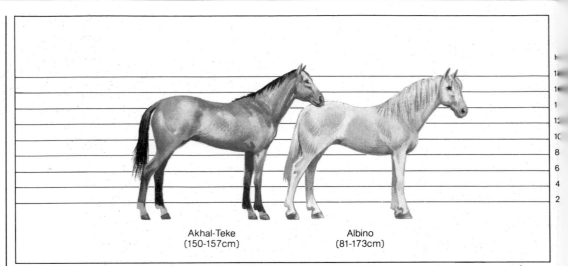

Akhal-Teke
(150-157cm)

Albino
(81-173cm)

The Akhal-Teke is an ancient Russian breed that has been bred in Turkmenistan, Central Asia, for centuries by the Turkmen tribes. This is an isolated area surrounded by mountains and desert. There is substance to the Russian claim that the Akhal-Teke has never been crossed with other breeds; it is a pure breed of ancient lineage (more than 4,000 years) protected by the tribesmen who took great pride in the purity of their horses. On the other hand, some claim it is a descendant of the horses left by the Mongols, who raided the occupied areas in this region during the 13th and 14th centuries. It *is* certain that the Akhal-Teke bears a close resemblance to the Turkoman from Iran, which was said to have

originated in this way. But it could be the Turkoman was descended from the Akhal-Teke.

Whatever its origins, this is a unique, eye-catching breed. It has enormous stamina and the ability to withstand great extremes of temperature. This may be due to its adoption for many centuries as the chief mount of the Turkmen warrior. The Akhal-Teke was used as a charger; so weak specimens were not allowed to survive. Food was difficult to come by in the arid Asian desert, and these horses were tethered and fed mixtures of alfalfa and barley by hand, rather than being set free to graze in herds, like most other breeds.

Is is believed the Akhal-Teke had an influence on the development of many breeds—the Byerley Turk (one of the Thoroughbred's

foundation sires) probably had Akhal-Teke blood. This can't be authenticated because it is too far in the past, but the Polish and West German Trakehner has some Akhal-Teke blood, as do many of the Russian breeds, such as the Don, Karabakh and Karabair. Today, one of the chief bases of the Akhal-Teke is the Tersk stud in the northern Caucasus, where it is being used to evolve new breeds.

The Akhal-Teke is fast, and has great powers of endurance. It has long been used for racing, and attempts were made at the beginning of the 20th century to make it even faster by crossing it with the Thoroughbred. The Anglo-Teke proved to be very fast over long distances, but it remained smaller than the Thoroughbred

and lost its distinctive features. More recently, breeding policies have focused on re-establishing the original type.

The Akhal-Teke's lack of size has restricted its value as a competition horse. However, there have been notable exceptions to this general rule. One of these was the stallion, Absent, who won the individual gold medal in dressage for the USSR at the 1960 Olympic Games. There have been many good show-jumpers, and in 1935 a group of Akhal-Tekes performed an outstanding feat of

Below: The ancient breed of Akhal-Teke is related to the Turkoman Horse. This mare and foal are being shown at the Moscow Exhibition.

endurance when they traveled 2,500 miles (4,000km) from Ashkhabad to Moscow. This epic journey included 3 days spent crossing a desert without water.

The Akhal-Teke is an elegant, narrow, light framed horse. The head is intelligent and beautiful, with a face that is usually straight but can be slightly Roman or concave below the forehead. The eyes are large and expressive, and the ears are long. The neck is straight, long and narrow. The withers are high, and the shoulder has good shape. The body tends to be shallow. The back is long. Often the back and loins lack strength and muscle. The croup is straight to slightly sloping. The tail is set low. The thighs are fine and strong. The forearm is long, the cannons are short and the hindleg is often sickle-shaped. The feet are small and strong. There is little hair in the mane and tail.

ALBINO

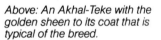

Country of origin
Albinos are found all over the world, but as a breed, they originated in the United States.
Height
32in-17hh (32-68in).
Color
Snow-white or cream with pink skin, and light blue, dark blue (nearly black), brown or hazel eyes.
Features
This unusual color may be found in a wide range of types, from miniature ponies to draft horses. The skin is often highly sensitive to the sun.

The Albino is a color but in the United States the American Albino Association has been formed to establish it as a breed. Although the Albino color (a complete absence of pigment from the skin and other tissues) does appear at random amongst many breeds, in this case, the horses breed true to color, and are *consistently* white. The ability to do this over a number of generations establishes membership of the breed.

The foundation sire of the American breed was Old King (1906), which was claimed to be of Arab-Morgan stock. Careful selective breeding of his offspring has led to multiplication of the Albino color.

Albinos come in all shapes and sizes. The criterion is color, not shape. They are used for general riding, but because of their striking appearance they are in demand for demonstrations and ceremonies. They are popular in parades as flag bearers and for circus work.

Above: An Akhal-Teke with the golden sheen to its coat that is typical of the breed.

Below: An Albino foal born to a Lusitano mare. The characteristic colors of the breed can be

seen—the snow-white coat and the pink skin that surrounds the muzzle and eyes.

ALTÉR REAL

Country of origin
Portugal.
Height
15-15·3hh (60-63in).
Color
Bay, brown and gray are most common.
Features
Athletic, intelligent horses that are popular for general riding. They are most famous as "high school" horses for demonstrating advanced horsemanship.

The Altér Real is a Portuguese breed based on Andalusian blood from Spain. In the mid-18th century, when high-school demonstrations were so popular amongst the courts of Europe, a royal stud was started in Alentejo Province, Portugal. More than 300 Andalusian mares were imported and used as foundation stock. The progeny were intelligent and athletic, which suited the requirements of the court. They wanted horses on which the nobility could ride and show off their skills as horsemen in exhibitions and carousels. These are similar to those now practiced at the Spanish Riding School in Vienna by the Altér Real's distant relative, the Lipizzaner.

The popularity of high-school work and the Altér Real did not last. With the coming of Napoleon at the beginning of the 19th century,

Right: An Altér Real trotting free to show its paces.

Below: Altér Reals being ridden in a display, showing their springy, collected gaits.

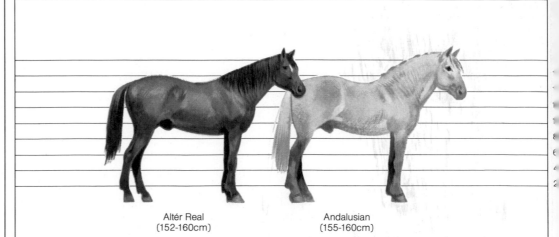

Altér Real
(152-160cm)

Andalusian
(155-160cm)

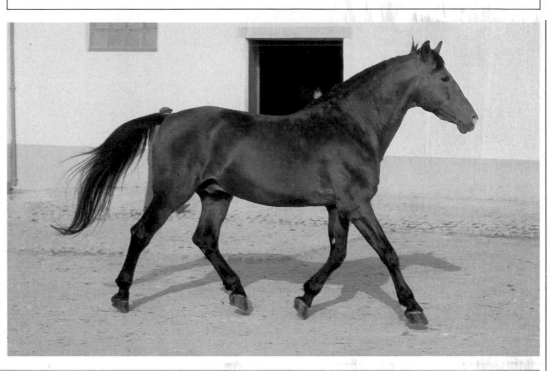

the stud was disbanded and the Altér Real was crossed extensively with other breeds.

By the beginning of the 20th century, the value of the breed began to be appreciated again. Existing Altér Reals were crossed with their original foundation stock, the Andalusian, to re-establish the features of the breed.

The Portuguese government now takes an interest and promotes selective breeding of their national breed. This has led to great improvements, and the Altér Real is again established as a breed famous for high-school work.

The Altér Real is similar to its founder, the Andalusian. It has an intelligent head, with eyes set well-apart, and it can have a convex face. The neck is muscular and crested, the shoulder slopes and the body is short and deep. The quarters are muscular and powerful, and the limbs are strong and well-set.

The action of this intelligent horse is highly valued. It is very athletic, with high knee and hock action. This enables it to take elevated strides, which are so useful in high-school work.

ANDALUSIAN

Country of origin
Spain (Andalucía).
Height
15·1-15·3hh (61-63in).
Color
Gray is most common but this breed can be found in bay, black or roan.
Features
This ancient breed has an eye-catching, high-stepping, athletic movement. It is most famous as a high-school horse but it is also popular for general riding.

The Andalusian is of ancient lineage. Cave drawings in the Iberian Peninsula, dating back 20,000 years to the early part of the last Ice Age, show a very similar type. The Andalusian probably is a direct descendant of the Steppe Horse (see page 8). But experts who believe all horses are descendants of Przewalski's horse claim the Andalusian comes from the Barbs brought over by the Moors in their invasion of the Peninsula in AD 711 and during their long occupation until 1492. It seems possible some of the Muslims' Arabs and Barbs were crossed with the indigenous Iberian horses in Andalucía, a province in southern Spain. But the shape of the Andalusian does not indicate that this breed possesses much Oriental blood.

The Andalusian is important. Its blood is found in the ancestry of many breeds. These include the Kladruber, Nonius, Altér Real, Lusitano, Lipizzaner and many German regional breeds, such as the Hanoverian and Holstein. It

was also the breed that went with the Spanish colonists to North and South America. The Criollo, Paso Fino, Mustang, Peruvian and Appaloosa were based on Andalusian stock.

The major reason for its popularity as a foundation breed was its fame as a high-school horse. From the Renaissance until the French Revolution, the nobility performed high-school work in their courts. All over Europe, carousels and exhibitions became part of court life. The Andalusian, with its tractable temperament, great presence and athletic

Below: Andalusians being ridden in a Pas de Deux in front of a huge crowd. They are extremely skilled performers.

Above: An Andalusian galloping free. This is a very athletic breed as shown by this individual's spectacular stride.

high-stepping paces, was ideal for this demanding work.

The Andalusian's athleticism also made it a good cavalry horse. From the departure of the last Muslims from Spain in the early 15th century until the end of the 18th century, it was in demand all over the world. Its breeding was enthusiastically promoted by the Spanish court.

With the dawn of the French Revolution, European monarchies ran into difficulties. The fashion for high-school was forgotten and, with it, the Andalusian, except by some

of the Spanish monks.

The Carthusian monks in the monasteries of Jerez de la Frontera, Seville and Castello, made an important contribution by selectively breeding the Andalusian for centuries. The Jerez monastery, in particular, maintained these activities when elsewhere the Andalusians' purity was in jeopardy due to crossbreeding to make it heavier. Many were exported, especially during Napoleon's rule. Fortunately, some purebred Andalusians were maintained at the Jerez de la Frontera Stud, and their progeny still live there today.

Today, there are other helpful promoters of the breed. The Spanish government is responsible for a number of studs, run by the army, and it controls private breeding. As a result of this extensive promotion the Andalusian flourishes.

However, the horse is not used extensively. The *Rejonedores (mounted bullfighters)* use them for high-school work in the bullring. They are also used in Spain for demonstrations and for dressage. They are gaining popularity in other countries because of their athleticism, which can make them good jumpers, dressage horses or simply excellent "fun" horses to ride.

The Andalusian's head is large. The forehead is broad, and it has a convex face. The neck is muscular and crested. The shoulder is long and sloping. The wither is prominent and the body is deep and close-coupled. The quarters are broad, muscular and rounded. The tail is set quite low. The limbs are normal length, but the cannons tend to be short. The mane and tail are very long and have an abundance of hair.

ANGLO-ARAB

Country of origin
All over the world, but the French Anglo-Arab is the only well-established breed.

Height
The French Anglo-Arab used to be no more than 15·3hh (63in), but its size has been increased, and some now reach 16·1hh (65in).

Color
Most solid colors, but gray is most common.

Features
A very athletic horse, which has excelled in all types of equestrian sports, from racing to dressage.

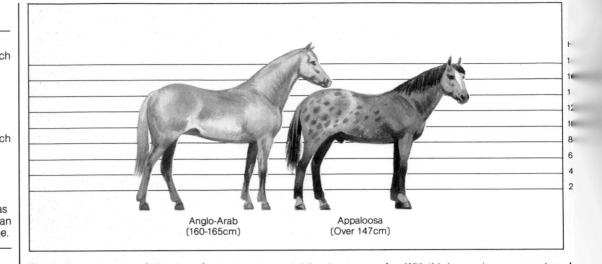

Anglo-Arab
(160-165cm)

Appaloosa
(Over 147cm)

The Anglo-Arab is found all over the world, but in most countries it is a crossbred animal produced by crossing an Arab and a Thoroughbred. In some countries, it has become so well-established that many Anglo-Arabs are the progeny of Anglo-Arab parents. This is the case in France, where they are one of the most popular breeds.

One reason for their development as a breed in France was the existence of foundation mares in the southwest and in Limousin, in central France. These were light horses that had been bred in these areas for centuries.

They had a very strong Oriental influence and appearance. They were known as the horses of Navarre, Bearn and Gascogne, and they were used to develop the breed of Anglo-Arab after its creation in 1843.

The center for the development of the Anglo-Arab was the Pompadour Stud. There purebred Arabs and Thoroughbreds were used, together with the local and south-western mares of Oriental type. From the 1920s, the breed was sufficiently established to use Anglo-Arab stallions.

The Anglo-Arab became popular, first as a mount for the cavalry,

then as a general riding horse and a specialist for competitions. It was the first French breed to be created and bred for use in a wide variety of sporting events, including jumping, eventing, dressage and racing. Races especially for Anglo-Arabs were started in 1874.

With this increasing success, two additional studs, Pan and Tarbes in south-west France, began concentrating on breeding the Anglo-Arab.

The two centers for Anglo-Arab breeding—Limousin and the southwest—produced different types. In the southwest, the breeding aim was speed for the racetrack, so the preferred type was light. In the Limousin, on the other hand, the aim was athleticism and power for competitions, so the resulting type was heavier and stronger.

The success of the French Anglo-Arab as a competition horse has led to it being used to breed France's other competition horses, the Selle Français and the Cheval de Selle. Only 31% of the Anglo-Arab stallions' progeny is Anglo-Arab; the remainder of their offspring are either Selle Français or Cheval de Selle.

In France, there are two divisions of the Anglo-Arab—the Anglo-Arab itself and the Anglo-Arab de Complement. This second division has less than 25% pure Arab blood in its veins.

The French Anglo-Arab has a more consistent build and shape than those in other countries, which quite often resemble their Arab or Thoroughbred parents. The French Anglo-Arab has alert eyes, open nostrils, long ears and withers well back. This gives "a good length of rein" to riders. The shoulders slope well, the back is short, the body is deep, the quarters are powerful and hocks are set low.

The outstanding feature of the French Anglo-Arab is its courageous temperament. Sometimes it is spirited. It also has supple, brilliant paces.

Above: The Anglo-Arab has Arab and Thoroughbred blood. This horse shows features of its forebears—the short, tapering head and flattish croup of the Arab and sloping shoulder of the Thoroughbred.

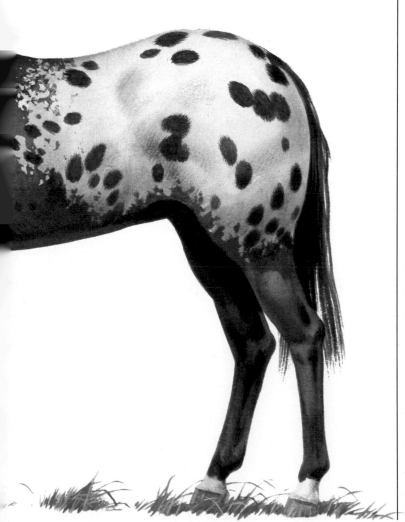

Left: Various spotted horses, all of which are representatives of the breed of Appaloosa.

APPALOOSA

Country of origin
The breed was established in the United States, but spotted horses are found all over the world.
Height
Over 14·2hh (58in).
Color
Spotted; for detailed descriptions of the various patterns, see the text immediately on the right; see also the painting of some of them on the left. Gray and pinto are not allowed.
Features
This strong, intelligent, docile breed has great powers of endurance. It is useful for all types of riding. Its unusual coloring makes each horse unique.

The Appaloosa dates back to the ancient spotted horse that is depicted in cave drawings of prehistoric times. One of the most famous is at Lascaux in central France. The first famous spotted horse was Rukash, the mount of Prince Rustam, who led the Persian armies to victory in 400 BC. Today Iranians claim Rukash was the founder of the spotted horse. This isn't easy to prove, but spotted horses became quite common as mounts of nobility. The Spanish and Neopolitan breeds were particularly noted for the beauty of their spots.

It is believed spotted horses came to America from Spain around 1600. The Indians captured some of them, and their most famous promoters, the Nez Perce tribe,

were riding them by 1730. They bred their horses so that they had the strength, speed and stamina to hunt and travel the mountains, yet the horses also possessed the docility to be handled in camps. This tribe's homelands were near the Palouse River and the horses they bred were first called *A Palouse* by the French. This eventually became "Appaloosa".

In 1877, when the Nez Perce surrendered to the U.S. Army, their horses were dispersed to be sold or left to wander free. Appaloosas were subjected to crossbreeding. The breed was not maintained until Claude Thomson of Oregon began to collect horses from all over the country and selectively breed the Appaloosa. He re-established the quality of the Appaloosa with the help of an injection of Arab blood, and in 1938 the Appaloosa Horse Club of America was established. Today the Appaloosa is one of the foremost American breeds.

The Appaloosa has several distinguishing characteristics. The sclera of the eye is encircled with white, like a human's. The skin is mottled with irregular spots of black and white. These are especially noticeable around the nostrils. Hooves are striped vertically with black and white.

The Appaloosa's coat is variable, and no two horses are identical. There are eight basic patterns:
  1. *Spotted blanket:* Dark forehand with a white blanket over loin and hips with spots.
  2. *White blanket:* Dark forehand and a blanket that has no, or very few, spots.
  3. *Marble:* Base color is dark when born. It eventually fades to nearly white, except for darker "varnish marks" on face and legs.
  4. *Leopard:* Base color is pure white, with evenly distributed black spots over the entire body.
  5. *Near-leopard:* Has leopard markings at birth, but head and legs and possibly even the shoulders are a darker color. This dark coloring usually fades as the horse matures.
  6. *Few spot:* Leopard, with only an odd spot but with some blue or red roan marks. The base color is still white.
  7. *Snowflake:* Base color is dark with white spots. It is often born as a solid color, and spots appear later.
  8. *Frosted tip:* Dark base color with either frost or white spots on loin and hips.

The Appaloosa's head is straight and lean. Shoulders are long and sloping, with a well-defined wither, deep body and strong limbs. The mane and tail have little hair compared with most horse breeds.

Action is free and smooth, which makes this horse good to ride. The variety of types within the breed mean it is used for many activities, including general riding, trail riding, showing, ranch work, parades and gymkhanas, as well as competitions and racing. Its eye-catching appearance makes it popular for exhibitions and circuses.

AUSTRALIAN STOCK HORSE

Country of origin
Australia.
Height
14·2-16hh (58-64in).
Color
Most colors.
Features
An agile, tough, kind horse, it is used for cattle and sheep work. Its type is varied, but it is gradually becoming more uniform.

The Australian Stock Horse Society is responsible for the registration of this group of horses. Its aim is to make them more uniform, but as yet they cannot be said to breed true to type.

The foundation stock was the Australian Waler. Although never a true breed, it was a famous cavalry horse. It served bravely as the standard mount of the Australian cavalry. It was exported to many countries, particularly India, from the time of Waterloo until the 20th century. The Waler was used also to herd stock, for riding and for light harness work, mostly in New South Wales, where its breeding was concentrated.

Original foundation horses came from South Africa and Chile in 1795, and these were of Dutch, Spanish, Arab and Barb background. Thoroughbred was added to establish the tough, agile Waler.

During the 20th century, the crossbred Waler has had more Arab and Thoroughbred added, together with some Percheron and Quarter Horse. It is now called the Australian Stock Horse.

This is a versatile horse and is used extensively on sheep and cattle farms and in rodeos. It is also used for jumping, polo, eventing, endurance riding and some racing.

The Australian Stock Horse is a robust version of the Thoroughbred. It has a light forehand, strong back and quarters and good limbs.

BADEN WÜRTTEMBURG

Country of origin
Germany (south-west).
Height
15·3-16·2hh (63-66in).
Color
Most solid colors.
Features
This athletic horse is based on the Trakehner, and is helping to meet the increasing demand for sports horses.

Apart from the Trakehner, all German warm-blooded breeds

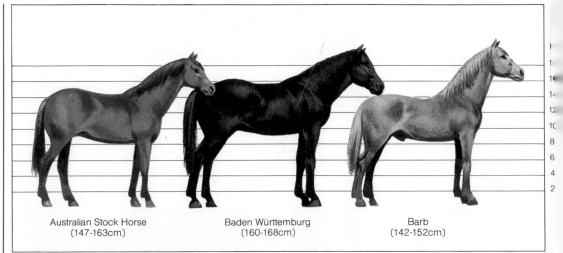

Australian Stock Horse
(147-163cm)

Baden Württemburg
(160-168cm)

Barb
(142-152cm)

Above: The most famous Australian Stock Horse, the World Event Champion Regal Realm. Bred in Australia, he came to Europe as one of the Australian event team and was bought by Lucinda Green.

Below: A Baden-Württemburg horse outside a traditional barn in its homeland of Bavaria.

are regional breeds. Consequently, these horses are given one of nine regional titles according to the area where they were born. For example, the horses born in Lower Saxony are called *Hanoverians* after the main town of this old region of Germany. Horses from the southwest of Germany are known as *Baden-Württemburgs,* and these form the third largest warm-blood breed in Germany, next to the Hanoverians (page 107) and Westphalians (page 144).

The center of the breeding of Baden-Württemburgs is the Marbach Stud. This is the oldest state stud; it was established in 1573. Through the ages, it has produced regional breeds to meet the demands of the time. Today, there are South German Cold-bloods to meet the demand for work-horses and the Baden Württemburg to supply the ever-increasing demand for horses for sporting and leisure activities.

The Baden-Württemburg is a refined version of the older dual-purpose cob type—the Württemburg. This horse was the result of many centuries of cross-breeding between horses from Hungary and Turkey, and later Andalusians and Neopolitans, Barbs and East Friesians, Anglo-Normans and Trakehners. The Baden-Württemburg is, therefore, derived from a variety of sources. In 1895 a stud book was started for the Baden Württemburg.

Today's version of this breed owes much of its athletic movement and elegant good looks to the Trakehner, or East Prussian (page 140). This breed has been used since World War II to give the Baden Württemburg more quality.

Above: A rider from Morocco in traditional dress mounted on a fine-looking Barb.

Below: A Fantasia display in Morocco in which Barb horses are ridden at a gallop.

BARB

Country of origin
Algeria, Morocco, Libya.
Height
14-15hh (56-60in).
Color
Bay, brown, chestnut, black and gray.
Features
An ancient, tough breed with great stamina and the ability to survive on little food. It has acted as important foundation stock for a wide variety of breeds, and is still valued as a purebred in its North African homelands and in other countries, too.

The Barb's original home—and the origin of its name— is the region of North Africa once called Barbary. This area is made up of the modern countries of Morocco, Algeria and Libya. It is likely that Barbs have lived there since prehistoric times, weathering out the cold conditions of the last Ice Age that affected areas as far south as North Africa, even though they were not gripped by ice. The Barb shares many similarities with the Arab, but these could well be due to frequent crossing between the two breeds. Since the time the Muslims invaded Barbary the Arab has been mixed with Barb blood. Yet there are some important distinguishing features between the two breeds.

The Barb has a ramlike head with a straight face and muzzle that is almost as broad as the forehead. This is very different from the small, fine head of the Arab, with its concave face and relatively small muzzle. The hindquarters, too, slope more than those of an Arab, and the tail is set much lower. Finally, the character differs, the Arab being much kinder and more tractable than the quick-tempered Barb.

These distinctions indicate a different background and derivation from the Steppe horse rather than from proto-Arab Oriental stock. Whatever its origins, this tough horse, which is so fast over short distances, has had a great influence on other breeds, most notably the Thoroughbred. Barbs were imported into England in the 17th and 18th centuries and played an important part in the foundation of this great British racehorse.

The Barb cannot be considered a purebred. There has been much crossing in the past with the Arab, and this has continued to the present day, as the crossbred tends to be a more easily trained riding horse.

Today, the Barb is still found in its original homelands. The King of Morocco keeps some of the best examples at his own stud.

The head is long and narrow with a straight face. The neck is crested, the shoulders are flat, the body is rounded and the croup slopes, with a low set tail. The limbs are long, fine and strong. There is an abundance of hair in the mane and tail.

BELGIAN HALF-BLOOD

Country of origin
Belgium.
Height
Minimum of 15·2hh (62in) but the aim is between 16-16·1hh (64-65in).
Color
Most solid colors.
Features
Although this breed originated in the 1920s, it is only since 1975 that these strong, high-quality horses have been bred in sufficient numbers to make an impact in international sports.

Belgian Half-Blood
(157-165cm)

British Warm-Blood
(160-170cm)

Brumby
(Height varies widely)

Belgium has been famous for work horses for a long time, but until recently it imported many of its horses for general riding and sport. A society for the Belgian Half-Blood has existed since 1920. But it was not until 1967, when it was given the right to add the adjective "Royal" to its title, that it began to make an impression and increase the quality and quantity of Belgium's national breeds of sports horses.

The most numerous and most influential stock has come from France. This has included Arabs, Anglo-Arabs, Thoroughbreds and Selle Français. Together they constitute about 60% of the stallions

Below: The Belgian Half-Blood Cyrano, representing Belgium in the 1982 World Show Jumping Championship, Dublin, Eire.

standing to produce Belgian Half-Bloods. There have also been some German and Dutch imports, but the majority of non-French stallions are home-bred Belgian Half-Bloods.

The Royal Society has followed the policies of most other European countries that have started a national breed of warm-blood. They have encouraged the importation of good stock and aided selective breeding through registration, grading mares, testing stallions and providing both financial incentives and prestigious awards for the producers of good breeding stock.

The aim is to produce an athletic horse that is comfortable when ridden. The head should have a broad forehead and small ears and the neck should be long. The shoulders should slope and the limbs should be straight and muscular, with good feet.

BRITISH WARM-BLOOD

Country of origin
Britain.
Height
15·3-16·3hh (63-67in).
Color
Most solid colors.
Features
This new breed of warm-blood exhibits great variations in type and does not breed true. This is due to the range of breeds among the breeding stock. They tend to be athletic and supple, which helps them excel in jumping and dressage competitions.

Britain has many significant breeds and types, but none are specifically bred to be sports horses as are

warm-bloods in continental Europe. From the end of the 1960s, increasing numbers of British riders began going abroad to find horses for jumping, dressage and driving. Import levels rose, and the British Warm-Blood Society was started at the end of the 1970s to offer the continental imports (mainly Hanoverian, Dutch and Danish, and their offspring by recognized British breeds) the same opportunities for selective breeding as exist in the rest of Europe. The aim of the Society is to gradually establish a recognizable and uniform type of British Warm-Blood.

The British Warm-Blood must have at least 50% of recognized continental warm-blood in its veins; for such horses, there are opportunities to register and for breeding stock to be graded and tested.

The result is the steady growth in Britain of high-quality horses with

athletic paces and the robust conformation needed in competitions.

Most British Warm-Bloods tend to be more refined than their European relations. A great deal of Thoroughbred blood is being used in the creation of this new breed of sports horse, which has done well in dressage and showjumping.

BRUMBY

Country of origin
  Australia.
Height
  Varies.
Color
  Most.
Features
  Brumbies are a collection of wild horses that are now close to extinction.

This wild Australian pony was established from imported stock turned loose after the great Gold Rush of 1851. The Brumbies flourished and multiplied, but they also interbred and had to live off poor grazing so their quality deteriorated. Brumbies also proved to be difficult to train so no valuable use was found for them.

Soon, the Brumbies became so numerous they posed a threat to agriculture, damaging fences, grazing land and water holes. For many years, Brumbies were drastically culled, and today few of these horses still roam wild in Australia.

Above: The British Warm-Blood is a new breed type and this horse, Dutch Gold, was one of the first to be registered. Ridden by Jennie Loriston-Clarke, he is a star in dressage and eventing.

Below: Brumbies have bred and run wild in Australia for more than a hundred years.

BUDYONNY

Country of origin
USSR (Rostov region).
Height
15·2-16·1hh (62-65in).
Color
Most are chestnut, but some are bay or brown. Budyonnys occasionally have a golden sheen to their coat that is typical of the Don and Chernomor breeds.
Features
This elegant, intelligent horse was purpose-bred for the cavalry. With the recent addition of more Thoroughbred blood, it is proving to be a high-class sports horse.

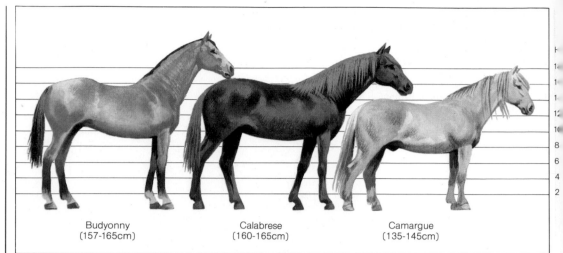

Budyonny
(157-165cm)

Calabrese
(160-165cm)

Camargue
(135-145cm)

The Budyonny is a 20th century Russian breed. Foundations were laid in the 1920s. It was largely encouragement from the Russian cavalry officer, Marshal Budyonny, that led to its official recognition in 1949. He wanted to create the ideal cavalry horse, and the army stud in the Rostov region became the center for the program.

Rigorous selective breeding methods were applied to develop the breed. All breeding stock was thoroughly tested for the features most needed in a cavalry horse—speed, endurance and a tractable character.

The foundation stock used was the Thoroughbred and the breeds of the Cossacks—the Don and the slightly smaller, lighter Chernomor. By 1948, these "outside" breeds were rarely used because the Budyonny had been established and was breeding relatively true to type.

Today, as the demand increases for a riding/sports horse, rather than a cavalry charger, the Budyonny is being refined by

Below: A Budyonny horse; this new breed is becoming very popular in the USSR.

re-crossing with the Thoroughbred. This has made it fast enough to race in steeplechases, and it has won the fearsome Pardubice marathon race in Czechoslovakia. It is also a good mover and is used in dressage, jumping and eventing.

In appearance, it is an elegant, muscular, light horse. Its head is harmoniously shaped, with a straight face. The neck is long, the withers prominent and the shoulder long and sloping. The body is

Above: A Calabrese horse. Today, relatively few are found in their home country of Italy.

deep and close coupled. The loins are muscular, the croup long and rounded. The legs are long and fine but with good dense bone and hard feet.

CALABRESE

Country of origin
Italy.
Height
15·3-16·1hh (63-65in).
Color
Any solid color.
Features
This was a popular saddle horse in the 19th century. Its numbers are now dwindling, although it is a good jumper.

The Calabrese is bred in the south of Italy and Sicily from a foundation stock that consisted of Oriental horses imported from Africa. During the 19th century, it was a popular saddle horse, but today there has been a great deal of interbreeding with the Salerno and the Thoroughbred. The result is there are few purebreds left.

The Calabrese has a fine, rectangular-shaped head. The shoulder is long and sloping, the back is strong and the croup has a medium slope. Limbs are strong and muscular. The hooves are correct and wide.

This is a lively horse but still easy to train. It is frequently used for riding and equestrian sport.

CAMARGUE

Country of origin
France (Rhône Delta).
Height
13·1-14·1hh (53-57in).
Color
Gray.
Features
An ancient breed, that still runs wild in herds in France. When caught and trained, it is an agile, tractable riding horse.

These shaggy, wild horses have roamed the swamplands of the Rhône Delta in the south of France for centuries. Their history is obscure. It is possible they are descendants of the prehistoric horses whose fossils were unearthed at Solutré in southeast

France. It is probable they have been subjected to crossbreeding from the horses brought into the area by Romans, Saracens and Moors. These influences probably included Arab and Barb because features of both are apparent.
In the 19th century some attempts were made to introduce Thorough-bred, Arab, Anglo-Arab and Breton blood. But none were effective in changing the rugged, wild features of this breed, which has caught so many people's imagination.

Today, Camargues still run wild on their damp, reedy homelands, which are hot in summer and bleak in winter. They roam in small herds, consisting of one stallion, mares of all ages and colts to 3 years old. There are regular roundups when foals are branded. Three-year-old colts not good enough to remain as stallions are caught and gelded. Stock is selected to be broken and trained. Catching and breaking Camargues is difficult. Initially they are wild creatures, but once they have been trained to accept human commands, they make good rides.

Trained Camargues are used extensively in the Delta. Their long-term use has been as cattle-herding ponies for the "Gardiens," the cowboys of the Camargue.

One of the most important agricultural activities in the Camargue is the breeding of small black bulls; the tamed, wild horses are used for herding, surveying and rounding up the bulls, and taking them to the bullring at local fairs.

The Camargue must be tough, strong and sure-footed to survive on the lonely marshlands. These qualities have made it a good work pony, able to carry heavy packs. It is also an ideal mount for tourists who take guided tours across the wild and beautiful Delta. It is good for this purpose, not only over the rugged area to which it is indigenous but also in other parts of France.

Since 1968, the Camargue has been officially recognized as a breed. Together with the formation of a Breeders Society, this has led to wiser selection of breeding stock. Even though they are allowed to run wild and breed, only the better stallions and mares are allowed to remain free when they reach the age for breeding. This is leading to distinct improvements in the quality of the stock.

The Camargue is robust rather than elegant. Its head is large and rectangular with a straight face. Ears are short with large bases

and are placed more to the side than those of other breeds. The shoulder is straight and short, and the back is short. The quarters are short, with a slightly sloping croup. Limbs are strong and of a good shape. The knees are large, and the feet are hard.

The Camargue is slow to mature, but lives to a great age. It can exist on very poor fare and is exceptionally robust. It is justly famous for its exceptional powers of endurance.

Above: A group of Camargue horses roam free in the wild region of south-eastern France in the Rhône Delta, after which they are named.

Below: A portrait of a typical Camargue horse.

CLEVELAND BAY

Country of origin
Britain (Cleveland).
Height
16-16·2hh (64-66in).
Color
Bay, with black points (black legs, mane and tail). No other color is permissible; only a small white star and gray in the mane and tail are allowed.
Features
This bay horse is the oldest established breed of English horse. It has great substance, stamina and strength, with a fine appearance and a tractable temperament. These characteristics make it suitable for riding and driving.

Cleveland Bay
(163-168cm)

Criollo
(142-152cm)

The Cleveland Bay has been bred in Cleveland, northeast England, for centuries. It is believed the original stock dates back to the work horses brought to England by Romans. It is certain that from medieval times a clean-legged bay animal was popular in this area. It was also called the "Chapman Horse" because before the advent of wheeled carriages, horses were ridden or used as pack animals. The chapmen, or traveling salesmen, used Clevelands to carry their wares.

Farmers also used them and valued them as all-purpose animals, for work on the land as well as

riding. When wool was Yorkshire's chief export, Clevelands were used as pack animals, carrying huge loads from the farms to the mills. It is thought likely that the pack and riding horses of these times had a little of the Yorkshire racing Galloway blood in them. It is certain two of the original Thoroughbred foundation sires had an influence through Manica (1707), a son of the Darley Arabian, and Jalap (1750s), a grandson of Godolphin Arabian.

Since the time of Jalap in the 1750s, there have been no further injections of Thoroughbred blood into the purebred Clevelands.

However, Thoroughbreds have been crossed with many Clevelands. The progeny became so popular that in the late 19th century, a

breed based on additional Thoroughbred blood was established and named the Yorkshire Coach Horse. This "classy" carriage horse became a fashionable means of pulling elegant, light vehicles until the era of carriages ended. The breed passed into extinction in the 1930s.

It is as a carriage horse that the Cleveland excels; its consistent color makes matching pairs and teams easy. Its tractable temperament facilitates training, while its strength enables it to pull large, heavy loads. During the 19th century it was popular for this purpose. By then farmers were using it for general riding, hunting, farm, draft and carriage work. In 1884, a Cleveland Bay Horse

Society was started to ensure the continuing purity of this multi-purpose breed.

With the demise of horse power in the face of tractors, trucks and cars, the Cleveland has been put to new uses. As a purebred, it is shown, hunted and driven, but partbreds are earning the most fame. They have made Olympic show jumpers, international dressage and event horses and combined driving champions.

Below: Cleveland Bays are most famous as carriage horses. This team of four is being driven by HRH Prince Philip of Britain.

HRH Prince Philip has successfully driven for Britain with a homebred team (consisting of 4 horses) of partbreds.

The Cleveland has long been important in breeding. It was used extensively in Germany during the 18th and 19th centuries to lighten the native breeds for use as high-class carriage horses. The Holstein, Hanoverian and Oldenburg all benefited from influential injections of Cleveland blood.

The Cleveland's head is large, with a straight face. Eyes are large, ears are long, the neck is long and lean and the shoulder is sloping and deep. The body is wide and deep, the back is muscular and not too long and quarters level, long, and powerful. Limbs are strong, with at least 9in of flat bone below the knee. Arms and thighs are muscular, and knees and hocks large and well-closed. The legs are clean with no superfluous hair. The feet are black in color, and good shape. Those that are shallow or narrow are undesirable.

The Cleveland Bay moves freely with true, straight action. Although the hock and knee flex, strides are sweeping and ground-covering rather than rounded and springy.

CRIOLLO

Country of origin
Argentina.
Height
14-15hh (56-60in).
Color
Dun with dark points, and a dorsal stripe, is most common, but Criollos can be red or blue roan, chestnut, bay or palomino.
Features
This compact, sturdy breed has great powers of endurance and the ability to withstand temperature extremes. It can survive on very little food.

The Criollo is Argentina's native horse. It was derived from stock brought to the country by the Spanish in the 16th century that was thought to be of Andalusian, Barb and possibly even Arab blood.

Legend has it that this foundation stock came from the cavalry horses that sailed across the Atlantic in a ship in 1535. Buenos Aires was sacked by the Indians soon after their arrival; the horses escaped to run wild on the South American pampas.

For over 300 years, these horses, which were probably joined by other escapees, bred naturally. The tough environment, with its temperature extremes, ensured that only sound individuals survived to continue breeding.

The Criollo developed into a very

tough horse, and it acquired a colored coat that aided its safety by camouflaging it. Dun became the predominant color among Criollos; the color blends in well with the sandy pastures of the Argentinian pampas.

The Argentinians discovered they had a tremendous asset running free in their country. Criollos were captured, tamed and bred as mounts for the Argentinian cowboys, or *gauchos*. The horse proved to be ideal for cattle herding, being quick, agile, maneuverable and intelligent. They also made strong ponies for pack work and were good mounts for those who wanted to ride for pleasure.

The Criollo has found another important use in the 20th century. It is often crossed with the Thoroughbred to produce the famous Argentinian polo pony.

A notable feature of the Criollo is its great powers of endurance. The most famous test of this was when Professor Aimé Tschiffely took two ponies, Mancha, 15 years old and Gato, 16 years old, on a 13,350 miles (21,485km) trek from Buenos Aires to New York, using them alternately as a mount and packhorse. This journey involved crossing some of the world's bleakest deserts and highest mountain ranges. Both horses coped with temperature extremes of well below freezing and higher than 100°F, (38°C) and they endured the thin air at altitudes of almost 20,000ft (6,100m).

The Criollo's head is broad, with

a straight face. Eyes are set well-apart, and the ears are alert. The neck is muscular, the withers clearly defined, the shoulder strong and the chest broad. The body is deep, the back short and loins are muscular. The croup slopes, and the quarters are rounded and muscular. Limbs are strong, with good bone and short cannons, and the feet of this tough breed are small and hard.

Below: this Criollo is being ridden in a demonstration.

Above: Criollos grazing free in their native lands of Argentina.

The Criollo has many close relatives in South America. Breeds were founded in other countries under the same conditions. The horses of the Spaniards and Portuguese were set free to adapt to local conditions and to breed in a wild state. These include a slightly smaller version in Brazil, called the *Crioulo*, and a lighter-framed horse in Venezuela, called the *Llanero*.

DANISH WARM-BLOOD

Country of origin
Denmark.
Height
15·3-17hh (63-68in).
Color
Bay is common, but horses are found in all solid colors.
Features
A new breed of warm-blood that has proved itself to be a top-class competition horse.

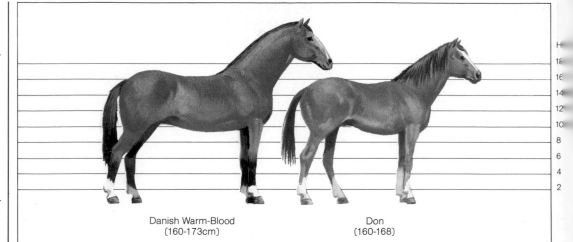

Danish Warm-Blood
(160-173cm)

Don
(160-168)

The Danish Warm-Blood is one of the new national breeds of sports horse. Denmark is famous for breeding horses, but in the post-World War II years, it had to rely on importations to mount most of its serious riders. In the 1960s, two societies, which later joined together, were established to lay the foundations for a national breed.

Unlike breeders in other European countries, the Danes could not rely on government assistance. Through private initiative, good foundation stock was imported from Germany, Sweden and Britain. Strict selective

methods of breeding were imposed, and the result was that by the 1980s, Denmark had become a foremost producer of sports horses. It has reversed its status from being an importer of horses to an exporter. Breeders produced great champions, such as Monacco (1979 European Three-Day Event Champion, 1980 substitute Olympic Champion) and Marzog (1983 European Dressage Champion, 1984 Olympic silver medallist).

Danish horses are famous for their generous, tractable temperaments and their athletic movement. As with most new warm-bloods, a variety of types are registered in the studbook.

Above: The Danish Warm-Blood 3-Day Event champion, Monaco.

Right: Marzog, the Danish Warm-Blood that won the 1984 Olympic Silver medal.

Left: A portrait of the Danish Warm-Blood.

DON

Country of origin
USSR.
Height
15·3-16·2hh (63-66in).
Color
Chestnut and bay are most common, often with a golden sheen.
Features
This Cossack horse has great stamina. It can survive extremes of temperature and live off frugal fare.

The Don is the famous Russian Cossack's horse. The extraordinary toughness and courage of this breed became renowned after Napoleon's Russian campaign. When Napoleon retreated to France in the dreadful winter weather of 1812, he lost many thousands of his French horses. Yet the Russian Cossacks, and their Dons, were tough enough to survive the appalling conditions, and continued to attack the French, driving them all the way back to their homeland, and then made the long return journey to Moscow. This feat is without equal in cavalry history.

At the time of this great achievement, the Don was a comparatively new breed. It had been developed in the steppe country around the rivers Don and Volga. It is still bred there. In this early stage in its development, it was smaller and more robust than it is today. It had been based on the horses of the nomadic steppe tribes but was refined with additions of Turkoman and Karabakh, and later the Thoroughbred and Orlov. In the 20th century, it has been purebred, with no additional outside blood added.

Part of the toughness and stamina of the Don must be attributed to the way it has been bred. Herds of Dons run free on the steppes and must be sound to survive the bleak and extremely harsh winter conditions.

The cavalry no longer needs large quantities of Dons. However, they are still in demand for general riding and endurance riding—a sphere in which they excel. In competitions, their successes have been limited because they are rather short striding.

The Don has been used to improve other breeds, in particular to give them greater stamina. The Don has been particularly influential as foundation stock for the development of the Budyonny, and in the improvement of the Kazakh and Kirghiz.

The Don's head is Thoroughbred-like, with breadth between the eyes. The neck is medium length. The shoulder tends to be upright. The back is straight and broad. Legs are long and strong, but there is a tendency for the pasterns to be upright. Feet are quite large.

Above: Don horses pulling a troika. This is a traditional means of driving them in the USSR.

DUTCH WARM-BLOOD

Country of origin
The Netherlands.
Height
15·3-16·3hh (63-67in).
Color
Most solid colors.
Features
This new breed of warm-blood is divided into types. This variety ensures there are Dutch horses available to fulfill a wide range of demands from riders and drivers.

The Dutch Warm-Blood is a new breed, which like its Danish equivalent, was started in the 1960s to meet the rising demand for sports horses. The Dutch used their heavy mares—the Groningen and Gelderland—as foundation stock. They also brought in Thoroughbreds, Anglo-Arabs and Arabs. In the 1980s seven Lipizzaner stallions were included among the breeding stallions.

The Dutch Warm-Blood Society covers a wide range of horses and aims to breed five types. There is the sport horse, which should be sound with excellent conformation and movement, good character and temperament, and capable of good performance in show jumping, dressage and eventing. The second type is the riding horse, with 25% or more Arabian or Anglo-Arab blood. The carriage horse, which is similar to the old Dutch breeds, with high-stepping gaits, great power and grace, is the third type. The fourth type is the basic horse, which is a heavier horse with the old Gelderland and Groningen lines, and is suitable for riding and driving. Finally, there is the Lipizzaner-bred type, used for riding and driving.

These types have one factor in common—the breeding stock is strictly graded, and rigorous selective methods are imposed.

Dutch horses are famous for their docile, likable characters, athletic, rounded paces and muscular quarters. The breeding aim is a noble, likable horse with an honest character. The constitution should be strong and the average height about 16·1hh (64in). Movement should be easy, supple, strong, balanced and rhythmical, with a natural forward urge.

Dutch horses have excelled in all competitive disciplines. Tjeerd Velstra won the World Driving Championships with a Dutch team. Other notable examples are Calypso, who won the World Cup Show jumping for America, Oran who won the European Three-Day Event Championship for Switzerland, and Limandus, who won the silver and bronze medals for Switzerland in dressage at the 1984 Olympic Games in Los Angeles.

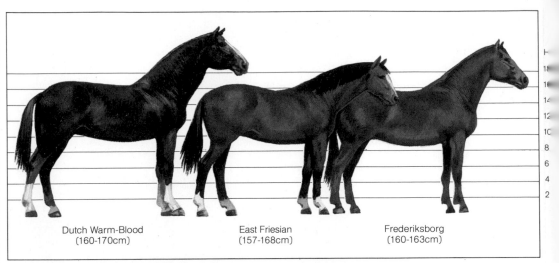

Dutch Warm-Blood
(160-170cm)

East Friesian
(157-168cm)

Frederiksborg
(160-163cm)

EAST FRIESIAN

Country of origin
East Germany.
Height
15·2-16·2hh (62-66in).
Color
Most solid colors.
Features
A powerful all-around horse, that can be used for riding and driving.

The East Friesian, from East Germany, is based on its neighbor from West Germany, the Oldenburg (page 123). It was developed in the 19th century, and a few other breeds were used to lighten it. These included British, Polish, Hungarian and Spanish horses. Since the partition of Germany, the East Germans have relied on the Arab and Hanoverian for this refining admixture.

The East Friesian is a handsome, strong, all-purpose horse used for riding, competition and harness work.

Left: The famous Warm-Blood, Calypso, being ridden for the USA.

Below: Dutch horses are famous as carriage horses.

foundation stock. Today, there is only a small number of purebreds left (about 250 mares), and few are good quality. The breed has been weakened by crossbreeding and attempts to lighten it to meet modern riding demands.

The Frederiksborg was named after the stud where it was bred, north of Copenhagen. It was founded in 1562 by King Frederick II. He was a keen horse breeder and developed this breed to perform the high-school work that had become so popular in the courts of Europe.

Andalusian and Neapolitan horses were used as foundation stock. Later, Oriental and British half-bred stock was introduced. The Frederiksborg became such a high-class horse that it was used all over Europe as a high-school, cavalry and harness horse. During the 18th century, the Frederiksborg was even used to upgrade Lipizzaner stock.

Frederiksborgs were so popular that many were exported. Stock became poor, and in the mid-19th century the Danish stud, which had survived for almost 300 years, was forced to close.

Today, efforts are being made to preserve this breed which has given Denmark so much prestige in the past.

The Frederiksborg is a strong horse, with a large, plain head, a straight face and big ears. It has a powerful shoulder, and a long, strong deep body with a flat croup. Limbs have good bone.

Above: A fine example of the all-purpose East Friesian breed.

Below: A typical Frederiksborg, with its flaxen mane and tail.

FREDERIKSBORG

Country of origin
Denmark.
Height
15·3-16hh (63-64in).
Color
Chestnut is most common.
Features
An honest, strong athletic breed that has been used all over Europe as a cavalry, high-school and harness horse. For the last 100 years, it has been close to extinction.

The Frederiksborg was a famous Danish breed during the 17th, 18th and 19th centuries, when it was exported to many countries and used for upgrading and as

Below: Frederiksborg horses have been used for many purposes, from serving as cavalry mounts to working in harness.

FRENCH TROTTER

Country of origin
  France (Normandy).
Height
  Varies, but an average is 16·1hh (65in).
Color
  Chestnut, bay and brown are most common. Gray is rare, but some are roan.
Features
  The French Trotter has competed against the best harness racers in the world. It is a more robust breed, with greater stamina, than other breeds of harness racers. It is used for jumping, general riding and breeding riding horses.

This breed was developed in the 19th century in France, although it was only officially recognized in 1922. The stimulus for its development was the growth of harness racing. The first French Trotting course was opened at Cherbourg in 1836, and it was so popular that within years, five more courses started in and around Normandy.

Horses were needed for this fast-developing sport. British stock was imported to supply speed and trotting ability when crossed with Normandy mares. The most influential examples of the British blood were the Norfolk Trotter called The Norfolk Phenomenon and a Thoroughbred named The Heir of Linne. These gave rise to Anglo-Normans; the foundation lines of the breed were Lavater, James Watt, Phaeton, Cherbourg and, most important, Fuschia. The development of the French Trotter and Anglo-Norman (later to be called the Selle Français) ran along a parallel, overlapping route during the 19th century and only became different breeds in the 20th century.

The sport of harness racing soon spread; courses opened around Paris, beginning in the 1870s. The fastest horses were most desired and some American harness horses, which had been so successfully developed into the Standardbred, were imported. The use of outside Trotter blood was limited, and in 1937 the French stud book was closed.

An unusual form of harness racing is practiced in France, which also helps the breeding of Trotters. In these mounted races, the horses must have the substance, strength and soundness to carry the weight of the rider. Therefore speed is not the only breeding criterion.

Consequently French Trotters are more robust than other national breeds of harness horses. This makes them suitable for a variety of activities. Some are used for general riding and jumping, and many are used to breed riding horses, particularly the Selle Français (see pages 132-133).

The Trotter is bred all over

French Trotter
(Average 165cm)

Friesian
(150-160cm)

Above: Close-up view of the head of a French Trotter.

France, but the original area of development of the breed in Normandy remains the most important. Two studs, at Haras du Pin and Haras de Saint-Lo, are still the centers for breeding these impressive horses.

The French Trotter varies in type, from those that closely resemble the Thoroughbred to the more old-fashioned type, which is much sturdier, with straight shoulders and rounded action. The one area they all are strong in is the hindquarters. These tend to be short, with sloping croups and tremendous muscle power. Limbs are well-formed, hard and sound.

Below: The French Trotter is a particularly robust harness horse.

FRIESIAN
(Frisian)

Country of origin
  Holland (Friesland).
Height
  14·3-15·3hh (59-63in).
Color
  Black. A small star is permissible.
Features
  This old breed is renowned for its great "presence" and its very fast trot, with showy high-knee action. It is a part of Holland's past and is often used in demonstrations of historical pastimes, as well as in driving competitions and for general riding.

The Friesian cow and horse were developed in northern Holland, in the province of Friesland, which is famous for its rich grasslands. Horses have existed in this

province for a long time—the bones of a heavy horse from thousands of years ago have been unearthed there. The Romans favored and used a horse from Friesland. It is believed they took it with them to England. There the horse influenced many breeds, including the Fell, Dales and Clydesdale (see pages 28-29, 22-23 and 56 respectively).

It is certain the Friesian was very popular in medieval times; there are many pictures of knights mounted on these showy, stocky, black horses.

One of their great assets is a very active, fast trot. They flex their legs very high, which is spectacular to watch. In the 18th and 19th centuries, this speedy trot was valued, providing a fast, fashionable means of travel. The Friesian was used extensively to inject this asset into other breeds. It was exported to Russia to influence the Orlov Trotter (page 124), to England to affect the Norfolk Trotter (page 195) and, through this latter breed, the American Morgan (pages 118-119).

Friesians were used in trotting races, but the development in the 19th century of specialized harness breeds (such as the French Trotter) led to their eclipse.

The demand for the Friesian for crossbreeding led to the adulteration of the purebred stock, so in 1879 a Friesian Herdbook Society was started to ensure the continuance of the breed. It was not an easy task because the demand

for Friesians fell with the approach of the 20th century. Mechanization led to their demise as a speedy means of transportation.

Another important demand for the breed had been from farmers who used them for pasture maintenance. But with the advent of tractors, the Friesian became redundant also in this sphere.

Recently the Friesians' fortunes have taken a turn for the better. Their ability as carriage horses has been put to good use; Tjeerd Velstra won a silver medal in the

European Championships with a Friesian team. They are also used for demonstrations.

Because they are always black, color matching is no problem. Their willing, gentle character means they are easily trained. Their showy action and spirited way of going makes them spectacular to watch. They can be ridden or driven and are often used in circus work.

The Friesian has a fine, long head with alert, expressive eyes and short ears. The neck is crested, shoulders and back are strong,

Above: The black Friesian horses from Holland are famous as circus and driving horses.

quarters are well-rounded and the tail is set quite low. Limbs are strong, with good bone. There is a lot of hair in the mane and tail and feather on the legs.

The legs are sometimes covered with hair right up as far as the knee joint.

Right: A Friesian horse, one of the oldest of all European breeds.

GELDERLAND

Country of origin
Holland (Gelderland).
Height
15·2-16·1hh (62-65in).
Color
Chestnut, bay or gray.
Features
Bred as a utility farmhorse, the Gelderland is a strong, willing worker. With little demand for it from mechanized farms, very few remain.

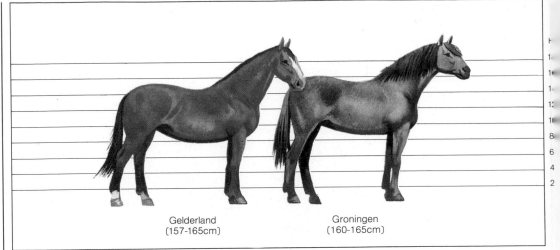

Gelderland
(157-165cm)

Groningen
(160-165cm)

The Gelderland is a utility farm horse bred in the Dutch province after which it is named. It was developed from the native breeds of the area and mixed with Thoroughbreds, Norfolk Trotters, Holsteins and Anglo-Normans. The intent was to provide farmers with a horse that could work the land, pull carriages and be ridden, similar to the Irish Draft and Cleveland Bay. The Gelderland was used extensively on the farms during the 19th century. The demand for it has declined, but until the 1950s it was used by many farmers.

As the demand from agriculture declined, the Gelderland was converted into a coach and riding horse. Holstein, Trakehner, Anglo-Norman and Thoroughbred horses were used to refine the breed. In the 1960s, another use was found for the Gelderland — it served as foundation stock for the Dutch Warm-Blood. This crossbreeding, together with the small demand for farm horses, led to near-extinction of the breed. Steps have now been taken to ensure its survival.

The Gelderland forms an important section (basic type) in the Dutch Warm-Blood studbook.

Today, Gelderlands are used for general riding and harness work. They are also popular as show horses in the Netherlands.

The Gelderland has a plain head but an honest, gentle outlook. The face is straight to convex, and ears are long. The neck is strong and crested, the shoulder is deep and sloping, the body is deep and powerful, the croup hardly slopes and the tail is set quite high. Limbs are clean, well-formed and have good bone, so that the Gelderland has the appearance of an animal of substance.

Below: With their quiet temperaments, Gelderlands can make good driving horses, as this splendid team of four shows.

GRONINGEN

Country of origin
The Netherlands.
Height
15·3-16.1hh (63-65in).
Color
Black, bay, brown or dark brown.
Features
This strong utility horse nearly became extinct in the 1970s when only one stallion remained. The Dutch authorities have ensured its preservation.

The Groningen is the Netherland's second utility farmhorse; its breeding areas are in the north of the country. The Groningen is larger and heavier than the Gelderland. It has been based more on the bigger Oldenburg and East Friesian breeds (the East Friesian is the East German version of the Oldenburg). Some British Suffolk blood was used in the 19th century. This made it into a strong

Right: A Groningen mare. This heavy breed of Warm-Blood often has a flat croup (or rump), as shown by this mare.

horse, greatly valued by farmers.
Like the Gelderland, mechanization meant less demand for it, and attempts were made to lighten it into a useful riding and harness horse. It is used for these purposes today. Like the Gelderland, it is used also as foundation stock for

Below: A Gelderland mare and her foal in the field.

the Dutch Warm-Blood. Its powerful quarters are an asset needed in a riding and competition horse.
Groningen numbers declined drastically in the 1970s, but this decline has now been halted. Oldenburgs are being imported and used to ensure against too much inbreeding. Today, the Groningen is being carefully preserved. Like the Gelderland, it is established as a basic type in

the same section of the Dutch Warm-Blood studbook.
The Groningen has a long head, with a straight face, and long ears. The body is deep and powerful. Limbs are a good shape with good flat bone. The feet are round and strong. The tail is set quite high and it is carried gaily. The croup of the Groningen is relatively flat and the quarters are muscular.

HACKNEY HORSE

Country of origin
England (Norfolk, Cambridge and Yorkshire).
Height
14-15·3hh (56-63in).
Color
Bay, dark brown, chestnut or black.
Features
The brilliant action of this elegant, small horse originally made it a fashionable, fast means of transport. Today it is a feature item at many shows.

Hackney Horse
(142-160cm)

Hanoverian
(160-173cm)

"Hackney" may be derived from the Old French word "haquenée" which means "horse for hire". That is how the ancestors of this spectacular high-stepping horse used to work. Harnessed to light vehicles, they were available for hire in London, just as taxi-cabs are today. The original hackneys were rather cobby trotters, and the breed was developed, like the Hackney Pony (see pages 30-31), from the older British regional breeds of trotter, the Yorkshire and Norfolk Roadsters (see page 195).

The Hackney was derived from some of the best of the Norfolk Roadster stock. One of the most famous sires was Shales the Original (1755). Shales could be traced back, via foundation stallions, to the Thoroughbred: he was by Blaze, the son of Flying Childers, who was by Darley Arabian, one of the chief ancestors of the Thoroughbred. Another famous sire was Fireways, whose son, The Norfolk Cob (1829), out of Shales's Mare, is reported to have trotted at 24 miles per hour. This high-class speedy Norfolk blood was crossed with Yorkshire Roadster mares, and the result was the Hackney.

The Hackney, together with the Roadsters, thrived from the early part of the 19th century until the advent of the railways. Horses provided a speedy, elegant means of travel along the newly macadamized roads. However, the railways reduced the demand for horses. The sturdier, less-spectacular breeds of Roadsters died out, but the Hackneys, with their high-stepping action, continued to be fashionable mainly as show animals.

In 1878, serious efforts were made to organize a society. The original meeting was at Downham Market in Norfolk, but it was not until 1883, at Norwich, that it was agreed to start a stud book for Hackneys, Roadsters, Cobs and Ponies. Eminent names were soon involved; the Prince of Wales became Patron to the Hackney Society. This helped to make the breed very fashionable, and the Society an active, prosperous organization.

Hackneys are still exported all over the world. Even after the automobile had superseded them

Below: Hackneys being driven to a carriage called a "unicorn" at the Royal Windsor Show, UK.

Above: The Hackney has great presence, with head held high and brilliant action.

as a means of transport, they were kept for demonstrations and showing. They became known as "the ballerinas of the show ring," with their volcanic personality and brilliant action. Today, they are a feature item in the show ring in many countries.

The Hackney has a small head, with a convex face, large eyes, small ears and a small muzzle. The neck is long and well-formed. The shoulders are powerful, with low withers. The body is compact, with a broad chest. The tail is well set on the quarters and carried high. The forelegs are straight, with gently sloping pasterns and well-shaped feet. The hocks are well let down. The coat is fine and silky.

The action is a striking feature of the breed. The legs must be raised high enough and thrown forward far enough to cover the ground, not just raised up and back. The head should be carried erect but not too high or too low. The ears should be pricked. The whole animal should be a living portrait of elegance and beauty.

HANOVERIAN

Country of origin
Germany (Lower Saxony).
Height
15·3-17hh (63-68in).
Color
Most solid colors.
Features
A strong, powerful breed of sports horse that is very athletic and has excelled as a show jumper and dressage horse.

The Hanoverian is the most famous and numerous of the regional German breeds. It comes from the state of Lower Saxony and dates back to the hefty War Horse of the Middle Ages. Its history is a classic case of adaptation to current needs. The make, shape and character of the Hanoverian have been modified to meet the demands of the time.

The first major step at organizing the breed came in 1735, when George II, Elector of Hanover and King of England, established by royal decree the Celle State Stud. This housed selected stallions that were available, at a nominal fee, to brood mares owned by local farmers. The aim was to upgrade and refine existing Hanoverians and turn them from the heavy, War Horse types into farm horses and carriage horses. The first stallions came from Holstein, but later some came from England (Thoroughbred and Cleveland Bay). Then some Neapolitan, Andalusian, Prussian and Mecklenburg stock was used. By the end of the 18th century, sufficient improvement had been made to use mainly stallions foaled in Hanover. The Hanoverian had become a very famous coach horse.

Celle housed 200 stallions, but many others were privately owned.

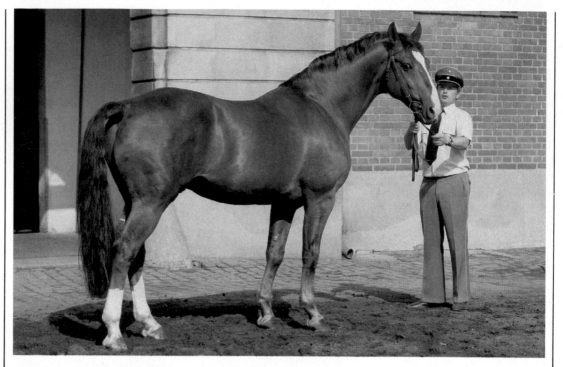

Above: A Hanoverian stallion from the state stud of Celle, in West Germany, which was founded in 1735 by King George II of England.

To raise the general standard of stallions in 1844, a *Kor-Ordnung* (Selection Rule) established that only those stallions passed by a commission could be used for breeding. Today, there is still an annual *Hengst Körung* (Stallion Selection) for 2½-year-old stallions.

In 1867, the private breeders formed a society. They laid down as their breeding aim "the production of a robust, strong horse equally well-suited to serve as a coach and as a military horse." This was followed in 1899 by the establishment of a stud book for mares. The results were impressive, and Hanoverians were used all over Germany as well as in Scandinavia and Switzerland.

After World War I, there was much less need for horses in the army. The breeding aim was restated as "a strong warm-blood capable of doing every kind of farm work, yet possessed of enough blood, nerve and gaits to be usable as a bold riding and coach horse."

To further this aim, a young stallion training and testing station was opened in 1928. All young stallions went through 11 months

Below: The Hanoverian gelding, Aramis, is shown here jumping for Canada at the 1984 Olympics in Los Angeles.

of training. Constitution, character and disposition were recorded before facing tests in endurance, jumping, speed and willingness. Only those that passed could be used for breeding.

World War II and the mechanization of farms changed the need again. A horse bred solely for riding was desired, and the aim became a "noble, correctly built warm-blood capable of superior performance—a horse with natural impulsion and space-gaining elastic movements—a horse which, because of its temperament, its character and willingness, is principally suited as an all-around riding horse.

This gradual conversion of the Hanoverian from a heavy agricultural-coach-military horse into an elegant, athletic, sports horse h[...] been achieved mainly by add[...] Thoroughbred blood. At pre[...] at Celle, about 10% of the 20[...] stallions are Thoroughbred[...] The other refining influence[...] been Trakehner and Arab[...] sentatives of these breed[...] make up 3% and 1%, res[...] of the stallions at Celle.[...]

With the breeding ai[...] trating on its characte[...] and soundness, the H[...] make and shape varie[...] distinguishing feature[...] sensible temperame[...] extravagant movem[...] strong body and g[...]

Hanoverians ar[...] and general ridir[...] excelled in com[...] include Olymp[...] gold medalist[...] Dressage C[...] and the W[...] Champio[...] success[...] pedigre[...] stock[...] year[...] use[...] Euro[...] also[...] horse[...]

HISPANO

Country of origin
Spain.

Height
15·3-16·1hh (63-65in).

Color
Bay, chestnut and gray are most common.

Features
This brave, intelligent, athletic horse is used for all types of riding.

The Hispano is Spain's Anglo-Arab. Spanish-Arabian mares were crossed with Thoroughbreds, mainly in Estremadura and Andalucia, to produce this all-around riding horse. It is popular with the Army, general riders and competitors in eventing, jumping and dressage. The Hispano is sometimes even seen in the bull-ring.

As a composite breed, the Hispano varies. Sometimes it looks more like a Thoroughbred, and at other times it looks more like an Arab. It usually has an elegant, light-framed body, with a good front. The limbs are long and slender but with dense bone.

Right: A Spanish Hispano performing in a display.

HOLSTEIN

Country of origin
Germany (Schleswig-Holstein).

Height
16-17hh (64-68in).

Color
Most solid colors.

Features
Over the centuries, this old German breed has played many roles, as a great war horse, a high-stepping, sturdy carriage horse and as an elegant competition horse.

---

probably the oldest German documents dated 1225 Holsteins were bred by in the pastures and along the River Elbe ern German state of Holstein. These lands very good breeding horses and cattle. Ages, a well-known produced from the 16th, 17th and Holsteins were were exported they were famous with high the Spanish, blood was

completed demand heavy

from base

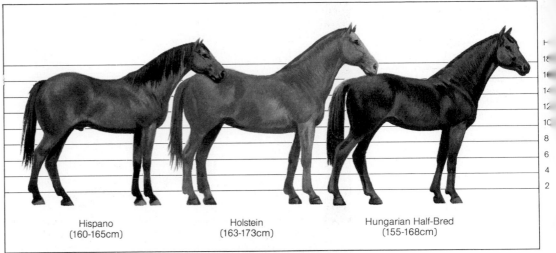

Hispano
(160-165cm)

Holstein
(163-173cm)

Hungarian Half-Bred
(155-168cm)

numbers. Sixteen horses were imported, but the most important blood came from three Yorkshire Coach Horses—all could be traced back to the Thoroughbred, Eclipse. Some interbreeding was practiced on these three sires, and the resultant carriage horse, featuring a high action to get out of the mud but also the ability to go a long way, became very popular. It was also useful to farmers as well as the Army. By the beginning of the 20th century, with the growth of competitions, the Holstein proved to be a powerful, heavyweight jumper and dressage horse.

After World War II, the demand by farmers for the Holstein fell. Although it was still sometimes required as a carriage horse, many thought it too heavy for

Above: The Holstein Montevideo competing at the 1984 Olympics, when it helped to win a gold medal.

competition. Numbers declined — in 1947 there were 20,000 registered mares, but by 1960 this had fallen to only 1,280. The Holstein Society decided to take steps to modernize and refine the breed. Twenty-five Thoroughbred stallions were imported from Britain. In 1960, the centre for breeding was moved from the Traventhal Stud to Elmshorn Riding School.

Since then, the breed has become increasingly successful. Numbers are still small (it is the smallest numerically of the German breeds), but quality is exceptional. At the 1984 Olympics 70% of the German horses in the dressage, jumping and eventing teams were Holsteins.

The modern Holstein is one of the most elegant of all sports horses. They are tall horses, with long, crested necks, strong, well-shaped backs and quarters, plenty of flat bone and elegant heads, with bold, honest expressions.

Holsteins have proved to possess great stamina and power, which has made them the most successful German breed in eventing. They have also excelled in driving, dressage and jumping.

The forelegs should be set well apart and the elbows should have freedom of movement. The feet should be open at the heel, dense and smooth. The tail should be carried well and not set too high.

Below: Hungarian Half-Breds have been successful in Combined Driving classes, winning many championships.

HUNGARIAN HALF-BREDS

Furioso, Gidran
Kisbér, Mezöhegyes

Country of origin
Hungary.
Height
15·1-16·2hh (61-66in).
Color
Most solid colors.
Features
Athletic, sound sports horse that varies in type from the light Kisbér to the stronger Mezöhegyes and the Anglo-Arab, which is known as the Gidran.

The Hungarians are famous horse breeders. They have bred great Thoroughbreds, such as Kisbér, which won the 1876 British Derby. Today, they are famous for their driving horses, which are exported all over the world. Horses are bred at state stud and stock farms. Each tends to specialize in a particular strain, type or breed of horse.

The officially designated major breed of Hungarian sports horse is produced at the stud at Mezöhegyes, after which it is named. The Mezöhegyes is a crossbred based on the older breeds of Furioso (originally Thoroughbred, Arab and local mares) and North Star (Thoroughbred and local mares). The Furioso and North Star breeds were named after their foundation Thoroughbred sires, which were imported from Britain in the middle of the 19th century. Both breeds are now merged into the Mezöhegyes. Since 1962, some Hanoverian and Holstein blood has been added to improve its sporting ability.

The Kisbér is the lightest Hungarian half-bred. It is produced at the military stud after which it is named. Holsteins and Mecklenburgs were used in its development during the 19th century, but the emphasis has been on adding Thoroughbred blood to make the Kisbér a useful event horse. Guy's Choice and Supreme Court were two recent Thoroughbred imports to Hungary from Britain.

The Gidran is the Arab-based half-bred. It was again developed in the 19th century from the Arab stallion, Gidran Senior, which was imported into the country in 1816. Local mares were used, then Thoroughbreds and some more Arab. The Gidran is the Hungarian Anglo-Arab. It is stockier and more robust than an Arab.

These breeds are used for riding and harness work, but it is an unnamed crossbred that is Hungary's most successful sports horse. It comes from the Kecskemet stud, where Lipizzaner mares are crossed with Trotter stallions (from the USSR and USA) and has become a world famous driving horse.

IOMUD
(Yomud)

Country of origin
USSR (Turkmenistan).
Height
14·3-15·1hh (59-61in).
Color
Gray is most common, but many are bay or chestnut.
Features
A slender, tough breed with the stamina to carry riders over long distances.

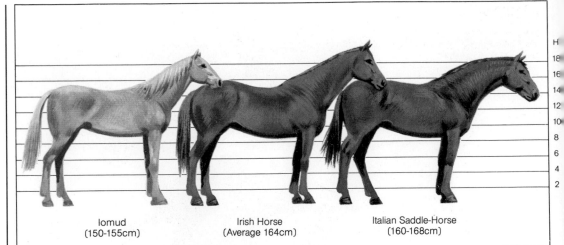

Iomud
(150-155cm)

Irish Horse
(Average 164cm)

Italian Saddle-Horse
(160-168cm)

The Iomud is similar to the Akhal Teke. Both share the ancestry of the Turkoman, or Turkmen, horse (pages 140-141) and have been bred in Turkmenistan for centuries. The Iomud's homelands are the Turkoman steppes that stretch from Russia into Northern Iran. It is sturdier, smaller, more compact and slower than the Akhal Teke, but it has more stamina. This is probably the result of some mixing with Arab horses and horses belonging to the nomadic steppe tribes.

The homelands of the Iomud are desertlike lands, so the horses have had to have a hardy constitution and an ability to live off frugal fare to survive. They were used as riding horses in the past by the Turkoman tribes and the cavalry. Today they are used for distance riding.

The Iomud has been raced over as great a distance as 30 miles (48km), but today it is usually tested over about 2 miles (3·2km). It has a very fast walk, a short, striding trot and a lightly balanced canter; each of these gaits is comfortable for the rider.

The Iomud's head is thin, with a straight profile, large eyes set far apart, wide nostrils and small, alert ears. The neck is long and straight, the body rather shallow and straight and loins broad, with a slightly sloping croup. Limbs are fine but with dense bone. There is little hair in the mane and tail, and the coat is fine and sleek.

IRISH HORSE

Country of origin
Ireland.
Height
Typically 16-16·3hh (64-67in).
Color
Most.
Features
These sports horses are still being developed as a breed. They are usually tough, and have proved to be outstanding jumpers and eventers.

The Irish Horse is a new addition to the sports horse group. It was formerly classed as a type, like the hunter and hack. It was a cross between a Thoroughbred and (usually) an Irish Draft. The Irish Horse did not have registration

papers and few, especially stallions, were ever used for breeding. Since the 1970s, selective breeding of the Irish Horse has been started, under the organization of the Irish Horse Board. Mares and stallions are graded, and stock is registered. More Irish Horses are being used as stallions.

There is still a variety of types among the Irish Horses, depending on the origins of the parents and the percentage of Thoroughbred blood. But most tend to have good heads and plenty of substance. Most are good, careful, sound hunters. Large numbers are talented jumpers, capable of going eventing and performing well in the show-jumping arena. Some have made good dressage horses.

Left: The Irish Horse, Rockbarton, ridden by Gerry Mullins.

Below: Irish horses competing for Switzerland in driving.

ITALIAN SADDLE-HORSES

Anglo-Arab Sardo, Maremanno, Salerno, Sanfrantellano, Siciliano

Country of origin
Italy.
Height
15·3-16·2hh (63-66in).
Color
Most solid colors.
Features
This breed group is in the early stages of its development. The large number of breeds playing a part in its establishment means that there are considerable variations in type.

Like so many European countries, Italy has merged her regional breeds of riding horses and imported stock to upgrade the new breed group into a useful sports horse. Importation has been from France, Ireland and Germany, with a few horses from the Netherlands and Eastern Europe.

The majority of brood mares for the Italian Saddle-Horse (more than 4,000 are now registered) come from the two Anglo-Arab types of Italian-bred horses—the Sicilian Anglo-Arab and the Sardinian Anglo-Arab. Both are based on Arab and Barb stock originally brought from Africa. These have been infused with other Arabs and Thoroughbreds. The Sardinian has some Andalusian blood added. The two breeds have shown talent in equestrian sports and are good foundation stock for the Italian Saddle-Horse.

In addition, Salernos (Salernitanos), were developed in the 16th century in Salerno province, close to Naples. They were infused with Neapolitan and Andalusian blood. The Salernos were popular cavalry horses and are now used mostly for recreation and competitions. Maremannos from the central and western areas of Italy, in and around Tuscany, have also been used in the breeding of the Saddle-Horse. It was originally a tough, frugal, fast horse with little quality. But the mixture of British Thoroughbreds has

increased its nobility. It is still used for work and riding, so the lighter Maremanno is crossbred to the Thoroughbred to make the best Saddle-Horses.

Sanfrantellanos, from Messina in Sicily, have also been used in breeding Saddle-Horses. The Sanfrantellanos are allowed to run wild in their native lands, but when caught they are used for riding and harness work. Crossing with the Thoroughbred has given a new perspective to the breed. It has enabled them, like the Maremannos, to be used for competitions. Foundation stock includes the Anglo-Normans, which came to Italy as cavalry horses in the 17th century, and Hackneys, Lipizzaners, Maremannos and Nonius, which have been introduced for breeding during more recent times.

This amalgam of different breeds is being used to develop the Italian Saddle-Horse. Numbers of this interesting breed group are steadily increasing in Italy.

Above: A representative of a new breed type in Italy, the Italian Saddle-Horse. It is being developed from a variety of different breeds.

Below: A fine Irish Horse with her foal.

KABARDIN

Country of origin
USSR (Caucasus).
Height
14·2-15·1hh (58-61in).
Color
Bay is most common, but they can be dark brown, black or gray.
Features
An active, strong, sure-footed mountain horse that can be used under saddle or in harness.

The Kabardin is a native of the northern Caucasus mountains in the USSR. It has all the assets of a mountain horse—sure-footedness, docility and intelligence. It is strong enough to serve as a pack horse and is good enough to be ridden.

The Kabardin has been used by the nomadic tribes of the region for a long time. They developed the breed by crossing horses from the south—Karabakh, Persian and Turkoman—with their own steppe horses.

Since the beginning of the 20th century, some Kabardin have been crossed with Thoroughbreds to establish the taller, finer, faster breed of Anglo-Kabardin.

The typical Kabardin has a long, thin head with a short muscular neck, a straight shoulder, a short straight back and a broad, sloping croup. The limbs are strong with dense bone and good feet.

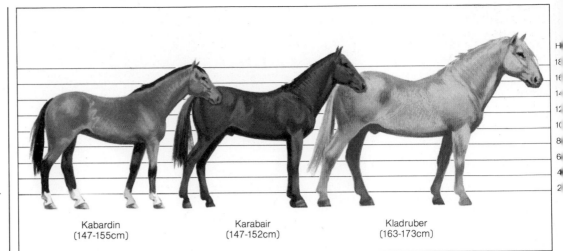

Kabardin
(147-155cm)

Karabair
(147-152cm)

Kladruber
(163-173cm)

Above: A jet-black Karabair horse from the USSR.

This is an ancient breed with a sparse mane and tail.

Below: The Kabardin is bred by nomadic Caucasus tribesmen.

KARABAIR

Country of origin
USSR (Uzbekistan).
Height
14·2-15hh (58-60in).
Color
Gray, bay and chestnut are most common, but other colors are found.
Features
A tough, lean breed adapted to hot climates. For centuries it has served as a riding horse for the tribesmen in Uzbekistan.

The Karabair is a very old breed based in Uzbekistan. It was developed from the steppe horses of the nomadic tribesmen and from horses that came from the south—the Turkomans, Persians and Arabs. It is a dual-purpose

horse and is useful for riding and harness work. The Karabair is also used for sport in local games such as *kokpar,* in which riders fight over a goat. When crossed with Thoroughbreds, Karabairs have proved to be talented at other equestrian competitions, such as jumping or eventing.

The Karabair is a small, thickset riding horse. The head is of average length, with a straight to convex face. The neck is straight and thick, running onto low withers. The body is broad but shallow. The back is short and strong, and the croup is rounded and muscular. The limbs are fine but with dense bone. There is a tendency for the hind legs to have cow or sickle hocks. The feet are tough, with good quality horn. The mane and tail have very little hair. The coat is fine.

KLADRUBER

Country of origin
Czechoslovakia (Bohemia).
Height
16-17hh (64-68in).
Color
Gray or black.
Features
Strong, kind horses with short strides and high knee action. They are famous as coach horses.

The Kladruber is bred at Kladrub, the oldest functioning stud in the world. It lies in the region of

Above: The noble-looking Kladruber is one of the largest breeds of sports horses.

Bohemia in Czechoslovakia, close to the steeplechasing course of Pardubice. The stud was started by the Emperor Maximilian II, who imported Spanish stock of Andalusian lines during the 1570s.

Horses from this royal stud were bred to provide coach horses for the royal stables. They are a heavier, taller version of their relations the Lipizzaners, which were developed at the Yugoslavian stud of Lipizza. Today, Lipizzaners are bred in Czechoslovakia at

the Topolcianky Stud. There has been some use of Lipizzaners in the breeding of Kladrubers, along with heavy native horses, Barbs, Turks and Neapolitans.

More outside blood was used after World War II, because stock was severely depleted by the fighting. Oldenburgs, Anglo-Normans and Hanoverians were imported to restore the breed, which was in danger of becoming extinct.

The Kladruber is bred in two colors. The most common is gray, but black was also developed in the 19th century. The base for the black Kladrubers was the state stud of Slatinany.

Today, the Kladruber is used for riding and driving but it is more famous as a driving horse. A spectacular attraction at international events is a team of 16 gray Kladrubers pulling a carriage.

The Kladruber's head has a noble look, with a convex face. The neck is muscular and crested, and the shoulder slopes. The body is long and shallow. The hindquarters are rounded and muscular and the limbs are clean.

Below: A team of Kladrubers being driven in a dressage arena.

KNABSTRUP

Country of origin
Denmark.
Height
15·1-16hh (61-64in).
Color
Appaloosa patterns on a roan base.
Features
A gentle, strong horse that is popular for use in demonstrations and exhibitions.

The Knabstrup is a spectacularly spotted horse from Denmark. Like the Appaloosa, patterns vary, and no two horses are identical.

The breed developed from one mare named Flaebenhoppen. She was allegedly brought to Denmark during the Napoleonic Wars. She eventually fell into the ownership of the proprietor of the Knabstrup estate. This chestnut mare, with a white blanket and white mane and tail, was put to one of the Danish Frederiksborg stallions; he had the palomino colour. The result was the foundation sire of the Knabstrup breed. He was called Flaebehingsten. Although similar in color to his mother, he had many more shades to his coat.

Recently, there has been much crossbreeding. Breeders have concentrated on producing better color patterns rather than consistent conformation. This has led to considerable variation in type.

The Knabstrup, with its spectacular coloring, has been much used as a circus horse, but it is valued also for general riding.

LIPIZZANER

Country of origin
Austria.
Height
15-16hh (60-64in).
Color
Usually gray but can be bay. They are born dark but lighten as they mature.
Features
For many years, these intelligent, athletic, strong horses have been famous as high-school horses. Today, they are also earning fame as harness horses in Combined Driving.

This famous breed of Austrian high-school horse has Spanish origins—hence the name "Spanish School" for the base in Vienna, where these gray horses demonstrate their gymnastic ability. The foundation stock of nine stallions and 24 mares was brought to the stud of Lipizza (now in Yugoslavia) by Archduke Charles of Austria in 1580.

The vogue for high school was just beginning in the courts of Europe, and the Archduke was determined that the Austrians would have the material to excel.

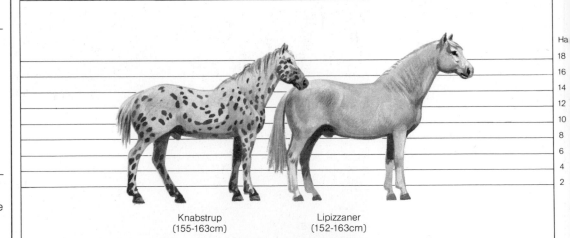

Knabstrup
(155-163cm)

Lipizzaner
(152-163cm)

Above: A Knabstrup, with its spectacularly spotted coat, galloping free.

Below: Lipizzaners are famous for giving high school demonstrations all over the world.

The Andalusians from the Iberian peninsula were recognized as top-class material for this form of riding, so these must have been the imported stock that was bred to local mares. It is likely that over the ensuing 200 years, more imports were made from Spain, and possibly some from Italy. The Neapolitan, from Italy, was the other fashionable high-school horse.

After the establishment of the school in Vienna, in 1735, the Lipizzaner's breeding began to be recorded. All Lipizzaners today trace back to six stallions imported in the late 18th and early 19th centuries. These are Pluto, a Frederiksborg; Conversano and Neapolitano, both Neapolitans; Maestoso and Favory, both Kladrubers; and Siglavy, an Arab. This was not such a heterogenous collection as it seems: Frederiksborgs, Neapolitans and Kladrubers are based on Andalusian stock, and there had been crossbreeding

before between these three breeds and the Lipizzaner. Attempts were made later to use other blood, such as Thoroughbred and Anglo-Arab, but their stock was not very successful at the Spanish Riding School. The best of the Lipizzaners have not had much outcrossing, because Andalusian lines are the most important.

The breeding of the Lipizzaners suffered great disruption with the break-up of the Austro-Hungarian Empire in 1918. The original stud at Lipizza became Italian territory, and the Italians did not make good use of the stock left there. After World War II, Lipizza became part of Yugoslavia, which has done much to promote the Lipizzaner.

The Yugoslavians collected stock from elsewhere, and today there are about 10,000 Lipizzaners in Yugoslavia. The Yugoslavian dressage team is the only one in the world to be mounted on Lipizzaners.

Lipizzaners are not only used in competitions and demonstrations. The Yugoslavs have discovered that farm mares crossed with Lipizzaner stallions make good

Above: A Lipizzaner being ridden by a member of the Spanish Riding School at a British show.

agricultural workers. These crossbreds are also often used by farmers in parts of Romania and Hungary, where the terrain is similar to that in Yugoslavia.

Hungary promotes her Lipizzaners for another reason. It has found that purebred and crossbred horses, bred with the Trotter, make high-class harness horses for Combined Driving. The Hungarians export these horses all over the world and use them to win major driving championships.

Despite the various uses for these intelligent, athletic, strong

animals, it is as the mounts of the members of the Spanish Riding School that they remain most famous. The stud for these school horses is now at Piber in Austria. The only stallions that can breed at the stud are those that have proved themselves to be outstanding high-school horses in Vienna. Even the mares are put through performance tests before they are allowed to breed. The Austrians still follow the principle that the best basis for selecting Lipizzaners is their performance ability.

Right: The Lipizzaner is one of the most intelligent and athletic of all horse breeds.

LUSITANO

Country of origin
  Portugal.
Height
  15-15·3hh (60-63in).
Color
  Gray is most common, but other solid colors are found.
Features
  A courageous, athletic horse which is famous in the bullring. It is also valued by farmers and the Portuguese cavalry.

The Lusitano is a relative of the Lipizzaner because it is believed to be founded on Andalusian stock. There are indications that some Lusitanos went to Austria as foundation stock for the Lipizzaner. The Lusitano's home country is Portugal. Together with the Altér Real, it has been the country's main riding horse for centuries. It is similar to its forbears, the Andalusians, but is thought to have more Arab blood.

The Lusitano was popular with the Portuguese cavalry. It is a very strong horse, and farmers used it for riding and light draft work. The Lusitano is most famous as the horse of the mounted bullfighters (*rejoneadores*). Horses are trained to advanced levels of high school, to make the fight more entertaining and to reduce the risk to horse and rider. Some horses are used in demonstrations prior to the appearance of the bull. Others, which are particularly skilled and fast, are used during the actual fight. In Portugal, unlike Spain, the bull is not killed.

The Lusitano has an Andalusian-type head, with a straight-to-convex face. Ears are small but alert. The neck is muscular, the shoulder slopes and the body is compact and deep. Quarters are rounded and very powerful. The mane and

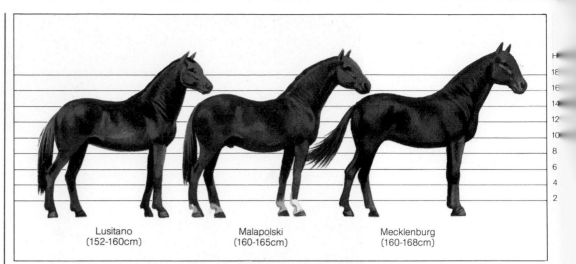

Lusitano
(152-160cm)

Malapolski
(160-165cm)

Mecklenburg
(160-168cm)

Left: A Lusitano being driven.

Below left: Lusitanos are famous as mounts of bullfighters.

Below: Lusitanos are as popular for hacking as for high school riding.

tail have an abundance of hair.

The Lusitano has great courage. It moves with relatively high, round strides which makes it easy to train for the exacting standards of high-school work that are required for the Portuguese bullring.

MALAPOLSKI

Country of origin
Poland.
Height
15·3-16·2hh (63-66in).
Color
Bay, gray, chestnut and black are most common.
Features
An honest, willing worker that is useful under saddle and in harness.

___

This all-around horse is bred in the southeast of Poland. It developed from primitive local horses (of Tarpan origins) that were crossed with Arab and Thoroughbred blood. This was largely through the use of such Hungarian and Austrian horses as the Shagya, Furioso, Gidran and Lipizzaner, as well as Poland's other riding horse, the Wielkopolski.

The Malapolski is an elegant horse with a lean frame. It has great powers of endurance and conserves its fodder. It is used

Above: A Mecklenburg. This horse is based on, and is similar to, the West German Hanoverian.

___

extensively by farmers as an all-around horse that can be used to tend the land, act as transportation and be ridden. The demand for it is extensive; at the state studs there are 300 stallions. Another 800 or so are privately owned.

The Malapolski has good width between the eyes and a tendency toward a concave face. The body is strong and muscular, but not deep.

MECKLENBURG

Country of origin
East Germany.
Height
15·3-16·2hh (63-66in).
Color
Most solid colors.
Features
A docile, trainable horse that is athletic and suitable for general riding and competitions.

___

The Mecklenburg is East Germany's version of the Hanoverian.

Blood lines are similar, and there has been considerable interaction between the two studs at Celle and Mecklenburg.

The Mecklenburg's main use has been as an Army horse. But today it is in demand as a general riding horse.

It has good substance, yet it is also a very athletic and powerful breed.

The head is medium-sized, the neck muscular, the chest broad and the body deep and compact. The hindquarters are muscular and the legs have substantial bone and short cannons.

MISSOURI FOXTROTTER

Country of origin
United States (Missouri).
Height
14-16hh (56-64in).
Color
Any.
Features
A reliable, gentle horse with an unusual shuffling gait called the *fox trot*, which provides a fast, comfortable means of travel.

The Missouri Foxtrotter was developed in the Ozark Hills of Missouri, at the beginning of the 19th century. Pioneers who settled the area brought with them their horses— mainly Arabs, Morgans and Southern Plantation Horses. These were used (later additions were the Saddlebred, Tennessee Walker and Standardbred) to produce a horse that provided a fast and comfortable means of travel. A horse of this type was in great demand from doctors, sheriffs, assessors and stock raisers.

Stallions were used that had shown the ability to perform an ambling gait that became known as the *fox trot*. The horse walked in front and trotted behind. In this type of gait, they could travel at 5 to 8 miles an hour and were very comfortable to ride. Careful selective breeding

Below: The Missouri Foxtrotter is one of the most comfortable rides in the United States.

Above: This Missouri Foxtrotter wears a bridle that is designed for Western riding.

produced the Missouri Foxtrotter.

Besides its distinctive gait, another feature of this breed is its docility. It was often described as "the common man's pleasure horse" because of its gentle disposition, ease of training, handling and feeding.

Today, it is very popular for trail riding because of its comfort, sure-footedness, speed and gentleness. It is also used as a show horse. A breed society, which began in 1948, promotes exhibiting of Missouri Foxtrotting Horses which are judged 40% on the fox trot gait, 20% on the flat foot walk, 20% on the canter and 20% on conformation.

The Missouri Foxtrotter's head is neat and intelligent, with pointed ears, large eyes and a tapering muzzle. The neck is well-shaped, the shoulder slopes and the body is deep. The back is short and strong, and the limbs are strong and distinctly tapered.

Missouri Foxtrotter
(142-163cm)

Morgan
(145-157cm)

MORGAN

Country of origin
United States (Vermont).
Height
14·1-15·2hh (57-62in.)
Color
Preferably dark with minimal white. Bay is most common.
Features
This is a versatile breed that is easy to handle, and endowed with great presence.

This versatile breed was founded in the 1780s in the United States by a single stallion, believed to be of Arab and Barb descent. It is possible he also had some Welsh Cob or Friesian blood. He took his name from his owner, a Vermont singing teacher named Justin Morgan. The teacher added to his income by using his stallion to pull logs. At only 14·1hh (57in) he was capable of outpulling all his rivals. The stallion was then given a chance at racing, and he beat challengers both in harness and under saddle. His fame spread and so did the demand for his services by the owners of mares in Vermont. Demand grew even greater when, whatever the standard of the mare, he stamped their progeny with his assets. With this demand, and because he lived well into his 20s, he was able to leave a large enough family to found a breed.

Justin Morgan's progeny soon became known simply as "Morgans". Some were used to found other major American breeds, such as the Standardbred and American Saddlebred.

The army quickly adopted the breed. Morgans were the best available breed in terms of ease of training, remaining calm under stress, enduring hard work, living off little food and coping with the demands of parade work.

Today, the Morgan is still popular, because its versatility makes it a high-class family horse. Its kind nature and sturdy physique combined with a relatively short stature enables it to carry a man or a child with equal comfort. It can also be driven and has a tremendous air of importance,

which is very eye-catching. The Morgan is used in dressage and endurance tests. It also is used as a cow pony or a roadster (speed trotter). It is still used for work on the farm.

The breed is divided into Park and Pleasure divisions. Both work in harness and under saddle. The Park takes time to train—about 7 years—and has higher action. The requirements are a combination of balance and light controls with animation and great spirit. The Park Morgan is expected to present a picture of great beauty, brilliance, animation and elegance. It can be shown under English or Western tack. The Pleasure Morgan has a lower action, is easier to train and has very good manners.

The Morgan's head is medium sized, tapering slightly from the jaw to the muzzle. The face is straight or slightly concave. Ears are small, alert and have fine points. The neck is medium length and well-crested. Withers are prominent and slightly higher than the point of the hip. Shoulders slope. The chest is broad and deep, and the

Above: A Morgan Horse pulling a buggy. This is just one of the many uses for this versatile breed, which can also be ridden. Its kind temperament, compact shape and athletic movement makes it valuable for many tasks, from farmwork to dressage.

back is short, broad and muscular. Loins are wide and muscular, the quarters are muscular, and the croup is gently rounded, with a fairly high-set tail. Limbs are set square, with muscular forearms and second thighs. Knees are wide and flat, hocks are wide, deep and clean, cannons are short, wide and flat, and the feet are round, smooth and dense.

The Morgan moves with flat-footed, elastic, rapid, long, straight and free strides at the walk. It moves with square, freegoing, collected and balanced strides at the trot. Smooth, easy, collected straight strides are usual on both leads at the canter.

Right: A portrait of the hard-working Morgan Horse.

MURGHESE

Country of origin
 Italy.
Height
 14·2-16·1hh (58-65in)
Color
 Usually chestnut.
Features
 This is a utility type of horse developed since the 1920s in the famous breeding area of Murge.

The Murghese comes from Murge, an area that was famous for its horses in the 15th, 16th and 17th centuries. There were two types: a heavier type used for agricultural

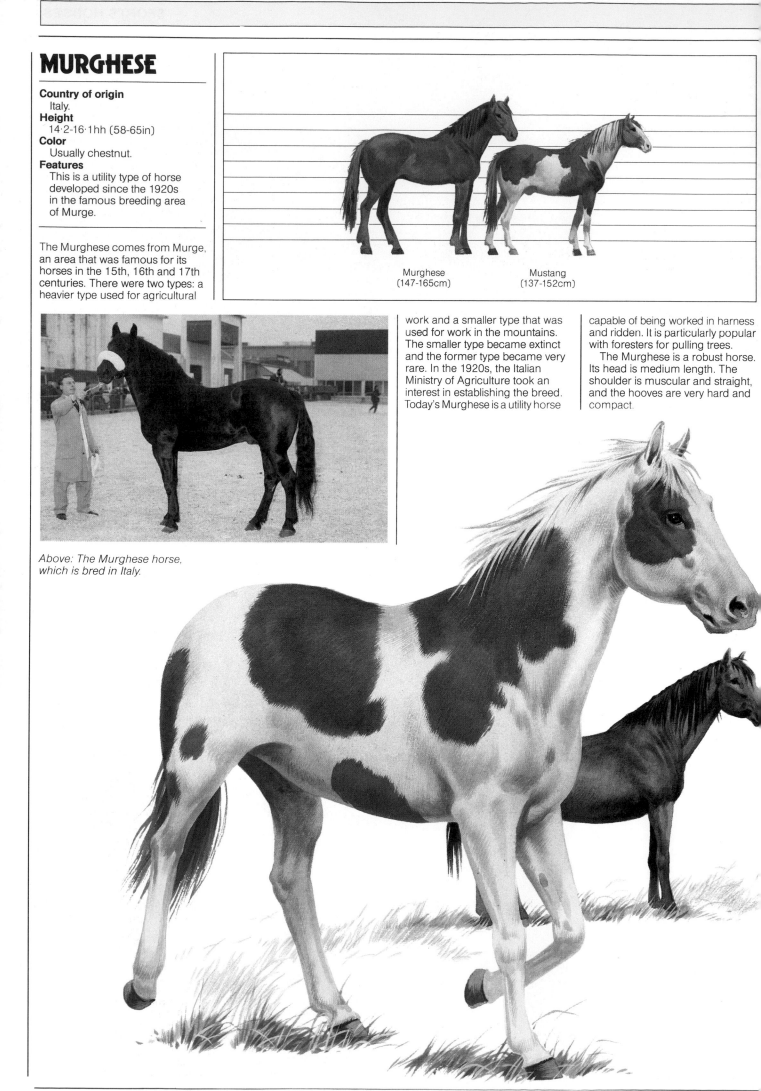

Murghese
(147-165cm)

Mustang
(137-152cm)

Above: The Murghese horse, which is bred in Italy.

work and a smaller type that was used for work in the mountains. The smaller type became extinct and the former type became very rare. In the 1920s, the Italian Ministry of Agriculture took an interest in establishing the breed. Today's Murghese is a utility horse capable of being worked in harness and ridden. It is particularly popular with foresters for pulling trees.

The Murghese is a robust horse. Its head is medium length. The shoulder is muscular and straight, and the hooves are very hard and compact.

Above: Mustangs, feral horses of the United States and the original mounts of the American cowboy, are shown in a demonstration at Lexington, Kentucky.

Left and Above: Mustangs are tough, wiry horses of every known color, with many unusual shades and combinations.

MUSTANG
(Bronco, Cayuse, Chickasaw)

Country of origin
United States.
Height
13·2-15hh (54-60in)
Color
Any.
Features
This is a feral horse with a tough constitution. It isn't elegant, but it has a romantic history, closely allied with that of the United States. It was the original Indian horse and cowpony of the American West.

The Mustang has Spanish origins, based on Andalusian and Barb stock brought to North America by the first Spanish Settlers. Escaped horses ran free and multiplied to form large herds. They were sometimes caught by the North American Indians, and later by cowboys. In California, Texas and New Mexico, these horses became known as 'Mustangs'. Farther north they were often referred to as 'Broncos' and sometimes 'Cayuse'.

Many earlier Mustangs were fine representatives of the Spanish Barb ancestry. The Indians used some of the best Mustangs to chase bison. They were also caught and tamed by the cowboys, and proved to have "cow sense", a valued ability to work livestock.

Many Mustangs were left to breed in the wild. The continuous drainage of the finest stock eventually depleted the wild herds of their best stock quality. The remaining Mustangs, while tough and wiry, lacked the original beauty and quality.

As settlers moved West, they brought carriage, draft and riding horses with them. Often they were taller, heavier horses; they were crossed with Mustangs to increase the size of the native western horses. The most successful of these crosses were the early Quarter Horses, from crosses of imported Thoroughbreds with the fast Chickasaw Horses of the Southeast. The Chickasaw Horses, also Mustangs, were probably survivors of horses lost by early Spanish explorers in the southeast area of the United States.

With their common ancestors and heritage, these Quarter Horses helped increase the size and substance of the Mustangs without diluting the "cow sense" desired in a stock horse. Today, most western American breeds, including the Quarter Horse, Appaloosa, Pinto and Palamino, owe a great deal of their stock-horse qualities to their Mustang heritage.

We can only estimate how many of the original Mustangs remained by the early 1900s, but it was certainly not many. Crossbreeding diluted most of the remaining herds. Because they were considered a nuisance to cattle ranchers, many remaining horses were rounded up and subsequently sold or shot.

Although the true Mustang has been crossbred almost to extinction, several registries have been set up to preserve those of pure Barb type and bloodlines. The term "Spanish Mustang" is used to refer to those animals of obvious Barb descent collected by Robert Brislawn and bred at the Wild Horse Research Farm in Porterville, California. These horses show the Barb characteristics of only five lumbar vertebrae (most horse breeds have six), a slab-shaped body that is narrow and deep, a sloping croup and low set tail. They have small ears, round bone to the limbs and the straight or convex profile typical of the Barb. They come in a variety of colors, including the "Medicine Hat" pinto (nearly all white over pinto, with dark markings over the ears), roans and various duns including grulla (black dun) and claybank (red dun).

Many of these horses are fine examples of the old Spanish Barb and make excellent riding and endurance horses. Another group, the Spanish Barb Mustang Registry, also registers horses with Barb characteristics. No claim is made that they are of pure Barb descent, but horses must prove to have desirable characteristics to achieve permanent registration.

Finally, there is the American Mustang. This is registered by the American Mustang Association, which was formed in 1962.

NONIUS

Country of origin
 Hungary.
Height
 Large: 15·3-16·2hh (63-66in).
 Small: 14·3-15·3hh (59-63).
Color
 Bay, brown or black.
Features
 A gentle, active horse that
 can be used for light draft
 work and riding.

The Nonius is the most numerous
and best-established of the
Hungarian breeds. It is produced
at Hungary's major stud for sports
horses, Mezőhegyes. The original
stock for this breed was brought
back by the Hungarians from
France in 1815. They were
Normandy horses, and the best
one was a stallion named Nonius.
He proved to be highly fertile when
put to local mares and also possibly
some others of Lipizzaner, Arab
and Turkish blood. The new
breed, to which Nonius gave his
name, was used extensively by
the Army and farmers.
 Toward the end of the 19th
century, more Thoroughbreds were
used on the Nonius mares. This
resulted in a lighter division to
the breed. Consequently, there is
the heavier light-draft type,
now used for driving and for
farm work, and the riding horse.
 The Nonius is a good-looking
horse with an attractive head,
a long muscular neck and sloping
shoulders. It has a broad back
and loins, muscular quarters and
strong limbs.

NOVOKIRGHIZ

Country of origin
 USSR (Kirghiz).
Height
 14·3-15·2 (59-62in).
Color
 Usually chestnut or bay, with a
 gold sheen.
Features
 This tough utility breed was
 developed after the 1930s.

The Kirghiz was the native pony
of the mountainous regions of
Kirghiz and Kazakstan. It was
derived from Mongolian stock and
used by the local tribes for many
centuries. During the 20th century
the demand grew for a larger
animal to work the farms, so
Kirghiz ponies were crossed with
Thoroughbreds and Dons.
Through selective breeding, a new
breed, called the Novokirghiz, was
established, and this was officially
recognized in 1954.
 The Novokirghiz has proved
to be a good horse under saddle
and in harness. It is also used
for pack work in the mountains.

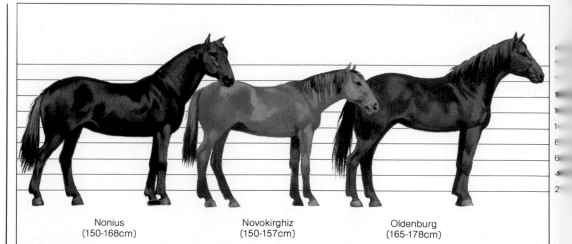

| Nonius | Novokirghiz | Oldenburg |
| (150-168cm) | (150-157cm) | (165-178cm) |

Mares continue to fulfill an
important traditional function of the
old breed by providing *kumis*
(fermented milk).
 The Novokirghiz type varies
from a type close to Thoroughbred
to one that is a heavy work horse.
All of them have a good-looking
head, a straight back, muscular
quarters and a short, sloping
croup. Limbs are strong and short,
although they often have cow or
sickle hocks. Feet are hard.

*Left: The head of a Nonius with its
honest expression.*

*Below: A Nonius horse stands
square to show its conformation.*

OLDENBURG

Country of origin
Germany (northwest).
Height
16·1-17·2hh (65-70in).
Color
Bay, brown and black are most common.
Features
An early maturing, even-tempered, strong breed, that has been famous as a coach horse. Now it is being adapted to make a sports horse.

The Oldenburg has been bred in northwest Germany for centuries. It has much in common with its neighbor, the East Friesian, whose breeding grounds are now in East Germany. Both breeds were based on Friesian blood from Holland.

The Oldenburg breed was named after Count Anton von Oldenburg (1603 to 1667). He organized importations of Spanish and Italian stock to improve local mares.

Farmers in the 19th century established today's breed. They organized themselves into a Breeders' Society and imported upgrading stock. These included Thoroughbreds, Cleveland Bays, Yorkshire Coach Horses, Normans, and some Hanoverians from Lower Saxony. The breed they developed was a large warm-blood capable of working fields, pulling coaches and being used by the Army.

Recently, the Oldenburg has

Above: A tall, handsome Oldenburg stallion at stud.

been further lightened with Thoroughbred and French blood to make it less of a coach horse and more of a sports horse.

The Oldenburg's popularity has not been confined to Germany. It is frequently seen in neighboring Denmark and has been used to restore and upgrade other breeds,

including the Kladruber.

The Oldenburg is the tallest, heaviest German regional breed, although the recent lightening process is bringing it more into line with the others. Its *métier* in the past has been as a high-class, strong coach horse, but it has adapted to the falling demand in this field and the rising one in equestrian sports.

Its head is plain, with a straight-to-convex face. The neck is long,

the shoulder sloping, and the body is deep and muscular. Quarters are strong, and the limbs are relatively short, with a good amount of bone.

Below: Oldenburgs are big, strong horses that are excellent for driving.

ORLOV TROTTER

Country of origin
USSR.

Height
16hh (64in), but it can grow much taller.

Color
Gray is most common, but black and bay are often seen.

Features
An elegant horse with athletic action and sound conformation. It is used in trotting races and as breeding stock to improve other breeds.

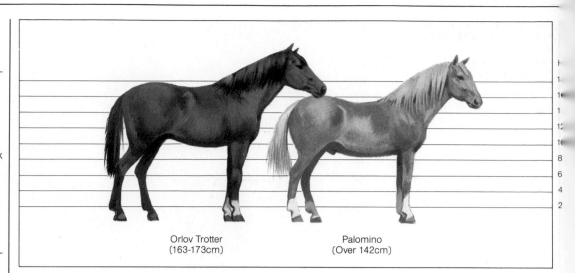

Orlov Trotter
(163-173cm)

Palomino
(Over 142cm)

The Orlov Trotter was the first of today's breeds to be bred for harness racing. It was developed at the instigation of Count Alexius Grigorievich Orlov (1737 to 1808). In 1777, he imported foundation stock and supervised the selective breeding of the progeny.

The first, and most important, stallion to be imported was the Arab, Smetanka. He was put to a Danish mare of Spanish origins to produce the stallion Polkan. When Polkan was put to a Dutch mare, the first important trotter and progenitor of the breed was produced in 1784. He was called Bars First. He was bred with more Arab, Dutch and Danish mares, and to Mecklenburgs and British half breds. There was considerable in-breeding to him, and most of today's Orlovs have Bars First in their pedigrees.

By the time harness racing was seriously under way, in the 1830s, the Orlov had been developed into a definite type. Use of stock on the race track and culling those with poor performance records led to further improvements in the breed. The Orlov became the world's supreme trotter, and by the end of the 19th century more than 3,000 stud farms in Russia specialized in its breeding.

The Russian Revolution in 1917 disrupted breeding. The Orlov's breeding was restored when peace returned, but it never regained its international supremacy of the 19th century. The American Standard-bred took its place. To speed up race time, Russians crossed some of their Orlovs with the Standard-bred to produce the faster Russian Trotter (see page 130).

The Orlov is a handsome, tall horse, and it has been used extensively to upgrade other breeds. It passes on its height and its strong light conformation. These are useful qualities for improving other breeds.

The Orlov's head is small, with an Arab influence. The neck is long, and the chest is broad.

Below: The Orlov Trotter was developed as a racehorse, but it is strong and robust enough to be used for general driving purposes.

The back is long and straight and the loins and croup are powerful. The quarters are rounded and muscular, and the legs are fine, with good, dense bone.

PALOMINO

Country of origin
Found all over the world, but America has the longest established breed society.

Height
Over 14hh (56in).

Color
Like a newly minted gold coin, with light mane and tail.

Features
Their beautiful color makes these horses in demand for general riding, showing and parades. Because they are categorized according to color, not shape, there is a great variety of types and an equally varied range of talents.

Palominos have coats the color of untarnished gold, with light manes and tails. They are some of the most eye-catching horses in the world but do not yet breed true to type. They are said to be a "color" rather than a breed. Consequently, there are Palomino Saddlebreds, Quarter Horses, half-breds or ponies. They are very popular.

Palomino societies are being established all over the world. In South Africa and Britain, there are thriving organizations, but it is the Americans who were the first to take an interest. This may be because of the Palomino's association with the cowboys. Palominos were found among the wild herds of Mustang horses that escaped from the first settlers.

The Palomino's origins precede the first settlers. It is believed that golden horses with silver manes and tails were ridden by China's early emperors. Achilles, the Greek warrior, rode Balios and Zanthos, who were "yellow and gold and swifter than storm winds".

For a while Palominos were called Isabellas after their most famous promoter, Queen Isabella of Spain. They were taken to the New World with Columbus or Cortez. Queen Isabella gave some to Count de Palomino, who was said to have named them after himself. However, there is another possible explanation for their name. It may have derived from the luscious golden grape called *Palomino*.

When the Spanish suffered military setbacks in America, most of their horses escaped to become Mustangs. It was from among these that the cowboys chose their Palomino cowponies.

Today, the Palomino has had another surge in popularity. It is much in demand in the show ring, for cutting, Quarter Horse racing, Western classes, pleasure and trail riding.

The Palomino's coat is never more than three shades darker or lighter than a newly-minted gold coin. It has a light mane and tail and should have dark skin, except under white markings. The eyes are dark or hazel. White markings are permitted on the legs to the knees or hocks and on the face. In addition, proof of breeding is required by most Palomino societies. Breeds accepted vary from country to country.

Above: The beautiful color of the Palomino makes it popular in the showring for many classes, such as Western Pleasure.

Below: A portrait of a Palomino. It is a color type rather than a true breed.

PASO FINO

Country of origin
  Puerto Rico.
Height
  13-15hh (42-60in)
Color
  Most.
Features
  A very comfortable riding horse with an unusual four-beat gait known as the *Paso*. It does not trot.

Paso Fino
(132-152cm)

Peruvian Horse
(147-157cm)

The Paso Fino is supposed to have been derived from stock brought to Santo Domingo (now known as the Dominican Republic) by Columbus on his second voyage. Allegedly he had on board Barbs, Andalusians and Spanish Jennets. A feature of the Spanish Jennet was its four-beat gait. It was a broken pace which was very fast and comfortable to sit to. This became known as the *Paso gait*.

Breeding farms for these horses were established on several of the Caribbean islands.Stock from them was used as remounts for the Spanish Conquistadores in their conquest of Mexico, Peru and other parts of South America.

Right: A Paso Fino performing the gait for which it is famous, the four-beat, lateral Paso gait.

Below: This view of a Paso Fino shows how the lateral pair of the right fore and right hind leg are lifted almost together.

Today, the Paso Fino is being brought to the United States from Puerto Rico, Colombia and the Dominican Republic. These horses, which have changed little in the four centuries since their ancestors were brought from Spain, are used for trail riding, pleasure, driving and exhibition.

In the show ring, the Paso Fino is shown at the *Classic Fino* (the speed of a slow walk), *Paso Corto* (the speed of a collected trot) and *Paso Largo* (the speed of a slow canter). In Versatility Classes, the horse may also be asked to canter and take a small jump.

The Paso Fino has great presence. Its head is Arablike. The back and hindquarters are short and strong. The limbs are small, but the bone is strong and dense. The cannons are quite short.

PERUVIAN HORSE
(Peruvian Paso)

Country of origin
Peru.

Height
14·2-15·2hh (58-62in).

Color
Bay, chestnut, brown, black or gray. Roan, once common, is now seen less often. Palomino and various shades of dun are found occasionally.

Features
This breed has flourished in Peru for over 300 years. Its growing popularity in other countries is based on its Paso gait, which is fast and comfortable, and its kind, easily managed disposition.

The Peruvian Horse was developed from the same origins as the Paso Fino: Andalusians, Barbs and Spanish Jennets brought to South America by the Spanish Conquistadores. Nearly 400 years of selective breeding have improved its harmonious gaits, fast, smooth ride and gentle disposition that are the unique characteristics of this breed.

In other countries, the development of roads led to the growing popularity of trotting horses. However, in Peru the need was for a smooth traveling ambler that could be used to cover the vast estates. The Peruvian Horse's unique gait is inherited by 100% of purebred foals and

Above: A Peruvian Horse at a show being ridden in the national costume of the country.

often by partbreds. It is called a *broken pace.*

The Peruvian Horse, with its distinctive Paso gait, swings its forelegs outward in an arc as it moves. The hind legs are very powerful and push forward with long, straight strides. The hindquarters are held low, and the back is straight. The horse can travel over very rough terrain in this gait and can keep up a speed of

as much as 15 to 18 miles an hour for a surprisingly long time without tiring. An indispensable breed characteristic, called *brio,* enables the horse to respond with energy and willingness and gives it great ability to withstand fatigue. The Peruvian is used in parades, endurance riding, pleasure riding and showing. At a show, the Peruvian is always "in gait" and is not allowed to walk or canter in the show ring.

The Peruvian has a stocky conformation of Criollo type, combining strength and elegance. It is broad and deep in the body,

with strong loins and hindquarters. Generally larger than the Paso Fino, the Peruvian has long, sloping shoulders to facilitate its longer stride. The bone is strong and dense, and the pasterns are long. The croup slopes, and the tail is set low and carried quietly. The mane and tail are full, and hair is long and fine. The neck is crested, but long, and the head is always carried high.

Below: A fine Peruvian Horse mare and foal feeding in a well-fenced paddock.

PINTO
(Paint)

Country of origin
United States.

Height
Varies widely.

Color
There are two Pinto patterns. In the Overo, white patches start from the belly and extend up. The back, mane and tail tend to be dark, the face white and the eyes "glass" (blue). The limbs are dark and white.

In the Tobiano, white patches have no regular place of origin but often start from the back. Patches are larger than on the Overo and are of solid color. White legs are common, but the white face and glass eyes are rare. Tobiano horses are usually larger than Overos.

Features
Tough, spectacularly colored horses. They were famous as mounts for Indians, but today they are used for general riding.

Like the Palomino, the Pinto was originally registered in the United States as a color rather than a breed. However, today, the name covers four conformation types because the Pinto coloration is prepotent and tends to reproduce itself. The mixture of black and white (called piebald) or of bay or brown and white horses (skewbald) is not found amongst purebreds, such as the Arab and

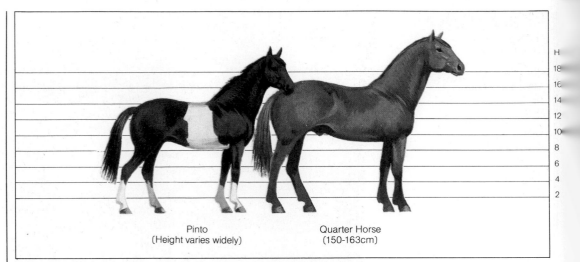

Pinto
(Height varies widely)

Quarter Horse
(150-163cm)

Above: A Pinto, or Paint as it is often called, standing square.

Below: Portrait of a Pinto horse.

Thoroughbred.

Pinto types are covered by three separate registries in the United States. The American Paint Horse Registry was founded to register horses of Stock Horse type, with Quarter Horse and Thoroughbred breeding and conformation.

The Pinto Registry registers four types—the Stock-Horse type,

Above: Pintos being ridden in Western Gear.

the Hunter type (an English horse of predominantly Arabian or Morgan breeding) and the Saddle type (an English horse of predominantly American Saddlebred breeding with a high head carriage and animated, high action).

The Moroccan Spotted Horse Cooperative Association registers gaited horses and also those of Hackney, Saddlebred, Tennessee Walker, Arabian, Morgan and Thoroughbred ancestry.

The Pinto Registry, started in 1956, now includes over 30,000 horses in the United States, Canada, Europe and Asia, but it is as an American horse that the breed is best known.

QUARTER HORSE
(American Quarter Horse)

Country of origin
United States..

Height
14·3-16hh (59-64in).

Color
Most, however white markings are not allowed. Horses cannot be registered if there are white markings.

Features
A tremendously strong, gentle, agile and versatile breed that is used for everything from racing to rodeos and trail riding. It is the most common breed in the United States.

The American Quarter Horse was developed in the 18th century in the United States by settlers in Virginia and the Carolinas. They wanted a horse to race, but the only easily accessible tracks were main streets and cleared ways through virgin wilderness. About ¼ mile was the usual length of

this type of track, hence the name given to the breed when the Society was formed in 1940.

Over this distance, great powers of acceleration were needed. It was discovered that the fastest horses were crossbreds between the British imports of the developing Thoroughbred and the local Chickasaw Indian pony. The Indian pony was wild Mustang stock of Spanish and Barb origins (see page 121) that had been caught by the Indians. Mustangs had tremendous powers of acceleration.

The most famous early Thoroughbred sire was Janus, which stood at stud in Virginia and North Carolina between 1756 and 1780. In England, he had raced over 4 miles, but his progeny won regularly over quarter of a mile sprints in the United States.

With the development of proper

courses and the advancement in Thoroughbred breeding, racing down main streets and through clearings became less common. But more organized Quarter Mile Horse Racing continued. Today, the world's richest horse race is the All-American Futurity for 3-year-old Quarter Horses.

It was discovered that the Quarter Horses had talents other than racing. They were strong enough to carry big men and heavy packs all day. With the spread of cattle ranches, these horses became known as *the* best cowponies and, later, rodeo horses. They were agile, fast and tough, which made them very popular with the cowboys for ranching and for rodeo work.

Today, the Quarter Horse is the most numerous breed in the United States, with more than two

million horses registered. Their export has resulted in more than 80,000 Quarter Horses being registered in 57 other countries. Their calm temperament, their great powers of acceleration and their strength and agility make them popular in so many spheres.

The Quarter Horse has a short, broad head with small alert ears, wide-set eyes, large, sensitive nostrils and a short muzzle. The head joins the neck at almost a 45° angle, with a distinct space between the jaw bone and neck muscles. The neck is medium length and slightly arched. Shoulders are deep and sloping. Withers are pronounced and medium to high. The chest is deep and broad, and the back and loins are short and very powerful. Quarters are broad, deep and heavy when veiwed from either side or rear. They are very muscular through the thigh and second thigh. Hocks are wide, deep, straight and clean. Cannons are short. Pasterns are medium length. The feet are round and roomy, with a deep, open heel. There is considerable substance to the limbs.

The Quarter Horse possesses great driving power in its hind-quarters and stands with its hindlegs well underneath its body. This use of the hindquarters continues in movement—the hocks are always placed well under the horse. This gives great collection to its action, and it can turn, stop and start with unusual ease and balance.

Below: These Quarter Horses are being ridden out. This is the most popular cowpony in the United States because it is agile, fast and readily trainable.

RUSSIAN TROTTER

Country of origin
USSR.
Height
15·3-16hh (63-64in)
Color
Most are bay, but some are black, chestnut or gray.
Features
A tough, muscular horse developed from Orlov and Standardbred blood to produce a fast trotter with good, strong conformation.

Russian Trotter
(160-163cm)

Saddlebred
(152-163cm)

The USSR led the world in the early stages of harness racing. It was the first to produce a specialized breed, the Orlov Trotter (page 124). This breed sustained its reputation as the finest harness racing horse until the late 19th century. The development of the American Standardbred ended this supremacy, and from 1890 on, American horses were imported and crossbred to the Orlov. A faster trotter was produced.

In the ensuing years, selective breeding with the Orlov and these crossbreds resulted in the official recognition of the Russian Trotter as a breed in 1949. In recent years, small additional infusions of American blood have been introduced.

The Russian Trotter has a light, robust frame. Its head has a straight face. The neck is straight and the shoulder long and sloping. The body is deep, the back muscular, and the croup sloping. The legs of the Russian Trotter are fine and hard.

Above: A Russian Trotter showing the breed's typical straight face.

Right: The Russian Trotter was produced by crossing Russian Orlov trotters with American Standardbreds.

AMERICAN SADDLEBRED
(Kentucky Saddler)

Country of origin
United States.
Height
15-16hh (60-64in).
Color
Bay, chestnut or gray, but occasionally roan, pinto, or palomino.
Features
An intelligent, versatile breed that can be used for many purposes. It is best known as a show animal with animated gaits. In the case of the Five-Gaited horses, two extra gaits can be taught, which are unique to the breed.

The Saddlebred, originally called the Kentucky Saddler, is the "All American Horse." The breed was developed by Kentucky pioneers as an all-around asset. It was comfortable and fast to ride the trails and plantations, stylish and eye-catching to pull fancy buggies, strong and tractable to pull a plough, and fast and courageous to race against other farmers' horses on special occasions. These were the demands, and the stock used was Thoroughbreds, Morgans, Trotters and the now extinct Narragansett Pacers.

Of the Thoroughbreds, the most famous was Denmark (1839), whose son, Gaines Denmark (1851) is the officially recognized foundation sire. The result was a horse with speed, action, style and stamina, that gained fame as the mounts of many well-known generals in the Civil War.

In 1891, in Louisville, Kentucky, the American Saddle Horse Breeders Association was formed—one of the earliest breed associations to exist in the United States. A register was started, and careful selection of parents with adherence to a recognized type was encouraged.

The American Saddlebred, as it is usually called, is used for many purposes. It is agile, fast, intelligent, responsive, strong and balanced. It is popular for pleasure riding, driving, hunting, jumping, and as a parade horse, but it is best known as a show horse.

The American Saddlebred has three divisions: The Three-Gaited, the Five-Gaited and the Fine Harness Horse. The Three-Gaited Horse is judged on its action, conformation, animation, manners and soundness. It should execute gaits in a slow, collected manner, with high action. The head should be high, with an overall impression of brilliance. The mane of a Three-Gaited Horse is always clipped.

The Five-Gaited Horse has a full mane. It is shown in its three natural gaits, walk, trot and canter, and two man-made gaits, the slow gait and the rack. The ability to learn these two gaits is inherent

in the breed, but it usually takes a good trainer for the horse to perform well. They are both four-beat and very smooth for the rider. The slow gait should be done very slowly with the legs lifted very high, particularly in front. The rack is a much faster version. Speed is desirable if done in form. The knee and hock action should be snappy.

The Fine Harness is shown in two gaits: the animated walk, and an airy part trot, when there should be plenty of action behind and in front. Extreme speed is penalized. The mane is full and the vehicle four-wheeled. Once again performance, conformation, animation, manners and sound-ness are judged.

These three divisions are sub-divided. In each of them there may be performance classes, where the emphasis is on activity and motion, pleasure classes, where the emphasis is on manners and the provision of a pleasant ride, (in this sub-division even the Three-Gaited have a full mane), and the equitation classes, where riders are judged for their skill in presenting their mounts.

The Saddlebred has great quality and substance. The head is well-shaped, with small alert ears. The large eyes are set well apart. The Saddlebred has a good muzzle and wide nostrils. The neck is long and arched. The withers are sharp, the shoulder is sloping and the back is short. The croup is level with the tail, which is set high. The quarters are muscular. The legs are straight with long sloping pasterns. The hooves are good and sound and they are open at the heels.

Above: A handsome Saddlebred trots out to exercise.

Below: The Saddlebred shows off one of its spectacular gaits, the rack.

SELLE FRANÇAIS

Country of origin
France.
Height
15·3-16·2hh (63-68in)
Color
Chestnut is most common, but all colors are permissible.
Features
This supple, active, robust sports horse was established in 1958 by the amalgamation of the French breeds of half-bloods.

Selle Français
(160-168cm)

Shagya
(147-152cm)

The Selle Français came into existence in 1958. It was a title given to the amalgamation of the French regional breeds of riding horses, other than Arabs, Thoroughbreds, and Anglo-Arabs. These regional breeds had been classed as half-bloods, and they were pedigree breeds with records tracing back many generations. Those with unknown or missing origins are now known as Cheval de Selle.

The most popular of these half-bloods was the Anglo-Norman. It had been bred in Normandy where the soil and climate help to produce horses with good bone and strong muscles. The breed traces back to the medieval Norman war horse, which was refined in the late 18th and early 19th centuries through the use of Arab, Thoroughbred and Norfolk Trotter blood. These refinements led to two branches—the trotter and the cavalry horse. The cavalry horse became known as the Anglo-Norman, which has proved to be the more influential blood for the Selle Français.

The other major breeding area for half-bloods was in the Limousin, after which the regional breed was named. The Limousin has had a strong Arab influence, beginning with horses brought to France by the Moors in the 8th century. Thoroughbred blood and Anglo-Norman blood has also been used.

Other regional breeds include the Vendeen Charollais and Angevins. Since the 19th century, they have been based on crossing native mares with Normans, Anglo-Normans, Thoroughbreds, Arabs, Anglo-Arabs and Norfolk Trotters.

With Anglo-Normans used often for crossbreeding, regional breeds of horses became more alike. The establishment of the Selle Français was a logical step.

The Selle Français remains an amalgamation of breeds, with 33% having a Thoroughbred sire, 20% Anglo-Arab, 45% Selle Français and 2% Trotter.

The Selle Français falls into three divisions. The most valuable are the competition horses. The Selle Français have shown their aptitude for jumping, dressage and eventing with such great horses as I Love You and Galoubet.

The second division is for race

horses. There are many French race meetings for horses which are not Thoroughbreds, known as A.Q.P.S.A., (*Cheveaux*) *Autres Que Pur Sang Anglais*, or "(Horses) of Other than Pure English Blood." Most of these races are over fences. Horses from this division have also excelled as Eventers.

The third division is for non-specialist horses, which are useful in riding schools and trail riding.

With such a variety of parents and uses, the Selle Français is not uniform. It is divided into middleweights and heavyweights, according to their substance and weight-carrying capacity. Middleweights have more Thoroughbred blood.

The ideal Selle Français is a strong, muscular horse, with a distinguished head, expressive eyes, a long neck and sloping shoulders. It should have a strong muscular body, large hindquarters, strong limbs with muscular forearms, well-defined joints and good bone. Its paces are supple, free and active.

Above right: A Selle Français has muscular, strong conformation.

Below: A team of Selle Français being driven.

SHAGYA

Country of origin
Hungary.
Height
14·2-15hh (58-60in).
Color
Usually gray.
Features
Similar to the Arab, this horse is famous as a cavalry and carriage horse and has proved itself capable of a wide range of activities, from farm work to general riding.

The Shagya is a Hungarian breed that is based on the Arab. It was developed at the Hungarian Arab stud of Babolna, which the state has owned since 1789, and which has specialized in Arabs since 1816. Like other Hungarian breeds, the Shagya is named after its foundation sire, which was born in 1830 and bought from the Bedouins to stand at Babolna. Other desert and Egyptian stock was imported around this time. Some Arab mares, together with local stock which was not always purebred, were put to Shagya to start a special type. Careful selective breeding and some inbreeding was practiced to establish this distinctive breed.

As the breed became established, and its value was realized as a light cavalry and carriage horse, it was bred elsewhere in Hungary. It was then exported to Poland, Austria, Romania, the United States and Czechoslovakia.

Today, at Babolna nearly half the stock is original Arab and the remainder are Shagyas. The breed has proved itself as a sports horse and as a good mount for general riding.

In appearance, the Shagya is similar to the Arab but a little more robust. It is a hardy breed and can thrive on poor food. It is a good mover, athletic and energetic.

Above: O'Bajan 1, a beautiful Shagya from Hungary.

STANDARDBRED

Country of origin
United States.
Height
14-16hh (56-64in)
Color
Bay is most common, but all colors are found.
Features
This is the fastest breed of trotter. It is used extensively for racing and to upgrade other breeds of harness racers.

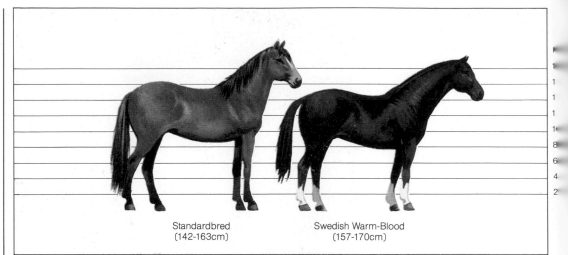

Standardbred
(142-163cm)

Swedish Warm-Blood
(157-170cm)

The Standardbred is the world's fastest breed for harness racing. It was developed principally from Thoroughbred stock. The most important of these was Messenger (1780), who traces back to all three foundation sires of the Thoroughbred. When he stood at stud in the United States he was put to a variety of local mares. But as the trotting races were held over well-ridden fields and were very amateur affairs, there was little thought of starting a breed of trotters from this sire.

Yet Messenger founded a dynasty of harness racers. He had four sons to which nearly every Standardbred can be traced.

The most important of his descendants was born in the era when the sport was fast gaining popularity and selective breeding

was being practiced to produce fast harness racers. This great sire was Hambletonian 10 (1849), who is considered to be the father of the modern Standardbred, producing 1,335 offspring.

The other important Thoroughbred sire was Diomed (1777).

Thoroughbreds were put to more robust strains and particularly those with the talent for trotting or pacing .These included Narragansett and Canadian Pacers and Cleveland Bays, but the most important breeds, apart from the Thoroughbred, seemed to be Morgans and Norfolk Trotters. The most

Right: A Standardbred shows its natural ability to pace.

Below; Standardbreds racing in Kentucky.

influential Norfolk Trotter was Bellfounder (1816), who stood in the United States in the 1820s and was the grandsire of Hambletonian 10.

In the 19th century, the informal, ridden trotting races began to be turned into increasingly official harness races. This saw the consequent growth of selective breeding to produce faster horses for the sport. An American Trotting Register was started in 1871 and the National Association of Trotting Horse Breeders laid down the standards for inclusion in 1879. A 1-mile speed standard was set of 2 minutes, 30 seconds for trotters and 2 minutes, 25 seconds for pacers, hence the name Standardbred. Pacers move their legs in lateral pairs rather than in diagonal pairs like trotters. Entry standards were adjusted with the passage of time, and today they relate to blood alone.

Harness racing has flourished in the United States with horses becoming as valuable as flat race horses. The American Standard-bred has become so good at its sport that it has been exported all over the world to improve other breeds of harness racer.

With speed being of primary importance, conformation of the Standardbred varies. It is usually shorter in the legs and stronger in the body than a Thoroughbred. It is more robust in appearance, with powerful quarters, and hind legs behind, not under, the quarters.

SWEDISH WARM-BLOOD

Country of origin
Sweden.
Height
15·2-16·3hh (62-67in).
Color
All solid colors.
Features
A highly intelligent horse, with spirit, yet tractable. It is athletic and has excelled in all Olympic equestrian disciplines, as well as driving.

The Swedish Warm-blood was developed as remounts for the Swedish cavalry. During the 19th century, native stock was crossed with carefully chosen imports, mainly Thoroughbreds, Hanoverians and Trakehners. A stud book was started in 1874, and more rigorous standards were laid down for entry into it. These began with veterinary, conformation and action tests. Temperament, performance and pedigree tests were added at later stages. The stallions must go through extensive tests in dressage, jumping, cross country and harness. Then they are given a full breeding license only after their 3-year-old progeny

has been examined.

This rigorous selection, together with continued importing of breeding stock when it is needed to counteract any weakness in the breed (the studbook is not closed), has led to the Swedish Warm-blood being one of the best breeds of sports horse in the world. Representatives of the breed have won gold medals at the Olympics in all three disciplines and have been very successful in driving.

The Swedish government actively supports the breeding of their Warm-blood. They run a national stud at Flyinge, where most leading stallions stand. Only a few stallions are privately owned.

The Swedes are very particular about the heads of their horses. The breed has an intelligent outlook, big, bold eyes and refined features. The neck is long and slightly crested. The shoulder is deep and sloping. The body and quarters are muscular and strong. Limbs are round, with short cannons. Feet are strong but tend to be narrow.

The Swedish Warm-blood is an athlete, with springy, free, powerful paces. This makes it much in demand as a competition horse.

Left: The Swedish Warm-Blood, Salute, does a pirouette in dressage.

Below: Jan Pahlsson drives his team of Swedish Warm-Bloods.

SWISS WARM-BLOOD

(Swiss Half-Blood)

Country of origin
Switzerland.
Height
15·3-16·2hh (63-66in)
Color
Any.
Features
This is a new breed of sports horse that is being promoted by the Swiss government, and is beginning to make its mark in competitions.

Swiss Warm-Blood
(160-168cm)

Tennessee Walking Horse
(152-163cm)

The Swiss Warm-blood is another post-World War II breed of sports horse. The Swiss are major importers of riding horses. But their national stud at Avenches has been directed by the government to produce riding horses, work horses and Army horses. This is leading to a successful new national breed.

The foundation stock were Swiss mares. Many of these can be traced to foreign origins (usually Holstein and Anglo-Norman). The main Swiss breed used was the Einsiedler, which is now merged with the Warm-blood. Records of the Einsiedler trace back to a stud started at the Benedictine Abbey of Einsiedler in 1064. The breed was a utility type for work, pleasure and the Army. But increasing injections of Anglo-Norman blood led to it becoming more of a sports horse, indistinguishable from the Swiss Warm-blood. In 1967 and 1968, some imported blood from Sweden and Ireland was added to these homebred mares.

Stallions were originally mainly imports, but today more Swiss Warm-bloods are standing at Avenches. The original stock

Above: One of the most successful Swiss Warm-Bloods is the dressage horse, Aristo. Here he is being ridden by the late Clare Koch.

Right: A Swiss Warm-Blood suckling her foal.

was mostly Selle Français, with some Thoroughbred, Hanoverian, Trakehner and Swedish Warm-blood.

Strict selective methods have been imposed. Stallions must go through two performance tests, one at 3½ years of age and another at 5½. Tests for conformation, action, soundness and pedigrees are also given. There are also progeny tests, and mares are strictly examined.

The aim of the Swiss is to produce a noble horse, large and correct, with a tractable temperament and a good character. It should be suitable for general riding, competitions and driving.

TENNESSEE WALKING HORSE

(Plantation Walker, Turn-Row)

Country of origin
United States (Tennessee).
Height
15-16hh (60-64in).
Color
Chestnut, (sometimes with flaxen mane and tail), black, bay and roan are common. Many often have white markings. Occasionally gray.
Features
An exceptionally comfortable and kind breed. This is a popular pleasure and show horse. Its unique "running walk" is a breathtaking spectacle. It once was a utility farm horse used in harness or for riding, but today it is used for showing, pleasure and trail riding.

The Tennessee Walking Horse is known as 'the world's greatest show, pleasure and trail-ride horse'. It was developed as a breed in the 19th century by the Tennessee plantation owners. They wanted a comfortable horse to ride around their properties. The horse needed to be agile to turn in plantation rows without injuring plants. Other names for this breed, *Plantation Walker* and *Turn-Row*, indicate how successful it was at these tasks.

The main foundation stock used were Narraganset Pacers and Canadian Pacers, both popular lateral-gaited horses of colonial times. Thoroughbred, Saddlebred, Standardbred and Morgan were also used in the formation of this unusual breed. The most influential stallion was Black Allan, a Standardbred, foaled in 1886.

The Tennessee Walker is highly versatile. As a pleasure horse, it can be ridden Western, English or plantation style.It can also be driven. It has a docile temperament which makes it highly trainable, and it is suitable both for novice and experienced riders.

One of the outstanding features of this breed is its comfortable

Above: The handsome head of a Tennessee Walking Horse, wearing a Western bridle.

and unusual gaits. These are the *flat-foot walk, running walk* and *rocking-chair canter.* All are natural to the breed, and even the running walk is performed by foals without any training. Yet it is unique to the Walker; no other breed has

mastered this gait.

The flat-foot walk is a 1-2-3-4 beat with each foot hitting the ground at regular intervals. With its right hindfoot, the horse glides over the track left by the right front foot, and the same with the left. This is called *overstride.* The horse nods its head in time with its feet.

The running walk is basically the same flat-foot walk but with an

increase in speed and overstride. It is a smooth gliding gait in which the horse pulls with the front feet and pushes with the rear. The hindfoot overstrides by 12-20 or more inches, and a speed of 6 to 9 miles per hour is sustained. In the show ring, the running walk is done at an extremely fast speed. Great elevation is obtained by keeping the horse's front hoofs long and having him wear heavily weighted shoes that must be attached with steel bands. Speeds of over 15 miles an hour can be obtained but cannot be maintained for long. Due to the manner of shoeing, a show horse can only be ridden in an arena.

The canter is often called the "rocking-chair canter." It is a high, rolling, collected movement that doesn't jar or jolt the rider.

This horse is used in the United States and abroad. Its success has stemmed largely from the work of the Tennessee Walking Horse Breeders' Association, started in 1935. The Tennessee Walking Horse is close coupled and robust. The head is large and plain, and the neck and back are short. The hindquarters are muscular and strong, and the croup slopes. The tail of the show horse may be artificially set to be carried high. The limbs of the Tennessee Walking Horse are strong, with good bone.

Below: The Tennessee Walking Horse displays its spectacular gaits.

TERSK

(Tersky)

Country of origin
USSR.

Height
14·3-15·1hh (59-61in).

Color
Gray, with a silver sheen, is the most common, but they can be chestnut or bay.

Features
A tough, robust version of the Arab, this horse is capable of a wide range of uses, from circus work to racing.

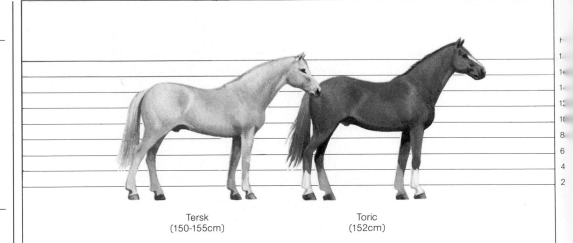

Tersk
(150-155cm)

Toric
(152cm)

The Tersk is a new breed developed in the Stavropol region (North Caucasus) of the USSR. The first steps in its creation were taken in the 1920s when some of the few remaining (now extinct) Strelets were collected at the Tersk stud. The Strelets were large Arab types, based on native Ukrainian mares and selected Oriental sires. These Strelets were crossed with Arabs, Arab-Don crossbreds, Strelets-Kabardin crossbreds, and Shagyas from Hungary. Selective breeding was imposed, and the breed was officially recognized in 1948.

The breeding aim was to produce a horse with the features of the Arabs (elegance, movement and endurance), combined with the robustness and toughness of native breeds.

The Tersk has proved to be gentle, intelligent, agile, athletic and capable of endurance. This has made it suitable for many purposes. It is entered in races for non-Thoroughbreds. It is used also for endurance rides and is popular with the Army, both for riding and harness work. It is used in competitions, particularly for dressage, and is popular in the circus. It is also used to improve other breeds, including the Karabakh and Lokai. Recently, there has been some crossing with the Thoroughbred to produce a larger horse.

The Tersk's head is of medium length, and the face is straight or slightly dished. The eyes are large, and the ears are long. The neck and back are medium length, the shoulder is sloping, the body is deep and the quarters are broad and muscular. The tail is set high. The limbs are fine, but the bone is dense. The hooves are strong.

Right: A herd of Tersks roaming free at Stavropol in the USSR.

Below: A Tersk stallion. This breed from the Caucasus in the USSR is based on Arab stock.

TORIC

Country of origin
USSR (Estonia).
Height
15hh (60in).
Color
Most are chestnut or bay.
Features
A high-class utility horse, capable of heavy draft work and general riding. It has great powers of endurance and unusual energy for such a heavy breed.

The Toric is probably the heaviest breed included in this section. It is used extensively for farm work, but lighter versions are used also increasingly for sport and general riding.

The Toric was developed in the late 19th and early 20th centuries from local ponies of Estonia, called Kleppers. These were the working ponies of Estonia, and a very small number still exist today. These dun ponies were prepotent for toughness and hardiness, which made them useful foundation stock. The Viatka (see page 47) also has Klepper blood. The Toric was officially recognized as a breed in 1950.

In the development of the Toric, many breeds were utilized in this upgrading of the Klepper. Arab, Ardennes, Thoroughbred, Orlov, Norfolk Roadster and Breton were used to increase its size and strength. The Norfolk Roadster Hatman seems to have been one of the most influential. Many Torics today trace back to him. Further crossbreeding was practiced in the 20th century with some German breeds, and the end result was a strong horse with unusually good paces and jumping ability.

The Toric's head is medium length. The neck is muscular and crested; this feature is especially noticeable in stallions. The back is long, broad and muscular. The limbs are short and strong.

Below: A strong, powerful Toric from Estonia, in the USSR.

TRAKEHNER
(East Prussian)

Country of origin
West Germany (East Prussia)

Height
16-16·2hh (64-66in).

Color
Any solid color, but they tend to be dark.

Features
Once renowned as cavalry horses, in the 20th century Trakehners have become leading competition horses. The serious depletion of their numbers, due to the destruction of their stud in World War II, has enabled other breeds to compete with them for the leading breed of sports horse.

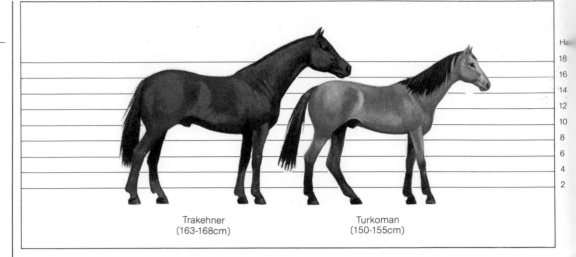

Trakehner
(163-168cm)

Turkoman
(150-155cm)

The Trakehner is one of the oldest, most elegant of the German breeds of warm-bloods. Its breeding was based at the Trakehnen stud, which was founded in 1732 by Frederick William I of Prussia. The stud consisted of a large area of drained marshlands, which proved to be ideal for rearing horses. The foundation stock was the local Schweiken horse, a tough, active, little horse used on the East Prussian farms for centuries. The Schweikens were put mainly to Arabs and later Thoroughbreds, but some Turkoman blood was

Below: The Trakehner Agent shows his handsome head.

used through the stallion, Turkmen Atti. This mixture and careful selection soon resulted in a high-class cavalry and coach horse.

The production was extended as the Trakehner's fame spread. Just before World War II there were more than 10,000 breeders and 18,000 registered mares. All the farmers in the area bred Trakehners, because it was profitable and the horses thrived well on their lands.

Breeding was strictly organized. The Trakehnen stud was the center where breeding stock was thoroughly tested. Three-year-olds were trained, and 4-year-olds tested by hunting with hounds and competing in cross-country races. The best stallions were kept at the Trakehnen stud. The second class went to the state studs, the third to private breeders

and the remainder were gelded and used as Army remounts.

The war disrupted the stud, and with the prospect of Russian occupation, a small group of refugees took 600 mares and a few stallions to the West. The majority of the breed was left behind in what became Poland. These formed the basis of the Mazury and Poznan breeds and were later amalgamated into the Wielkopolski breed.

The small nucleus of Trakehners that crossed the River Elbe into West Germany in 1945 was carefully built up. The Trakehner is the one national breed of warm-blood in Germany with bases all over the country. Neumünster in the northwest is used as the auction and training center.

Care was taken in this multiplica-tion of the breed, and today's

Trakehner breeds are truer to type than most warm-bloods. Its distinctive characteristics are passed onto the new generations, which proves the purity of the blood.

The Trakehner features of elegance, courage and stamina are in demand, and it has been used to upgrade stock in Germany (particularly the Hanoverian and Baden Württemburg) and abroad in the United States and Sweden.

The Trakehner has an elegant head, which is broad between large eyes and narrows toward the muzzle. The neck is long and crested, the shoulder slopes and the withers are prominent. The back is strong and medium length, and the quarters are muscular and gently rounded.

The Trakehner's supple paces and its tractable but spirited temperament make it a good competition and riding horse.

TURKOMAN
(Turkmen, Turkmene)

Country of origin
Turkmenistan (Afghanistan/Iran/USSR).

Height
14·3-15·1hh (59-61in).

Color
Gray, bay, chestnut or dun.

Features
This is an ancient horse that has tremendous stamina and speed over long distances. It was used for racing more than 2,000 years ago.

The Turkoman is not a breed in the strict sense of the word. It has no breed society. It is a horse that has been bred for centuries in Turkmenistan, an area of mainly desertlike land, that now forms the southeast corner of the USSR. It is bordered by the Caspian Sea on the west, Afghanistan to the southeast and Iran to the south. Today, the Turkoman is represented by the Russian breeds of Akhal-Teke and Iomud, which were established from the horses of Turkmenistan.

The Turkoman is a legendary

horse, which was supposed to have been used in Persia in ancient times by the great leaders Darius and Alexander. It was then called the Bactrian or Turanian horse. Darius was believed to have had 10,000 horsemen mounted on them. It also became known as the "heavenly" horse of Chinese legend. In 126 B.C., the Chinese attacked the Bactrian Kingdom (made up of the northern slopes of Afghanistan, which had formerly been part of the Persian Empire) to collect these extraordinary "blood-sweating heavenly horses"; such was their reputation.

The origins of the Turkoman are controversial. Some authorities, such as R. S. Summerhays, claim it is a mixture of Mongolian and Arab blood (mainly Persian). Others, such as Michael Schafer, believe it descended from the wild horses of the Steppe type and it is this group of Steppe Horses which settled in Asia. The other horses went to the Iberian Peninsula and are represented today by the Andalusian (page 87).

The Turkoman was said to have been similar to the mount of the Scythians in the first century A.D. It was certainly the horse of the Turkoman tribesmen. Descriptions of the Turkoman tribes' horses from the 16th century on say it was larger and longer striding than the Arab. It is also said it had a rather big head, was lean, angular and fast, and did not have the beauty of the Arab.

These Turkoman horses were important foundation stock for other breeds, particularly in the USSR. Turkomans were also used in the founding of the Trakehner. Turkmen Atti was an important early sire of Turkoman descent. Turkish horses were definitely used in the development of the Thoroughbred, and these must have had some Turkoman blood.

J. Osborne, in *Horsebreeders' Notebook,* claims there were 32 Eastern sires of Turkoman origin used in the founding of the Thoroughbred. However, it is questionable whether the most famous one, Byerley Turk, was pure Turkoman. He was believed to have had a large proportion of Arab blood. However, the Turkoman has founded breeds that are based on its stock. The Akhal-Teke (pages 84-85) and Iomud (page 110) from Turkmenistan in the USSR have been developed from it.

One of the Turkoman's original homes was Persia. It is still being bred on the Turkoman Steppes in northern Iran that border the USSR.

Below: A portrait of a Turkoman.

Above: The most successful Trakehner stallion, Abdullah. Conrad Hornfeld rode him in 1984 to win the Olympic Silver medal.

UKRAINIAN RIDING HORSE

Country of origin
USSR.
Height
Around 16hh (64in).
Color
Most are bay, chestnut or black.
Features
This is a new breed group of purpose-bred horses for general riding and sport. They have been developed since the last war, and nearly 50,000 are registered today.

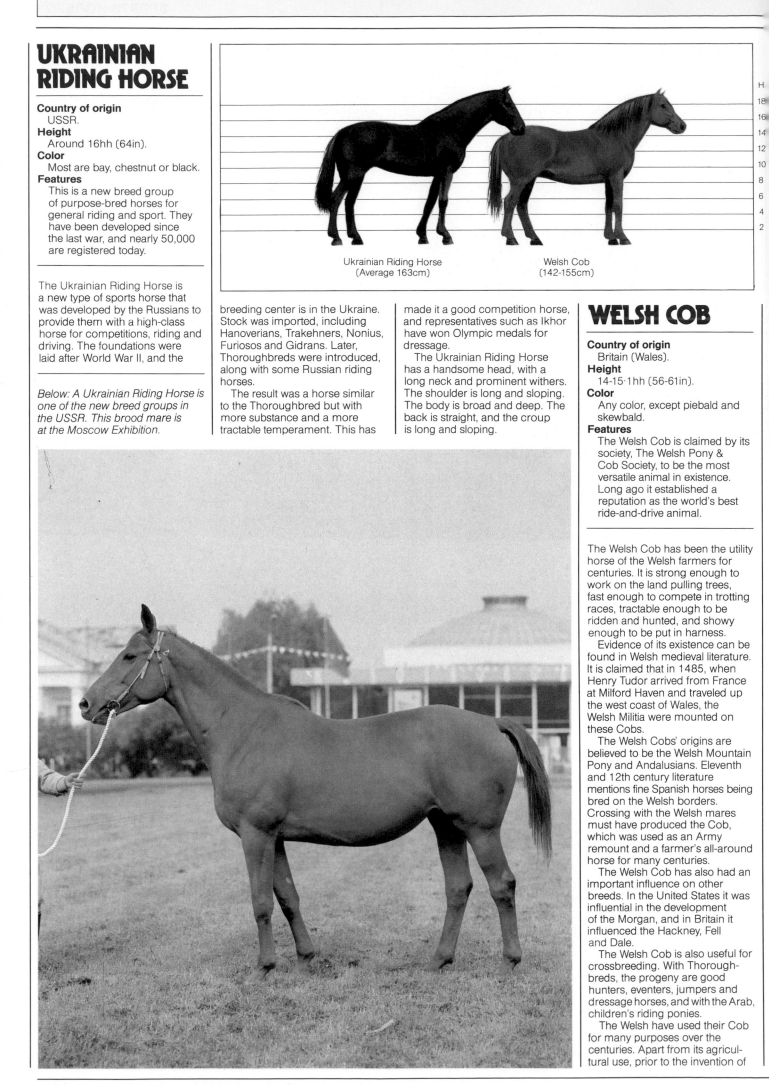

Ukrainian Riding Horse
(Average 163cm)

Welsh Cob
(142-155cm)

The Ukrainian Riding Horse is a new type of sports horse that was developed by the Russians to provide them with a high-class horse for competitions, riding and driving. The foundations were laid after World War II, and the

Below: A Ukrainian Riding Horse is one of the new breed groups in the USSR. This brood mare is at the Moscow Exhibition.

breeding center is in the Ukraine. Stock was imported, including Hanoverians, Trakehners, Nonius, Furiosos and Gidrans. Later, Thoroughbreds were introduced, along with some Russian riding horses.

The result was a horse similar to the Thoroughbred but with more substance and a more tractable temperament. This has

made it a good competition horse, and representatives such as Ikhor have won Olympic medals for dressage.

The Ukrainian Riding Horse has a handsome head, with a long neck and prominent withers. The shoulder is long and sloping. The body is broad and deep. The back is straight, and the croup is long and sloping.

WELSH COB

Country of origin
Britain (Wales).
Height
14-15·1hh (56-61in).
Color
Any color, except piebald and skewbald.
Features
The Welsh Cob is claimed by its society, The Welsh Pony & Cob Society, to be the most versatile animal in existence. Long ago it established a reputation as the world's best ride-and-drive animal.

The Welsh Cob has been the utility horse of the Welsh farmers for centuries. It is strong enough to work on the land pulling trees, fast enough to compete in trotting races, tractable enough to be ridden and hunted, and showy enough to be put in harness.

Evidence of its existence can be found in Welsh medieval literature. It is claimed that in 1485, when Henry Tudor arrived from France at Milford Haven and traveled up the west coast of Wales, the Welsh Militia were mounted on these Cobs.

The Welsh Cobs' origins are believed to be the Welsh Mountain Pony and Andalusians. Eleventh and 12th century literature mentions fine Spanish horses being bred on the Welsh borders. Crossing with the Welsh mares must have produced the Cob, which was used as an Army remount and a farmer's all-around horse for many centuries.

The Welsh Cob has also had an important influence on other breeds. In the United States it was influential in the development of the Morgan, and in Britain it influenced the Hackney, Fell and Dale.

The Welsh Cob is also useful for crossbreeding. With Thoroughbreds, the progeny are good hunters, eventers, jumpers and dressage horses, and with the Arab, children's riding ponies.

The Welsh have used their Cob for many purposes over the centuries. Apart from its agricultural use, prior to the invention of the automobile, businessmen and tradesmen found the Cob to be the speediest means of transportation. In the Army it was considered so valuable for mounted infantry and for pulling guns and equipment over rough terrain, that the government paid premiums for the best stallions.

Today, these handsome Cobs, with their spirited nature, are popular for driving. Welsh Cob teams have been very successful in international events. They are also used for trail riding. At shows, particularly in Wales, classes for Welsh Cobs are very popular. They are shown in hand, and their handlers have to run very fast to demonstrate their spectacular high-stepping trot.

The Cob's head is ponylike and full of quality. The eyes are bold, prominent and set well apart. The ears are neat and well-set. The neck is lengthy and well-crested in stallions. The shoulders are strong and laid back. The body is deep. The back and loins are muscular and strong, and the quarters are lengthy and strong. The limbs are muscular, with well-defined joints and good bone. The feet are well-shaped and dense. The hind leg should not be too bent nor the hock set behind a line falling from the point of the quarter to the fetlock joint. There is a moderate amount of fine silky feather on the limbs.

The Welsh Cob's action is free, true and forcible. The knee should bend, and the whole foreleg should extend straight from the shoulder as far forward as possible in the trot. The hocks should flex under the body, with straight, powerful leverage.

Above: The Welsh Cob, Llanarth Flying Comet, galloping free.

Below: Llanarth Flying Comet is from Section D of the stud book.

Here, he shows off his stocky, strong conformation.

WESTPHALIAN
(Westfalian)

Country of origin
Germany (Westphalia).
Height
15·2-16·2hh (62-66in).
Color
All solid colors.
Features
An athletic, strong breed of sports horse that has excelled at show jumping and dressage. It has also done well in eventing and driving.

The Westphalian is Germany's second most numerous regional breed after the Hanoverian. Like the other German warmbloods, it is not purebred. The stud book is not closed. At the state stud of Warendorf, there are Thoroughbred and Hanoverian stallions and Westphalians. The neighboring Hanoverian breed has played a major part in the Westphalian's 20th century development and its adaption from a farm and army horse into a sports horse.

Today, Westphalians are one of

Below: A handsome example of the Westphalian breed.

Westphalian.
(157-168cm)

Wielkopolski
(163-165cm)

the world's leading breeds of competition horses. Roman was their first major victor when he won the 1978 World Show Jumping title. In 1982, Fire won for them the same title. At the 1984 Olympics, Ahlerich took the individual gold medal and team gold medal in dressage.

The success of the breed is due to the rigorous methods of selection that were applied to a large number of horses. The Breeders Association was formed in 1826. At the Warendorf state stallion depot, horses are only permitted to stand after they have been through pedigree, conformation, character and riding tests. Stallions are tested for tractive power at 3½ years, for riding ability and jumping without a rider at 4 years, and for jumping and dressage with rider, plus veterinary examination, at 4½ years. These tests include observation of temperament, character, constitution, feed utilization, willingness to work, riding ability, jumping ability, working style and general

efficiency. Each horse is given a "training score" for these factors. Only the best are allowed to stand at Warendorf.

The Westphalian is a heavier, more substantial version of the Hanoverian. The head has an intelligent outlook, with good width between the eyes. The neck is well-shaped and harmoniously attached to a well-proportioned, deep, muscular body. The quarters are strong, but the croup can be straight. The Westphalian's limbs have good bone.

Above: The Westphalian show jumper, Fire, won the individual title for Germany at the 1982 World Championships in Dublin, Eire.

Below: Poland's riding horse, the Wielkopolski, standing square.

WIELKOPOLSKI

Country of origin
Poland.
Height
16-16·1hh (64-65in).
Color
Chestnut is most common but it can be bay, black or gray.
Features
This breed is based on the Trakehner stock left after the original stud was destroyed in World War II. The breed makes good riding, competition and draft horses.

This breed was established after the amalgamation of the Mazury (Masuren) and Poznan. Both these breeds were based on Trakehner/East Prussian stock. (The original, but now destroyed, stud of Trakehnen lies today in Poland.) With this common foundation and because they have been crossbred, it was logical to put them in one stud book.

The Wielkopolski is a utility breed and it is a good riding horse. Many have done well in competition. They are also used on the farms for draft work, particularly in western and central Poland.

Selective breeding of the Wielkopolski is practiced at 13 Polish state studs, and five of these concentrate on horses for sports purposes. Through this selective breeding, the height of the Wielkopolskis has been increased.

The Wielkopolski is a gentle horse, with a well-proportioned conformation. It is a muscular and strong middle- to heavyweight horse. Limbs have good bone.

145

TYPES

COB·HACK HUNTER POLO PONY RIDING PONY

Types differ from breeds because there are no stud books and no authenticated pedigrees. Also, because it is normal for the colts to be gelded, they are not used for breeding. Mare types are bred from, but rarely stallions. Types are produced by crossbreeding and there is no breeding true to type.

Types originated in the English-speaking world in response to a particular demand for horses or ponies. Most have a Thoroughbred or Arab as one of their parents. The abundant supply of Thoroughbreds that have relatively disappointing track performances and are therefore not in demand for breeding racehorses has meant crossbreeding is an economical way of producing the types of horses needed. There has been little incentive to turn them into a breed, as is usually done on the European continent.

The most important types produced today are the Cob, Hack, Hunter, Polo Pony and Riding Pony. In the United States, the Hunter is called a Jumper when it is used purely for jumping fences in an arena.

These types are used mainly in Britain, the United States, South Africa, Australia and New Zealand—countries that have not been so concerned with selective breeding and organizing societies (other than for racehorses and established purebreds) as in Europe.

Right: This Hunter is being exercised by the Master of the Taunton Vale Foxhounds, Somerset, England.
Below: Polo Ponies in action in Spain.

COB

Country of origin
 Britain.
Height
 14·2-15·2hh (58-62in).
Color
 Any.
Features
 A dumpy, strong, gentle horse
 that is popular for hunting,
 showing and general riding.

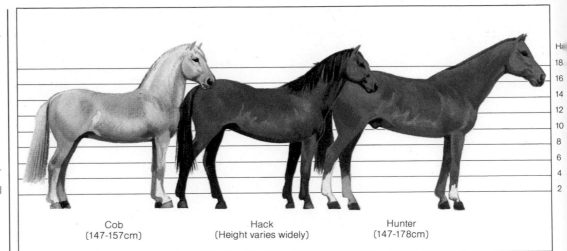

Cob
(147-157cm)

Hack
(Height varies widely)

Hunter
(147-178cm)

Cobs are compact, muscular, small
horses, with tremendous bone.
Although the term did not come
into use until the 18th century, the
type was used long ago in feudal
times when squires rode them in
battle and estate stewards rode
them in peace time. They were
called "rouncies".

Apart from the Welsh Cob, they
are not a breed and are produced
usually by chance. They are quite
often the by-product of Hunter
breeding. They did not grow large
but had great substance. The
breeding stock for Cobs is highly
varied, but some examples are
a Highland and a small Thoroughbred, a Suffolk Punch and an
Arab, or a Hunter mare and
an Arab. (See also Welsh Cob,
pages 142-143.)

The Cob has a ponylike head on
a muscular crested neck and a
strong sloping shoulder. It should
also have a deep, broad body, a
short back, rounded quarters,
short limbs with plenty of bone
and very short cannons. Feet
are hard and round.

The other feature of the Cob
is its temperament. It is supposed
to be very tractable and have
high-class manners. This makes it
a good ride for older and nervous
people. It is also used by racehorse trainers to watch their horses
work. It is an excellent hunter over
rough country or for heavy riders
who do not want to go too fast.

Its other use is as a show
horse. Classes are held for Cobs
at most major British shows.

HACK

Country of origin
 Britain.
Height
 Varies from country to country.
Color
 Any.
Features
 A refined, elegant horse that
 is a pleasure to ride and has
 great "presence".

"Hack" is a term that has been
used to describe a variety of
horses. It once meant a horse for
hire. Then it came to mean the
horse ridden to the meets (covert
hack) before transferring to the
hunter that was brought by the
groom. Later, it was the name
given to the elegant, refined horse
ridden by fashionable people.
Today, it covers different types of

*Above: The head of a Cob, which
is small and of good quality.*

horses in different countries. In the
United States, "Hack" usually
refers to a riding horse. It can also
refer to a pleasure-type American
Saddlebred or Hunter. A Bridle-
path Hack is usually a Saddlebred
type; a Hunter Hack is typically a
Thoroughbred and a Road Hack
can be a Morgan, Saddlebred or any
good-trotting English pleasure
horse. In Australia it is a Thoroughbred, and in Britain it is a smaller
horse, occasionally a Thoroughbred, but usually a crossbred.

Today's Hacks are showy
animals, which are well trained,
responsive to the aids (means of
controlling the horse) and very
easy to ride. They are supposed

*Below: A prize-winning Cob at the
1984 Royal Show, Stoneleigh, UK.*

to be horses which give pleasure
to riders who like non-competitive
activities, such as hacking, but
who also like to look good. To be
an enjoyable ride, the Hack should
have impeccable manners and
light, easy gaits.

Classes are held for Hacks in
various English-speaking countries.
Although terms of reference vary
(height, work required, etc.),
all are for lightweight, elegant
riding horses.

The principle criteria for judging
Hacks is conformation, "presence",
action, training, manners and ride.
Contestants are required to give a
short demonstration of their
correct training.

The head should have great
quality and be small. The neck
should be elegant and crested, the
body deep, quarters rounded
and limbs correct and fine.
Action should be light, straight
and true.

HUNTER

Country of origin
 Britain.
Height
 14·2-17·2hh (58-70in).
Color
 Any.
Features
 A courageous type, bold enough
 to get across country, yet clever
 enough to stay out of trouble.
 The Hunter must also have great
 stamina and provide the rider
 with a comfortable, smooth
 means of following hounds. In
 addition, Show Hunters need to
 have correct, harmonious
 conformation, "presence" and
 good free paces.

The Hunter carries a rider behind
hounds. It will vary greatly
according to the requirements, i.e.
the weight of the rider, the type of
quarry being chased, and the
type of terrain over which the
hunting takes place. All Hunters
have some features in common;
these include intelligence,
"handiness" (the ability to get out
of trouble when going across
country), stamina, jumping ability
good temperament, good con-

In Britain there are classes for Small Hunters, which are 14·2-15·2hh (58-62in); Light-weight Hunters, typically capable of carrying up to 175lb (79kg); Middle-weight Hunters, typically capable of carrying over 195lb (88kg); and Lady's Hunters which are horses suitable for carrying a lady side-saddle. In all of these classes the Hunters are judged upon how they perform on the flat. They should show free, straight, correct paces, particularly in the gallop. They should also have good manners, give a good ride to the judges, be sound and have a conformation that is likely to keep them this way, with harmonious proportions to the body, correct limbs and sufficient bone.

In the United States and in Britain's Working Hunter classes they are also required to jump. In the United States style is very important, and it is essential to maintain a constant rhythm into the fences.

The American classes are also split into divisions, some according to weight-carrying capacity, others according to the experience and previous successes of the horses. A Green Hunter is one in its first or second year of showing. A Working Hunter is one regularly hunted to hounds, and a Heavyweight Hunter one capable of carrying 200lb (91kg) or more.

The Hunter often turns out to be a good showjumper and, with the growth of this sport, the Jumper has become an important subdivision of the Hunter type.

Above: The champion show Hack, Tenterk, ridden by Robert Oliver. This fine horse has the elegant action of a true Hack.

Below: When young, Hunters are also shown in hand. This is Celtic Gold, which was champion young Hunter at The Royal Show, Stoneleigh, UK, in 1982.

formation and soundness.

In grassy country where there are plenty of fences to jump, a fast horse is needed, and the Thoroughbred or near Thoroughbred is considered the best.

In country where the going is deep and holding, a short-legged and powerful animal is more suitable. In hilly country, a balanced sure-footed horse with the stamina for the hard work of climbing up inclines is needed. In rough country, where there are many obstacles and little open land, a clever, handy horse of Cob type is suitable. Consequently, there are various subdivisions within the Hunter type. In addition, there are many other separate classes of Hunters that are used in the show ring.

POLO PONY

Country of origin
Argentina is the most successful producer.

Height
14·2-15·3hh (58-63in).

Color
Any.

Features
Courageous, spirited, tough, agile, fast types, that are usually almost Thoroughbred.

Polo Pony
(147-160cm)

Riding Pony
(Maximum 147cm)

Some of the original Polo Ponies, such as the Manipurs from India, were true breeds. Over the last century, when the game was introduced to Europe and North and South America, the height of these ponies has increased. They now usually range from 14·2hh (58in) to 15·3hh (63in). Although they have become horses, they are still referred to as ponies.

No single breed has been established as *the* Polo Pony. A number

Below: Polo Ponies in action on the unusual surface of snow.

of small Thoroughbreds are used, but it is the crossbred which has excelled. Argentina's Polo Pony is generally recognized as the best in the world. It is produced by crossing tough Criollos with Thoroughbreds.

In the 1890s, efforts were made in Britain to establish a good Polo Pony by using pony blood from some of Britain's native Mountain

and Moorland ponies, and the Thoroughbred. World War I disrupted this program, and it was never re-established. Instead, most countries have used imported Argentinian mares that have been crossbred to the Thoroughbred.

The Polo Pony is judged by its performance on the field. It must be able to gallop, to accelerate and stop very quickly, and to turn

on a dime or sixpence. It must be bold and strong enough to ride off the opposition. Polo Ponies do not need to be beautiful, but they must be tough and athletic, with a robust conformation.

Most Polo Ponies tend to have long thin necks, angular bodies with very strong quarters, correct sound limbs and quite upright pasterns.

RIDING PONY

Country of origin
Britain.
Height
Up to 14·2hh (58in).
Color
Any.
Features
Types with good conformation, action and manners, that are suitable for children to ride.

Most pony breeds evolved in the wild over the centuries. They had to be tough to survive and usually have a touch of native cunning, which makes them less tractable and trainable. Their robust bodies tend to be broad, which makes it difficult for children to get their legs around them. They are not ideal children's ponies.

A more athletic, gentle, elegant pony is required, and this has led to crossbreeding between native ponies and Thoroughbreds and Arabs. The Thoroughbred and Arab added the "class," elegance, athleticism and harmonious conformation.

Above: One of the many uses of the Riding Pony is showing. These are the prizewinners in a riding class at a major show.

Below: Most of the world's Riding Ponies are used for hacking out and general riding, and do not ever enter shows.

Many countries have followed this procedure. Some have followed the principles of selective breeding and have started a stud book such as those for the Australian Pony and German Riding Pony. In other countries, the process has been left to individual efforts. These ponies remain types, not breeds.

A riding pony has a good temperament, with the manners needed to give children confidence. Its conformation is harmonious and correct, and its paces are free, straight and true.

Most countries hold show classes for riding ponies. These are usually divided up to 12·2hh (50in), 12·2-13·2hh (50-54in), and 13·2-14·2hh (54-58in). Ponies that do well in these classes tend to be elegant, near-Thoroughbred types. In addition, most countries hold classes for working ponies. They are required to jump, when style and way of going is important. These working ponies do not need to be pretty as long as they are good performers and often these good performers have more substance and less Thoroughbred blood.

GUIDE TO
HORSE BREEDING

This chapter deals with all aspects of the fascinating and rewarding subject of horse breeding, and gives sound practical advice on how best to go about it.

It opens with a guide to the selection of suitable parents, then goes on to the specific tasks of choosing a stallion and a mare. There follows an account of planning a stud, from the design of buildings to the choice of grass, and then a concise account of the biology of horse reproduction.

The next sections deal with stallion management and mare management, and these are followed by a comprehensive account of the all-important processes of trying and covering.

Proper treatment of the pregnant mare is vital for successful breeding, and this is fully explained. The process of foaling is described in detail, with the help of step-by-step pictures, and possible complications are covered, too.

Finally, there is a full account of the care of youngstock, from the newborn foal to the two-year-old.

SELECTION OF PARENTS

Facing the Facts

Breeding is one of the most rewarding of equestrian activities, and it has the advantage that it can be done at all levels from multimillion dollar investments in a Thoroughbred stud to having a pony in a backyard paddock. Breeders have the satisfaction of watching the youngsters grow from fragile, fluffy creatures into animals they can ride and drive, or at least whose progress can be followed, especially if it is a racehorse, competition horse or show horse.

To those contemplating these romantic-sounding activities, there are some hard facts to be faced. Although native breeds of pony that have long bred in the wild can be left very much on their own, most of the more-refined breeds need regular attention, adequate facilities, occasional veterinary treatment, feed and knowledgeable handling. Although a pony may involve little expense, the higher the quality of the horse, the greater the expense involved in breeding. It is vital that the type of horse you choose to breed is one you have the knowledge, experience, facilities and finances to cope with.

The breeding of most horses involves considerable time and expense. It is worth making the best possible preparations and, in particular, taking careful consideration over selection. The higher the quality and ability of the horse bred, the greater the returns in terms of pleasure and finance when it is old enough to be shown or ridden.

The selection of parents is a fascinating study and one that has intrigued breeders of quality stock, especially racehorse breeders. The major requirements are common sense, a clear idea of the type of horse or pony to be bred and the application to gather and use data about the parents.

It is surprising how many people go into breeding simply because they take pity on some mare. They think of the joys of seeing her with a foal. They don't bother too much about the selection of a stallion and are happy to use one nearby. They think little about the future of the foal or what purpose it will serve. It often ends up valueless, rather a nuisance to its breeders, and the only person who will buy it is the meat man. Apart from the unhappy ending, the breeder has missed out on one of the most fascinating aspects of breeding— the selection of parents that are complementary so the breeder has the greatest possible chance of producing a horse that is both sound and talented.

The Goal

It is much more fun and interesting to start from another angle, and to decide what type of horse or pony it would be interesting to breed. Establish a clear goal, whether it is to be a racehorse, a show jumper, riding pony or a

purebred to be shown. List the qualities needed to achieve this goal, such as athletic ability, substance, power, courage, trainability, good temperament, good looks, elegance, good conformation, correct size or pretty movement. See which of these qualities are necessary for the breeding of a chosen type of horse or pony.

The only common feature to all goals is soundness, otherwise the requirements needed to achieve the goal vary considerably. The important factor is to clarify the assets needed.

Breeding Criteria

The next stage is to find parents that will reproduce these assets. There are four sources of data to help breeders ascertain if a horse or pony is likely to do so. These are the appearance of the parents, their records when performing, the pedigrees of ancestors and their progeny records.

When searching for suitable parents, it's important to realize the perfect horse or pony is *never* found. There will always be defects, but as long as the defect is not serious and the other parent does not suffer from it, then it can be accepted. Consequently, if a mare has a long back, look for a short backed stallion and one that passed on this particular feature to its progeny (offspring). The matings should be complementary.

Appearance

The appearance is the easiest criterion to investigate. The conformation, temperament and action of prospective parents can be examined to see if they behave, move and look like the type of animal you are aiming for. If one has a weakness, such as stiff movement, the other should be a particularly athletic mover and known to be prepotent for it. (*Prepotency* is the tendency in a horse to pass on its features to its offspring.)

Pedigree

Appearance is important but it cannot be taken as the sole criterion. It does not reflect the ▶

Left: Ben Faerie, the stallion that proved himself through such progeny as Priceless (Olympic Silver Medal) and Night Cap.

Above: This mare's progeny is too young to be judged on anything other than its conformation, but in less than 2 years it should race.

Below: The long-backed stallion (left) would be more suitable for the short-backed mare (center) than the long-backed mare (right).

Above: The most successful purpose-bred purebred is the Thoroughbred. It is a breed that was developed to race.

▶genetic makeup of a horse and it can be affected by the environment and feed. A tall mare may produce only small offspring because the genes for being tall were present in her parents only in minute quantities. For example, both parents were small but by some fluke the tall genes happened to be dominant and they produced a tall daughter. The few tall genes in her makeup were ineffective, and her progeny were small.

It's important that the genetic material of the parents has a high concentration of the required assets. This is best ascertained by consideration of two further criteria—the pedigree and the progeny. If the parents' ancestors and any offspring have the required traits, there must be a high

concentration of them in their genetic material.

A study of the pedigree for the above-mentioned tall mare might have revealed that her parents were small, and she was carrying a diluted quantity of genes for height. It is important to study the pedigree and determine if the ancestors possess the required assets.

Type of Breeding

The type of breeding (inbreeding, linebreeding or crossbreeding) is also important. If it is found that the potential parent is inbred (such as mother and son or brother and sister matings) or linebred (relations mated but a larger generation gap), and that the ancestor which consequently appears two or more times in the pedigree is prepotent for specific assets, there will be a high concentration of those traits. However, it is important to ensure that the stock to which it is inbred or linebred is prepotent for desirable, not undesirable, traits. Inbreeding can consolidate weaknesses and strengths. Also inbreeding leads to a loss of vigor, so this effect must be considered. If both parents have an asset in large amounts, and so do all their ancestors, then the offspring is likely to inherit that asset. The problem arises when one wants to breed a number of assets into a horse, and no purebred exists that possesses them all. Such has been the case this century in the escalating production of competition horses. The breeding goals are athleticism, suppleness, a tractable temperament, good size and substance. No single breed fulfills all these requirements, so crossbreeding (the mating of two entirely different breeds or types) becomes necessary.

When crossbreeding, it is important to select fairly similar types. A cross between a Shire and a Thoroughbred, if unlucky, might produce a huge-bodied horse on fine legs, or, if lucky, a good heavyweight with the required features of each in the right proportions. When the genes are such opposites the make, shape and ability of an offspring cannot be forecast and breeding with such extremes can be dangerous.

It is wiser to crossbreed fairly similar types, such as a small Thoroughbred with a Connemara. This crossbred (which should be bigger than the Connemara) can be put to a larger Thoroughbred, and a good-sized competition horse will be the likely progeny. Crossbreeding of similar types can help you forecast the make and shape of the offspring more accurately. And when that offspring is used as breeding stock itself, a lack of extreme genes means its genetic material is reasonably

Left: Connemara foals. This breed is good foundation stock with Thoroughbreds for producing competition horses.

Above: Overton Amanda, an Olympic team silver medalist for Britain in 1984 and an ideal mare with which to breed.

well-concentrated.

Consequently, pedigrees must be examined carefully to see if there has been any outcrossing, and if so, how extreme, because this affects the ability of parents to pass on their own traits.

Crossbreeding has another advantage; it restores vigor, so if there has been a great deal of inbreeding, then an outside cross gives an invigorating effect.

Progeny

The progeny are the best indicators of a parent's ability to pass on its traits. Unfortunately, this criterion cannot be used until the parents have produced many offspring. For mares with a maximum of one foal a year (and most mares fail to get in foal every 3 or 4 years), it takes many years before a fair assessment can be made. With stallions, particularly those that are popular and have many mares in a season, an assessment can be made earlier, when the stallions are still young.

Making a serious analysis of a stallion's progeny is the best means of finding out which assets he will pass on, although this is easier for racehorses who run at 2 years than it is for competition horses.

Performance

The final criterion for breeding is performance. Like appearance, this is usually a good indicator. But, on occasion, it can be misleading. There are always freak horses or ponies that are brilliant in themselves but which do not have a concentration of the genetic material to pass on to their progeny. Making allowances for these exceptions, in most cases examination of performance records is an aid and does increase the chances of achieving the breeding goal. The likelihood is a horse that jumps in great style is more likely to produce a talented jumper than one that jumps poorly.

The important factor when making a selection is to remember none of the four criteria are reliable on their own. It is only by studying all of them—appearance, performance, pedigree and progeny—that a reasonable assessment can be made as to the type of progeny a mare will produce if put to a similarly studied stallion. There are bound to be exceptions to the predicted results, but by making a careful selection you are shortening the odds in favor of producing the breeding goal, and increasing the chances of breeding a talented horse or pony. This makes the effort worthwhile, and the process involves fascinating studies. No breeder should ever rely on haphazard selection of parents.

CHOOSING A MARE

A brood mare is selected on the basis of her appearance, performance and pedigree, as well as progeny, if she has any. There has been less emphasis on performance for mares than for stallions, usually because a mare's performance is considerably affected when she comes into season. For this reason, many mares never realize their full potential. Also the effects of a mare's breeding are less widespread. The average mare produces about five foals in her lifetime, while a stallion may sire as many as a thousand.

When judging appearance, there are the specialist factors to be considered, such as a springy, elastic trot for a dressage horse, a free sweeping walk for a race horse, black color for a Friesian or a spotted coat for a Knabstrup. But there are also many general qualities that every brood mare should possess. The first of these is soundness. If the mare has a physical problem, it should not be an inherited one. Many people breed from an old mare they can no longer ride because she has

Below: This brood mare has a deep body and an air of femininity. She has a harmonious, well-proportioned body, an elegant head and a convex curve to the neck that smoothly joins the withers and the deep sloping shoulders. The withers are defined, the back gently curved, the hindquarters strong and the hind legs neither too straight nor too bent.

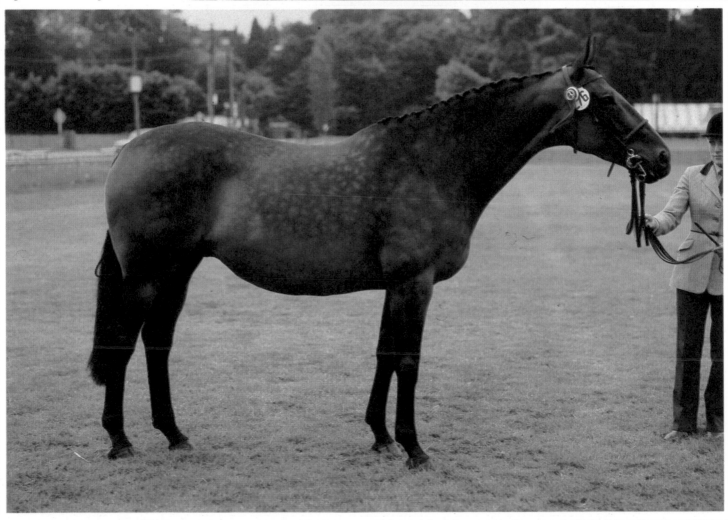

navicular or has gone in the wind, but she is likely to pass on these same defects to her progeny.

The next consideration is conformation—the make and shape of the horse. For a purebred, there will be specialist features the breeder tries to ensure are passed on to the progeny, such as the flat croup of the Arab. But generally there are certain factors everybody would like to see in their foals. A horse with good conformation is more likely to stay sound and work better than one with weak points. Such a horse will also be more valuable.

Despite this, it is worth remembering that weaknesses in conformation, as well as deficiencies in movement and temperament, can be accepted in a mare if she is put to a stallion that is particularly strong in these points and will therefore offset these defects. A weakness is more acceptable if surrounded by strong points, so a relatively straight hind leg is more permissible if the hock is broad and has a good shape, and the quarters are powerful.

A mare must have particular features if she is to be a good breeder. Her heart and lung capacity is important when she is feeding her foal, so she should be deep and broad in the chest and body. It is also important to have her breeding organs checked by a vet if she has not produced a foal, to ensure she is capable of doing so.

The last factor that can be judged simply by a horse's appearance is an air of femininity and grace. Sturdy masculine mares tend to be much more difficult to get in foal. It is also vital for a mare to have a good temperament. If she is unreasonable, she will be difficult to look after, and it is likely to make the progeny difficult to handle and train. Allowances can be made for mares being more flighty and unpredictable than geldings, but their general approach should still be bold, generous and gentle. The movement is also important, but it is more of a specialist's feature. A work horse might be wanted with short strides, a Hackney with high strides, a racehorse with long strides or a dressage horse with free, supple, rounded strides.

Above: Brood mares graze in a well-fenced field, Ballykisteen stud, Eire

Below: A well-proportioned mare by the Cleveland Bay, Forest Superman.

Above: This brood mare has proved her fertility by producing a foal; its good looks give confidence in her as a brood mare.

CHOOSING A STALLION

The stallion, also called an *entire* or *stud,* is selected using the same criteria as the mare—appearance, performance, pedigree and progeny. In his case, there usually are performance records, either on the race track or in specific performance tests. If he is old enough, the most reliable test of all can be used—looking at the appearance and performance of his progeny. The ideal stallion is prepotent in the aims of the breeding goal, so he stamps his stock with the desired traits. Seek out his progeny, find out what they have done, and see what their appearance is like.

It is important to look at the appearance of the stallion, and when putting a mare to him, ensure that his conformation, temperament and movement are complementary to hers. It does not matter so much as in the mare if he is deep through his body, but this is still an asset. In contrast to the mare, he should give an impression of masculinity and an air of precociousness and pride.

There is an additional criterion for the selection of stallions—fertility. There is no point in choosing a stallion that rarely gets his mares in foal because he will not be commercially viable if you buy him. He may prove to be an expensive waste of time if

Below: A Thoroughbred Stallion that has a precious, masculine air. He is a compact horse with a bold, intelligent outlook, and the stallion's typical crested neck.

you send your mare to him. It is important to check fertility rates before making a final choice.

Most breeders will select stallions for use with their mares, not for purchase. Stallions need more skillful handling than mares, as discussed in a later section on stallion management. For those embarking on breeding horses, begin with mares or employ an experienced stud groom who knows how to deal with stallions.

Paying for the Stallion

The services of a stallion must be paid for, and the amount varies from nominal sums for pony stallions to hundreds of thousands of dollars for a top Thoroughbred. Payment can be made in many ways. A syndicate share can be bought in a stallion and up to 40 are issued, entitling owners to

Above: A handsome stallion with its vital air of precociousness.

one service per year. Alternatively, there are nominations, which are usually sold at special auctions, entitling the purchaser to send his mare for service that year. Shares and nominations are the usual procedure for top racehorses, but for the less valuable, stud fees are

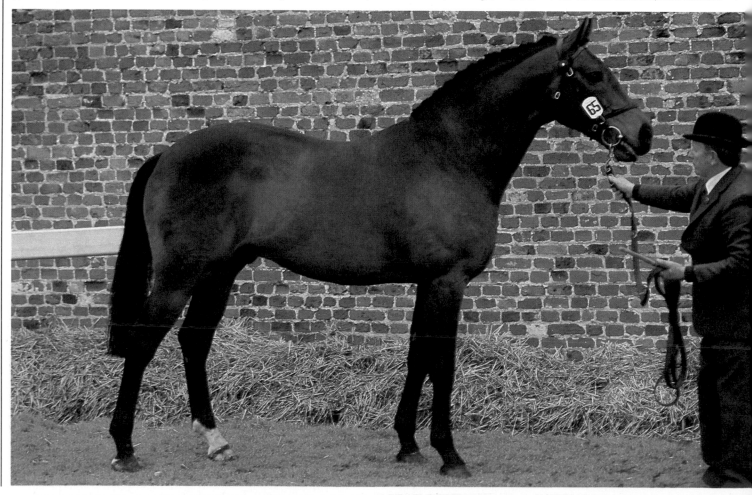

normally paid. This can be a straight fee that is due after the service. "No foal, no fee" is payable a few months after the season ends, unless a veterinary certificate is produced stating the mare is not in foal. "Live-foal guarantee" or "no foal free return", as it is known in the UK, means that the fee is due after service but the mare can return to the stallion for a free return if she is barren or has a dead foal.

The size of the fee affects selection, but breeders should remember that the costs of breeding are high (feed, vets, livery fees when at stud). A little more paid for a good stallion is small compared with these costs, yet it is likely to yield much higher returns in terms of talent and value of progeny. The price paid for youngstock is determined largely by the sire.

The final factor in selection of a stallion depends on where he stands. High-class management is important if the mare is to get in foal and return in good shape. Complaints are all too common about poor attention given to mares, so careful investigation of the stud facilities is absolutely necessary for good results.

Right: A handsome Welsh Section B stallion, a winner in his class.

Below: These stallions' stables have been built separately from the stables for other horses.

Grassland

The facilities at studs vary from a few fields in which two or three mares run free all year to luxurious, double-fenced paddocks, stables, barns and covering facilities. Studs that house stallions as a commercial business must give a good impression to mare owners, but all stud owners need serviceable facilities for the well-being of their horses. One vital facility is sufficient grassland. As a rough guide, 1 acre should provide enough pasture and space for two to three ponies, or 2 acres should be enough for three horses.

It is not enough to let grass grow naturally. Horses do a lot of damage to grass. If this damage is not taken care of, the grass will turn sour, or it will lead to excessive growth of weeds so the land becomes "horse sick" (see opposite page).

Grassland management is an important, but often neglected, part of stud work. Good grazing makes healthy stock.

The most productive types of grasses for a stud are bluegrass (ryegrass) and timothy. The ideal type of land has a limestone subsoil, that is rich in the phosphorus and calcium needed for the growth of healthy horses. The soil can be analyzed for any elements that are lacking. These can be added easily. Lime should be at a pH level of 6 to 6.5, and the phosphorus should be at ADAS Index 2. There must also be adequate potash (usually deficient in sandy soils) and nitrogen in the soil. Additions of lime or other fertilizers can correct the chemical composition of the soil, but it is also advisable to spread farmyard manure on the land. This helps the humus level and provides extra phosphate and potash.

Applications of specific additions to the land should be done at specific times. Lime is best spread in November, usually about every 5 years. Apply phosphates, which stimulate growth of the nutritious clover, in the spring. The potash salts are most effective if administered after a hay crop but *never* with a nitrogen application in the spring or before the autumn growth. Apply nitrogen, which will be most effective if phosphate-lime and potash levels are correct, 3-6 weeks before growth of the grass is required. When spreading manure, which must be stored for at least 6 weeks, don't graze the field for another 6 weeks.

To ensure the highest productivity of grass, a soil analysis is advisable every 4 to 5 years. This can be done by contacting your local agricultural agent.

Grass cannot grow efficiently in waterlogged fields, so drainage must be considered. Sand, chalk or gravel-type soils may drain naturally. But for clay lands, in particular, a drainage system is needed. This can be expensive, but it is a long term economy in terms of fertility and consequent yield. If

Above: A collection of mares and foals grazing on green grass. There are few weeds and no clumps of tough grass in this field.

a field remains ungrazed for such a period of time, due to waterlogging, it isn't an asset at all.

Drainage and adding correct elements are basic requirements, but there is other work involved in grassland management that needs to be done more frequently.

The first of these is harrowing. This drags out dead moss and grass and prevents a mat from forming. For this purpose, the spokes of the harrow must be long, and heavy enough, to dig into the grass. Harrowing also helps scatter droppings. Do it often because droppings sour the ground; only tough grass, which the horses will not eat, grows in their vicinity. Scattering droppings also reduces worm infestation because worms which thrive in damp piles of droppings tend to dry out and die in the sun and air. However, no matter how frequently you harrow, it will not totally eradicate worm infestation. Most high-class studs pursue the time-consuming but effective work of picking up droppings daily to ensure against

Below: A foal grazing on what appears to be poor grassland. There is little length to the grass; the foal is eating thistles.

Above: This lush, green pasture should provide the good keep that is so important for the mare and foal.

Left: Picking up droppings is the only way to stop worm infestation when acreage is limited and there is no crop rotation.

the worm hazard.

Rolling is another activity best done with a tractor (although both activities can be done with a pony or work horse in harness). This is not as essential to maintaining or increasing productivity, but it helps improve damaged pasture, and consolidates topsoil after frequent frosts, thaws or floods.

Understocking a field can be damaging. If the grass grows too quickly for the horses to keep it grazed, they won't eat the long grass. If this occurs, the higher, unpalatable grass needs to be cut.

Topping the grass is often necessary, even in fields that have been well grazed, because horses tend to leave patches of long grass. To make these areas more palatable requires regular cutting.

Efforts should be made to keep weeds down. Among the most common weeds are buttercups and thistles, which can be sprayed in late spring. Cut

burdocks (docks) in July after flowering, but before seeding. Spray ragwort in late spring. Other than chemical prevention, some weed control can be achieved by maintaining a correct stocking rate, good drainage and a rotation of land use. Where all else fails, reseeding may become necessary.

The alternate use of good pasture is vital. If the grass is used only for horses it is difficult to avoid "horse sickness". This occurs when the pasture is infested with worms and they are eaten by the horses. In large numbers the worms can greatly affect the horses' health causing loss of condition, colic and even death.

As mentioned above, horses are bad grazers, concentrating on certain areas and not touching others, so the grass length becomes very uneven, with "rings" of long coarse grass. The ideal solution to these problems is to rotate horse grazing with cattle grazing. Cattle reduce the worm count by eating the horse worms, and they will graze patches of grass left by the horses. It's better if the horses graze the land first and the cattle follow. Don't keep them both in the same field at the same time.

Sheep can also be used as alternate grazers, but, although better than nothing, they are not as effective as cattle.

Alternating a hay crop with horse grazing is another beneficial rotation method worth trying. ▶

▶ Fencing

Good fencing is necessary to minimize accidents. Horses, particularly youngstock, have an unfortunate tendency to gallop or slip into things that hurt them, so all sources of danger must be removed. Use common sense to ensure that there are no sharp-angled corners into which horses can gallop. Smooth the edges of troughs, stakes and old trees. Gates should be solid; never use barbed wire.

Ideally a paddock fence should be high, strong and solid. Wood rails are the most suitable material for fencing, but they are expensive. There is some special wire available, designed specifically for stud fences, that seems safe. Chain wire, as long as it is pulled taut between strong posts, is relatively safe. Natural, thick hedges are also usually an effective barrier as well as making the paddock look attractive.

The ideal size for an enclosed paddock is about 6 acres. It is best to have smaller areas rather than huge fields because it's easier to catch stock and inspect it. The availability of a number of paddocks makes alternate use easier as well as the safe division of horses.

It is best to separate barren mares and mares with foals. Geldings should be kept well apart from mares and foals, and only one gelding should be allowed to graze with barren mares: two or more tend to fight. Separate young horses from older horses; colts and fillies can usually run together until they are 18 months old, then they need to be separated. Stallions must always be kept away from all other stock.

Shelter

Another facility needed in a field is shelter. The type depends on the weather and stock. Native breeds in most weather and refined breeds in summer need only a few trees and perhaps a high hedge or wall to protect them against strong winds and rain or flies. For horses out the year round, a hut is advisable. One that is provided with a wide entrance is best, so horses can move freely in and out.

Water

There should be an abundant supply of fresh water at *all* times. Stagnant pools are dangerous. If there is no running stream in the field, a piped supply to a trough with an automatic filling device is necessary.

The Buildings

The quality and quantity of buildings depends on the type and size of the stock. Studs for Thoroughbred stallions have the most luxurious facilities, because investments are high, and these are delicate creatures. For native ponies, little is needed other than storage facilities for food, a tack room and some stables for veterinary care. Even a foaling box is rarely essential because ponies are usually best left to follow their natural instincts,

Above: These Thoroughbred yearlings are enclosed by sturdy wood posts and rails; this is expensive but safe fencing.

Below: A mare and foal in front of a good shelter that has a broad entrance and an adequate amount of space inside.

Below: The well-designed stables for stallions at the Irish National Stud.

Above: Cold-blood stallions have equitable temperaments and are kept in stalls at Le Pin State Stud, France.

Right: Baron Blackeney, a Thoroughbred stallion, being ridden for exercise.

and foal out in the field.

Storage facilities for feed must be designed so hay can be kept under cover and grain is protected from the damp and from vermin, such as rats or mice.

Stables need to be large enough to house the horses but designs vary considerably, from barns where all the stalls are inside, looking onto a central passage, to yards where all the horses look out. It's advisable to have some isolation boxes in case of diseases or contagious skin infections. Most studs have one or more foaling boxes that are larger, approximately 12 x 16ft (3·7 x 4·9m) in area, and easily observable.

For expensive stock, it's advisable to have a peep hole through to an adjoining room where stud hands can keep watch. Some studs now use closed-circuit television to provide this observation facility.

At a stallion stud, a covering yard is necessary where mares can be tried and covered with optimum ease and safety. Stallion studs should always have special exercising areas. An indoor school or outdoor school with a high fence is best. Horses can then be set free, lunged or ridden. For highly-strung stallions that cannot be turned out in a field, a small paddock with a special high fence is advisable.

THE BIOLOGY OF REPRODUCTION

Physiology of the Mare

To be able to give the mare the best possible care and opportunity to get in foal, it helps to know a little about her physiology and anatomy. The amount of knowledge needed will vary. If native ponies are the breeding stock they can be left to run free and little assistance is needed. But the more refined the stock, the closer it is to being Thoroughbred, the more knowledge of breeding is required.

The important organs are the two ovaries that are connected to the Fallopian tubes. This is where fertilization occurs. These tubes lead to the uterus, which is able to expand and house the foal. Beyond the uterus is the cervix, the vagina and the vulva, which together make up the birth canal. At the lower end of the vulva is the small, round clitoris, which may sometimes harbor venereal microbes. Sex hormones are produced by the anterior pituitary gland, the ovaries and the uterus.

The Estrus Cycle

When a mare matures to achieve puberty—usually between 15 and 24 months, although she can be as old as 4 years—cyclical changes start to occur in these organs. The correct terminology for this is the *estrus cycle*. The estrus cycle is also referred to as being "in heat," "in season," "on," "in use" or "showing," and it usually lasts for 5 days. During this time, the mare will accept the stallion, but for the following 15 days she will not. She is then said to be in *diestrus,* "out of season," or "not showing." The cycle lasts for about 20 days.

This cycle is controlled by hormones. A *follicle stimulating hormone* (FSH) produced by the growth of follicles (fluid sacs that form around the eggs just below the surface of the ovary). These follicles produce estrogen that affects the mare's behavior. She will then come into season and accept the stallion.

Signs of Estrus

There are several distinct signs that a mare is in season. The tail goes up, the cervix relaxes, the

genital track becomes moist and "winking" occurs: this is when the vulval lips open and close. The mare also passes urine frequently. Stretching her neck up and out and raising her upper lip is another sign a mare is in season and ready to be covered.

Usually on the fifth day of being in season, one follicle that has grown larger than the others (about 1-1¼in) ruptures from the stimulation of another pituitary hormone called the *luteinizing hormone (LH)*. The egg is released, and the ruptured follicle becomes a yellow body that secretes the hormone *progesterone.* This hormone then induces the typical behavior of a mare "out of season". The cervix closes, the genital track becomes dry and she is likely to kick the stallion if he gets too close. The egg passes into the Fallopian tubes where fertilization can occur.

If it is fertilized, it moves into the uterus. There the uterus starts preparations for pregnancy, but if the egg is not fertile, these will be

stopped about the 15th day of the cycle. The hormone that stops these activities is *prostaglandin,* which is secreted by the uterus and stops the yellow body on the ovary from producing progesterone. About the same time, there is a switch in secretion from LH to FSH by the pituitary. Another cycle is then started.

Changing the Cycle

It is possible for veterinarians, to use hormones to control the cycle and increase the chances of difficult mares becoming pregnant.

The estrus cycle does not occur normally all year round. Native mares running free tend to come into season in late spring and summer only. They produce their foal at the best possible time, when the grass is growing and the climate is most conducive to the foal's well-being. More-refined breeds, in particular racehorses and show horses, have been encouraged to come into season earlier so they can produce foals that will be more

Above: A veterinarian irrigating a mare's uterus.

Below: Equipment used by vets to facilitate mare examinations.

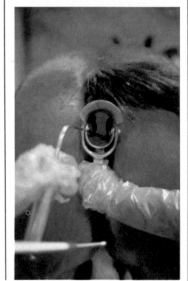

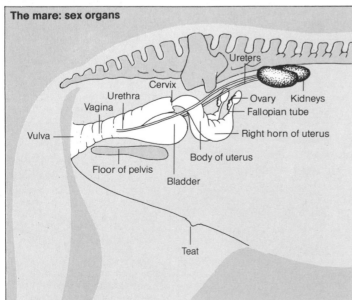

The mare: sex organs

- Ureters
- Cervix
- Urethra
- Vagina
- Ovary
- Kidneys
- Fallopian tube
- Vulva
- Right horn of uterus
- Body of uterus
- Floor of pelvis
- Bladder
- Teat

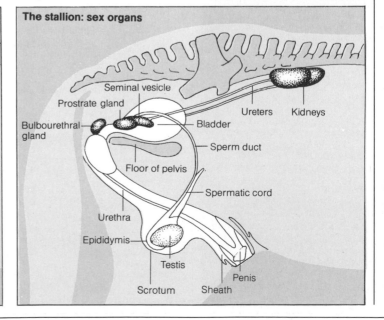

The stallion: sex organs

- Seminal vesicle
- Prostrate gland
- Bulbourethral gland
- Ureters
- Kidneys
- Bladder
- Sperm duct
- Floor of pelvis
- Spermatic cord
- Urethra
- Epididymis
- Testis
- Penis
- Scrotum
- Sheath

mature when they are needed to race or show.

The artificial life of horses who are stabled and are given an abundance of feed has been proved to have led to an earlier annual start to the estrus cycle. The use of artificial aids, such as light and hormones, can be used to induce an estrus cycle even in winter.

Variations in the Cycle

Most mares come into season every 3 weeks for 3 to 4 months every year, but there are many variations. Ovulation may not occur the first few times the mare comes into season each year, or ovulation can occur when the mare is not in season. A mare can be out of season for more than 15 days, which usually means she did not ovulate in the previous season. Alternatively, she may come into season and ovulate without showing any of the behavioral signs. Then there is the "normal" variation, when the mare with a new foal comes into season about 9 days after foaling. She is considered to be exceptionally fertile during that season. Pregnant mares will not come into season, although they have been known to accept the stallion, but then they usually lose their foal.

Length of Pregnancy

Pregnancy last about 11 months (336 days), but smaller breeds tend to have a shorter gestation. There are considerable variations; 10 days either way is not unusual, and there can be normal births 2 weeks early and 3 or 4 weeks late.

Fertilization and Development

Pregnancy occurs when the egg is fertilized by the sperm in the Fallopian tubes. Eggs die within 24 hours and are at their most fertile when they first enter the tubes. It is best for the mare to be served by the stallion *before,* not after, ovulation. The fertilized egg passes into the uterus or womb. The egg grows by dividing into an increasing number of cells and becoming loosely attached to the lining of the uterus. Differentiation of the cells occurs so the embryo gradually changes from a one-celled fertilized egg into a miniature horse. About 60 days after fertilization it is called the fetus.

Embryo and Fetus

Membranes form around the embryo as it develops into the fetus. The outer one is referred to as the "bag of waters" at birth. The placenta is the membrane through which the embryo receives oxygen, nourishment and removes its waste material. It is also where the fetal blood comes into close contact, but does not actually mix, with the mother's. The placenta is loosely attached to the uterine wall, and to the embryo by the umbilical cord, but it is not part of the foal's body so it can be discarded at birth.

The umbilical cord contains two major arteries and a vein, together with a duct connected to the foal's

Above: A mare grazing peacefully with her foal. It is important to give mares as natural an existence as possible.

bladder. The placenta contains the allantoic fluid which escapes at birth with the rupture of the placenta and the "breaking of waters". It consists partly of waste material not yet removed through the placental-uterine contact, and it is kept separate from the embryo by another membrane called the "amnion". This membrane protects the foal during pregnancy from the allantoic fluid. During birth, its slippery surface helps delivery through the birth canal. The amnion contains the amniotic fluid that bathes the airways of the fetus' head, neck, eyes, skin and ears. The fetus also swallows it to lubricate the stomach and intestine. Both the allantoic and the amniotic fluids act as shock absorbers to the fetus. Both the amniotic and placental membranes make up what is known in the foaling as the 'afterbirth'.

Development of the Fetus

As the embryo grows into the fetus, the walls of the uterus stretch, but the uterus walls are sealed from the outside by the cervix. The organs develop, and all internal ones are present after 1 month gestation but most do not function until birth. The exception to this is the heart, which provides blood circulation and nourishment. There is clearly some activity in the intestines because these contain waste material at birth.

The embryo

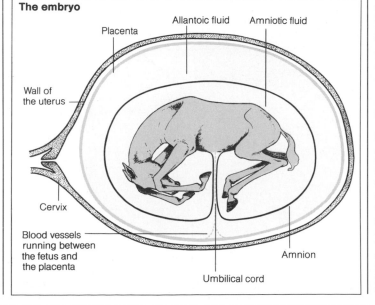

Placenta — Allantoic fluid — Amniotic fluid

Wall of the uterus

Cervix

Blood vessels running between the fetus and the placenta

Amnion

Umbilical cord

STALLION MANAGEMENT

Handling

A high-quality stallion is the most majestic and noble of horses. In his natural habitat he is the custodian of a herd of mares and youngstock. For this he needs courage and intelligence to ward off competitors and predators, and pride, strength and high spirits to establish and maintain his supremacy. These features, retained even by those breeds of stallion that have experienced centuries of domestication, make him the most admired and eye-catching type of horse and one which is quick to learn—both to obey and to disobey. If handled by someone who understands these traits, who is confident and who only makes reasonable demands, a stallion can be a very co-operative partner. Equally, he soon realizes who is frightened of him: a timorous pat, or a hesitant or unreasonable command, and he is quick to display his high spirits and courage in willful disobedience. Stallions need handlers who are relaxed, confident, positive and sympathetic in their work; they must grow to trust their handlers, who must never show fear.

This handling is relatively easy in the case of ponies which are small and affable in character, and it is

Right: Stallions, particularly Thoroughbreds, are high-spirited animals, as this horse shows at the St Lô Stud in France.

168

not too difficult even for the huge but gentle work horses, and for Arabs and warm-bloods which are specifically bred to have a good temperament. But for the most valuable breed of stallion—the Thoroughbred—it can take great skill. In the past, many high-spirited stallions were cooped up in boxes away from other horses, never ridden, and controlled with a big stick. They were treated as savages and usually became so. Now the trend is to treat all stallions, even Thoroughbreds, as normally as possible, so they are ridden, turned out to grass and kept in stable yards with other horses.

Housing

Where the stallion is kept will depend on his breed and character. There are breeds which still roam wild. They need little help from man because they have acres of land to graze and have never been softened by domestication. Today, most of these wild breeds are also bred in captivity, and as long as they are sturdy, tough types, then a stallion can be left at grass with his herd of mares. Attention needs to be paid to the fencing to ensure it is not likely

Below left: The stallion barn at Airdrie Stud in Kentucky, USA.

Below: A stallion in his stable at a Kentucky stud. The hot weather makes a fan (on right) advisable.

to cause injury or be broken down, and there should be no other ponies or horses in adjoining fields. A stallion is likely to treat these as competitors and try to fight them. Stallions should always have sufficient fodder (hay if necessary). Stock should be regularly transferred to other fields under a rotation system, to avoid horse-sick grass (see page 163). There must be

frequent checks to ensure that there are no injuries or illness.

Pony stallions can be allowed to run free with their mares, because they are tough, virile and not too valuable. Other types of stallions may also be let free with their mares, but if the breed is more refined, is one which has never (or has not for centuries) run wild in herds and is valuable, it is usual

Above: Hardy breeds like these New Forest Ponies can breed in the wild.

to let them out with only one mare at a time. Most horse breeding is now practiced in a very controlled and artificial manner to reduce the risk of injury, to maximize the chances of problem mares getting in foal and to ensure the ▶

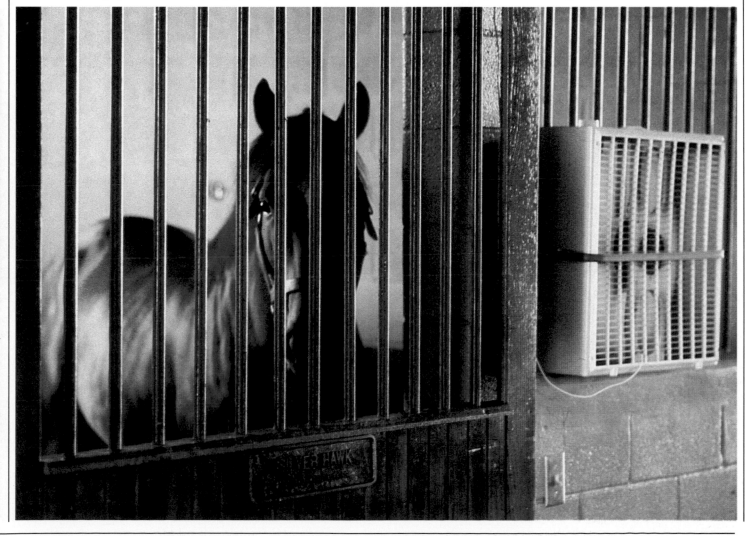

▶well-being of horses which after domestication no longer thrive when exposed to a rigorous outdoor life.

Stallions' stables should be strongly built because the animals tend to be more excitable and stronger than other types of horse and can easily demolish fragile buildings. A top door, or a grille for a top door (so that the horse can still see out), is needed: this can be closed in an emergency to stop him trying to jump free. The stable should be at least 12ft x 14ft (3·7 x 4·3m) for a 16h (64in) horse, because stallions like to move around. They like, too, equine company, so most are happiest in yards with other horses. It is important, however, that they cannot smell other horses and that mares in season are not put in an adjacent box.

Exercise

Stable-kept stallions need exercise. Their more fiery natures make it vital that they do not become frustrated through boredom and excess energy, or they will be extremely difficult to handle. The more placid pony and warm-blood stallions are often exercised in the same manner as mares or geldings and are hacked out, hunted and competed. Thoroughbred stallions tend to be more difficult, and only skillful horsemen can use them as riding horses, especially as they grow older. For stallions that are very high-spirited, exceptionally precocious and unmanageable in the company of other horses, or where a rider good enough to control them is unavailable, there are alternative means of exercise. All of these methods can be used for the ridable stallions too.

The first is to turn them out to grass. A small paddock of not more than 2 acres (0·8ha) is generally advisable so they cannot gallop around too wildly. It is essential that the fencing is sturdy and at least 5ft (1·5m) high, since most stallions are prone to jump or crash through fences if they see or hear other horses. There should be no horses in an adjoining paddock, but it often settles the stallion if he can be turned out with a pony, a gelding or a donkey, as long as the latter has been tested to ensure that it has no lung worm. It is also advisable to pick up droppings (see page 163).

Turning the stallion out is good for him psychologically, helping him to loosen up, but is not a means of getting him fit; consequently, although this may be the only form of exercise during and after the covering season, fittening work is needed beforehand. In order to ensure the highest possible fertility, stallions *must* be fit—some cover 100 or more mares in a season. The traditional means of getting a more refined breed fit was for the stallion man to lead the animal out at a walk for 1 to 1½ hours, but this method is time consuming. These days, lunging is a more common method of fittening. Ideally lunging is done in an indoor school or an enclosed outdoor arena. This helps to keep the stallion's concentration

Above: This stallion is being exercised as he is led by the stud groom. This was the traditional means of keeping stallions, but because it is time-consuming, it is rare today.

Right: Lunging is another way to exercise a stallion.

Below: This handsome Andalusian stallion runs free in a field.

and also serves as a place to turn him loose before or after his work.

The stallion starts his fittening work about 2 months before the season begins. The actual dates of the season vary according to the hemisphere (Australia's are in the opposite part of the year to Britain's), the breed, and the planned use of progeny. The racehorse season in the Northern hemisphere starts in February, because early foals are needed to enable maximum maturity for 2- and 3-year-olds. Similarily, sires used to produce in-hand show horses (Thorough-breds and Warm-bloods) have an early start, as a yearling born in March or April will be bigger than one born in June. For those breeders who allow their progeny to mature before use (as in the case of competition horses), the foals are best born when the grass is growing and it is warm enough to turn them out between April and June. In this case, the stallion's season is much later, from May to July.

Feeding

As for exercise, energizing feed should be increased when the season approaches and reduced when the stallion rests in the fall (autumn). Health, well-being and fertility depend on skillful feeding. The stallion must be given the proteins to enable him to muscle up; the energizing foodstuffs to enable him to carry out his work (but not so much that he becomes stupid); enough fattening foods to make him look healthy (but not so much that he becomes fat); the necessary vitamins, salts and addi-tives to maximize his well-being.

Other vital duties for the owner of a stallion are worming, teeth filing and foot trimming, which must be carried out at regular intervals: any pain or indigestion will make a stallion reluctant to serve mares.

Right: Stallions need skillfull care. One annual or biannual duty is to file the teeth so that none have any rough edges.

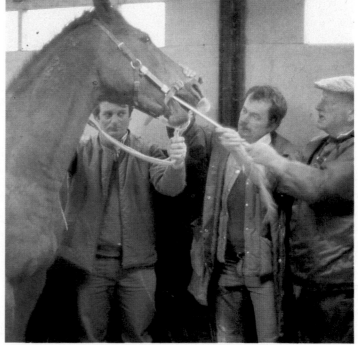

The skill, time and expense needed for mare management depends on the refinement of the breed. Ponies can be left on their own, but Thoroughbreds usually need a great deal of attention. The more we have interfered with a breed's environment, providing warm stables and hard feed, the less able the horses have been to look after themselves.

Condition

The more-refined breeds tend to be more difficult to get in foal and need to be well-prepared. The first concern is the condition of the mare. She is best when left in a natural condition, either having been turned out or, at the least, exercised a little. Fit mares, which are lean and muscular, are hard to get in foal and so are fat mares who have gorged themselves on the spring grass.

Cultures

Most studs today require mares to be swabbed, to ensure they are "clean"—free from contagious infections—and fit for service. A small piece of sterilized cotton is used to collect material that can be studied in the laboratory to check for infectious microbes. The outbreak of contagious equine metritis in 1977 led to much more stringent regulations about checking for infections. Cultures can be taken by the vet from the clitoris at any time or from the cervix when it is relaxed and the mare is in season. It is important to check with the stud whether culturing is required and if so, of which kind. This is then completed before the mare goes away to the stud.

Above: This mare examination box is part of the sophisticated equipment at Ballykisteen stud, Eire.

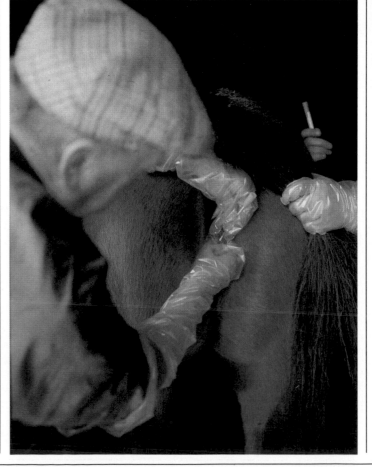

Right: A vet takes a swab for examination from a mare at the Ballykisteen stud.

Above: A brood mare grazes contentedly on good pastureland.

Below: A laboratory technician examines swabs from mares.

Worming

Studs where many horses graze the land are always liable to worm infestation. It is important, to help prevent this and for the sake of the mare herself, to ensure she is regularly wormed.

Removing Shoes

Prior to service, the mare's back shoes are always removed for safety. Front shoes can be left on.

The Cycle

For barren mares that have had a foal but are not at present in foal, and for maiden mares, which have never had a foal, it helps to establish a clear, regular cycle. Often these mares will not ovulate for their first and maybe second season and will not be fertile. It is wise to ensure a definite cycle before going to the stallion and to keep a record of the dates she comes into season. If an April, May or June foal is desired, and this is the most advantageous timing because grass and climate

Above: Worming tablets can be given in the feed but are often left untouched; oral application is the most foolproof method, and need not be difficult if done calmly.

are best, starting a cycle can usually be left to Nature. However, some mares are required to produce early foals so they will be sufficiently mature to run on the racetrack early in their second year or be shown as young stock. For these mares, artificial aid may be given to encourage an early start to the cycle.

The cycle is affected by season, nutrition and climate. It starts in late spring when the days get longer and the grass gets richer. If the mare is given a good protein diet, if she is kept warm, and if a light of 200 watts is left on in her box for about 6 hours after it gets dark, (so her day is lengthened progressively over about 2 months), her system

should tell her it is spring when it is still winter. This should ensure she comes into season early.

The veterinarian can provide help. He can prescribe a hormone treatment to encourage the start of the cycle. He can also examine her and check the functioning of her organs if she does not start to cycle or if there is any doubt about her fertility. Time and money can be saved if problems are corrected *before* she goes to the stallion. It is less expensive to incur some vet fees than to have the expense of a barren mare, which will involve paying her stud fees, living and keep for the year.

Deciding the Timing

Deciding when she goes to stud depends on when the foal is needed, except in the case of the mare due to foal. In this case, the mare should go to the stud about a month before foaling to be foaled there, or on the 5th day after foaling to catch the foal heat that usually occurs after the 8th day.

With the maiden or barren mare, it is less expensive, in terms of stabling and feed, and best for the foal to be born when Nature prescribed in April, May or June. This means going to stud in May, June or July. But, as in the case of racehorses and show horses, there may be other priorities.

The Stud

Once the cycle of the maiden or barren mare has been established, it's best to send her to stud about 5 days before she comes into season. Otherwise, the journey might upset the cycle. When she goes to stud, send her with a halter that has her or the owner's name on it for identification purposes. If she needs a culture certificate from the vet this should go, together with other details of the mare, such as age, breeding, previous foals, maiden, if in foal, the service dates, vices and idiosyncrasies.

For a mare that is difficult to get in foal, it's helpful to have full details of past veterinary treatment and the regularity of her cycle.

It should also be clarified how long the mare is to stay at the stud. It's a false economy to make her stay too short as this makes it more difficult to ensure the mare is in foal. The normal minimum is 3½ weeks, but it is wisest to allow 6½ or 9½ weeks and have 2 or 3 tests done.

The stud is responsible for keeping the owners informed. They should let them know when their mare has been served and when she has been tested. Owners have the right to enquire about this if not informed, but telephoning should be kept to a minimum because studs are busy places during the breeding season. Those in charge must work very long hours with many foalings in the middle of the night and a tremendous concentration of work. The stallion's quota of mares tends to come over a very short period of the year, and the stud hands have to work exceptionally hard at this time.

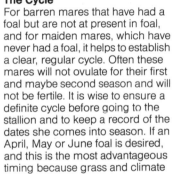

TRYING AND COVERING

Trying (testing whether a mare is ready for covering) and covering can be done naturally when a stallion runs with his herd of mares. No human interference is necessary because there is a well-developed natural system. Mares in season show distinctive signs (see page 166). The stallion smells and notices this and will approach such a mare. She will stand quietly. But a mare out of season will put her ears back and kick at the stallion if he makes any advances; he soon learns the difference.

Running a stallion with a mare is most effective when the breed is tough enough to stand up to the climate, does not require large quantities of hard feed and is not so valuable that the odd kick or accident will be expensive. Herds still need frequent checking for injuries. They need good fencing, and care must be taken that no geldings or stallions are put in adjoining fields, because it could lead to fights.

Trying

With the increasing value of horses, today mares are kept separate from stallions. Most of the trying is done in a more controlled fashion. It is best to keep it as natural as possible; one of the best methods is to lead or ride the stallion close to the mares' paddock. To avoid any kicking it is important not to go beside the fence. The mare's behavior must be carefully observed. Those that take no notice are out of season, those that follow him are likely to be coming in, and those that are 'in' will show the signs. This is a useful method but is not entirely reliable in the case of timid, nervous mares.

One reliable method is to use a trying board that is usually in a yard but can be within a fenced paddock. Ideally, this should be about 8ft 3in (2·5m) long and 6 feet (1·8m) high, padded on the top and on the side where the mare will stand. The ground should be firm and not slippery. Chalk or rough concrete is best. There should be plenty of room on both sides of the board. Alternatively, the stallion can be put into a large stable with a high door looking out onto a yard where the mare will be led.

Any arrangement is feasible, as long as you remember if the mare is not ready, she may react with strenuous kicking. It is important for her not to be able to hurt herself against a rough surface. There must be enough room for her handler to keep clear. The stallion may get excited, so there must be room to keep him safely under control.

The mare is led up to the stallion, head to head with the board or door between them, and reactions are noted. A mare that is strongly "in" will stand quietly. A mare that is pregnant or not in season will be aggressive, putting her ears back and striking out. Occasionally, a mare in season takes time to accept the stallion, and sometimes his attention helps bring her into

Above: A mare being tried. She stands behind trying boards to protect the stallion.

Below: When herds run free, like these Shetlands, trying and covering is naturally accomplished.

Right: Some modern equipment used in the examination of a mare by a veterinarian.

season. The mare should be broadside along the board; if she leans against it and generally inclines towards the stallion, she is ready.

Using a "Teaser"
If a single stallion is used too many times in one day for trying he will become tired; the over-exertion can reduce his fertility. Consequently, when a stallion is popular and valuable, a second, less-valuable stallion, called a *teaser,* is used for the task of finding out when mares are ready for covering.

Trying is a vital task, because it determines the optimum period for fertilization. If the covering is done too early or too late in the cycle, the mare will react aggressively, which can be very dangerous to the handlers and the stallion. Trying also minimizes the number of coverings needed and cuts down the risks of infection. It avoids tiring out the stallion and reducing his fertility.

Another method of trying is used at some studs. A teaser, which can be a pony, is kept in a paddock that is fenced well enough to prevent escape but permits contact between him and the mares in an adjoining paddock or paddocks. The behavior of the mares towards the stallion can then be observed and acted upon.

The Importance of Observation
Observation is a vital part of successful stud work, because cycles can be irregular in timing and intensity. Experienced stud hands have an instinct for when a mare is ready. All changes in behavior are carefully noted.

Maximizing the fertility of the stallions depends on the ability of those running the stud to catch the mares when they are fully in season and to cover them on the optimum day for fertilization.

Optimal Timing
The optimal time for covering is 24 to 6 hours before ovulation (see pages 166-167). There are only 24 hours during which the egg is fertilizable. There are no outward signs to indicate ovulation other than the mare being "very well in season". The only positive sign she has ovulated is when she goes out of season 24 to 28 hours later.

It is important to notice when a mare first comes into season. The covering then takes place when she is "well in"—2 to 3 days after the start. Some people advocate a second covering 24 to 48 hours later, but most experts feel this is unnecessary unless the first covering did not go well. Frequent coverings will tire the stallion, lower his fertility and increase the risk of infection. They are of doubtful value, especially if they are carried out after ovulation.

Veterinary Aid
A veterinary examination is the best way of finding out when there is a chance of conception and when covering will be as effective as possible. It can also determine when a mare is close to ovulation and whether a horse is free from any infections that might hinder fertilization. At many Thoroughbred breeding studs, where for mare owners expenses are minimal relative to the costs of not getting a mare in foal, veterinary examinations are the norm. By feeling the ovaries and the size, position and tension of the follicles, the vet can ascertain whether and when one (or two in the case of twins) of them is likely to rupture. The vet can then advise as to the best possible covering day. Also internal massage of the ovaries can help weak or cystic ovaries.

Another aid is the use of an instrument called a *speculum,* through which the veterinarian can see the condition of the vagina and cervix and forecast when ovulation is likely. He can also check for infections that could inhibit fertilization. Some discharges destroy sperm or a fertilized egg.

Veterinary aid can also help optimal timing by prescribing hormones that will hasten or delay ovulation or help bring a mare into season.

All these techniques help to increase a mare's fertility, so that there is no need for a stallion to cover the mare many times. This is such an important aspect of breeding at major Thoroughbred studs, they may employ a team of veterinarians full-time.

In-foal Mares
In-foal mares are normally easier subjects for optimal timing. They usually show around the ninth day after foaling, and this tends to be a strong season unless they have had twins, a bad foaling or they are so preoccupied with ▶

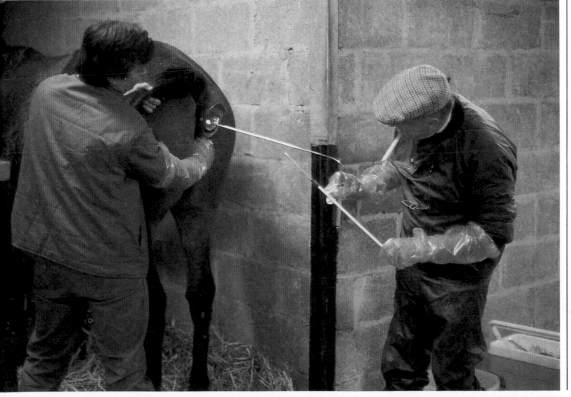

▶ their foal they do not come into season at all. Some mares only produce foals every other year. The mare with foal is normally most fertile in her first season, but if this is missed, the mare should return to the normal cycle, showing every 20 to 21 days.

The Covering

Stallions may be very valuable and must be protected from any cantankerous behavior by the mare. There once was a practice of tying two legs of a mare together with straps called *hobbles* to prevent her kicking or moving. But the realization that if a mare is "covered" (mated) at her optimal time she will be ready and willing to accept the stallion has meant hobbles are almost unnecessary. The normal precaution is to fit felt-and-leather-covered boots over the hind feet of the mare to minimize the effects of any kicks.

The mare is led to the trying board by a bridle, wearing a tail badge. At the board, she is tested with the stallion to make sure that she is "well in". She is then taken to the covering yard. The leader of the mare should have an assistant who can help keep the mare steady and position her.

A maiden mare or a nervous one needs plenty of reassurance. If she has a foal at foot during the service, some studs shut it away in a stable, but most have the foal held at a safe distance from the mare and stallion in the covering yard. In this way the mare is not disturbed by its absence. It's best to lead the stallion around a nervous mare so she can adjust to the situation. On the rare occasion when she is still difficult and may hurt the stallion or helper, yet she is definitely close to ovulation, a *twitch* (a device used to hold the attention of the horse) can be used.

The stallion is led on a bridle or halter with a lead rein 9 or 10 feet, to be positioned behind and to one side of the mare. He is allowed to touch the mare's quarters but not bite or mount her before he has dropped. This preparatory stage may take some time, but as soon as he shows the signs, the rein is loosened so he can mount the mare, still slightly to one side. When the service is finished, he is allowed to dismount and is taken back to his box where his sheath and hindlegs can be washed down with a mild solution of non-irritating disinfectant. The mare should be led around for 10 to 15 minutes after covering.

The key to successful covering is a calm, relaxed, disciplined handling of the mare and stallion. Everybody involved (usually three people) must know exactly what their role is. They must be experienced enough to know when to be firm and when to be gentle, when direction is needed and when to keep clear of flying hooves.

Artificial Insemination

The alternative to covering is artificial insemination (AI). This has many opponents, particularly in the Thoroughbred world, because it is believed it could lead to malpractice and overuse of popular stock. However, it is used on Standard-breds in the United States, where a single collection of semen from one stallion may be split into as many as 20 portions and inseminated daily into mares on the stud. This makes

Above left: The covering of two Percherons. The mare wears hobbles, to stop her kicking.

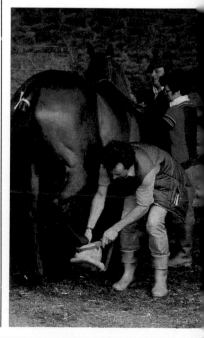

Below left: Hobbles are rarely used today; instead protective boots are put on, as this mare shows.

Below: Covering being done in a yard with the recommended number of three helpers.

Above: This covering is being done in the open. Only two helpers are necessary in this case.

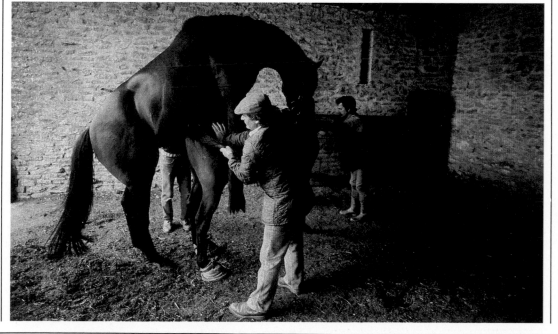

it possible for more mares to receive semen, and the daily administration close to ovulation helps relatively infertile mares to conceive. It is also an aid when mares are very difficult to serve, and it reduces the risk of spreading contagious diseases, which infected mares can pass on.

Frozen Sperm
Semen can also be frozen; this method is being used for international matings, particularly for competition horses.

Advantages and Disadvantages
Artificial insemination does have the undeniable advantages of containing disease, increasing the chances of an infertile mare having a foal, increasing the numbers of mares to any one stallion and making international matings less expensive. However, it also has problems of control, and these are realized by the most valuable breeding market of all, the Thoroughbred industry. It is for these reasons that no Thoroughbred conceived by artificial insemination is allowed to be registered.

THE PREGNANT/IN-FOAL MARE

The Tests

The first test of pregnancy is when the mare does not come into season when tried. She is said then to have "held" to the stallion. Procedure varies as to how often she is tried. Some advocate she be tried on the 9th, 15th, 21st, 28th, 31st and 42nd day after service. Others simply try on the 21st, 42nd and 63rd day. It is important not to assume she is in foal the first time she "holds" because mares can be 8 weeks between seasons. It is also easy for a mare to "slip" (abort) her foal in the early stages without anybody noticing because the fetus is so small.

On the other hand, less-frequent testing is not only labor-saving, but it is also less disturbing to the mare. It is advisable to make the tests as short as possible if the mare is believed to be in foal, because it is all too easy for her to abort if she gets very upset. Take her away from the trying board as soon as she shows any aggressive reactions.

Trying is the first means of checking pregnancy. It is not an infallible system because infertile mares may not come into season. Other methods are usually used in addition because it is important to know the state of the mare.

The more traditional methods are rectal palpation, blood tests and urine tests. A manual examination, 19 to 21 days after the last service, can determine whether pregnancy is or is not likely. At 30 to 35 days, it is more reliable, also the vet can feel if there are twins. At 39 to 42 days it can be considered an accurate diagnosis and at 60 days a check is carried out to make absolutely sure there has been no abortion.

There are anxieties that this manual examination can lead to an abortion. Evidence points to this only being the case if the mare is particularly susceptible to abortion.

Besides the manual examination, other traditional methods of determining pregnancy are blood and urine tests. The blood test, which should be done between 45 to 90 days from the service, is not 100% reliable. About 10% of those mares diagnosed as pregnant turn out not to be so. The urine test is more reliable and can be taken any time after the 120th day after service.

The newest, most reliable method of pregnancy testing is by ultrasound scan.

If a mare is barren, then veterinary assistance is probably advisable to help fertility. If she is pregnant, then her feeding, work and environment need to be monitored to promote healthy growth and ensure against the loss of the foal.

Most in-foal mares change in appearance about 6 months after service. Their bellies start to drop, and they swing slightly when they move. This is not an absolute rule for all mares. Those with their first foal may change little, and some barren mares carry a typical "in-foal" belly.

Abortion

Abortion, which is the expulsion of the fetus before the 300th day, is a disappointing and depressing occurrence. After this time, the foal is said to be premature.

When a mare aborts, it may lead to other fertility problems in the following season and then the advice of the veterinarian is advisable.

Some say abortion can be caused by stress, such as a disturbing experience or a sudden change in circumstances. This is why journeys must be undertaken with care and not too close to the expected date of the birth.

The diet should not be changed too dramatically, and the mare should not be deprived of water. Her food should never be musty, frozen or fermented. Take every precaution that she does not develop colic or a chill. She should not be subjected to frights or made to overexert herself.

Twins are often aborted; this usually occurs in the 6th to 9th month of pregnancy. The mare's uterus doesn't have the capacity to house and nourish twins, and as a consequence she aborts. Only about 20% of twins that are conceived are born and those that do last the full term rarely survive the first few days. If one does, it is usually weak and small. Great efforts are therefore made to avoid twins. Only about 2% of Thoroughbreds conceive twins.

Veterinary examinations can be carried out before service to see if two follicles, rather than one, are developing. Diagnosed twins are often washed out (artificially aborted) in the early stages, but they still occur in large numbers.

Abortion also occurs due to problems that can arise in the womb, causing death of the fetus. There can be a shortage of oxygen, the

Above: A head-on view of a Thoroughbred mare, heavy in-foal. Pregnancy usually lasts about 336 days (11 months).

Below: Thoroughbred mares being fed hard feed. This is needed by nearly all Thoroughbred horses.

Above: This mare, heavy in-foal, is viewed from the side to show the distinct drop in her belly.

umbilical cord can twist and cut off supplies, blood pressure and heart problems in the mare can result in under-nourishment of the fetus, there may be a hormonal imbalance or the fetus may be deformed.

Nutrition can also be a cause of abortion. It is vital for the mare to receive sufficient protein and amino acids in the early stages of pregnancy. Some drugs, such as cortisone and prostaglandins, can have serious effects in the first 6 weeks of pregnancy. Avoid the use of drugs during this period if possible. Some plants, such as ragwort, horsetails, bracken, poppy, flax, locoweed, oleander, jimson weed and bryony can be toxic to horses and may indirectly cause abortion.

Then there are infectious causes. The most serious of these is viral abortion, also called *equine herpes virus* and *rhinopneumonitis*. In young horses, it simply results in a runny nose, but in mares it will result in abortion in the 7th to 9th month of pregnancy. Vaccines have been developed to combat this

serious disease for mares. Bacteria living in the uterus are another cause of abortion and infertility. There is also a fungus that enters the uterus through the vagina after foaling or when a mare is in season. It grows on the placenta, adversely affecting the nourishment of the fetus.

The vet can prescribe preventative measures to reduce the chances of abortion. If a mare has previously aborted, or if it is believed she was exposed to any virus, bacteria or fungi associated with abortions, it is wise to seek consultation.

Health

The other concern during pregnancy is the healthy develop-ment of the fetus. It is believed the healthy development of the fetus depends on freedom from stress factors, such as sudden changes in the environment. Dramatic changes seem to radically affect the mother's ability to nourish her foal. A more direct effect on the fetus' healthy growth is the mare's food supply, although the mare's body will sacrifice itself for the foal, growing emaciated, rather than depriving the fetus.

The essential factor is to keep her looking healthy. Her coat should be in good condition and her body shouldn't be too lean or too fat. Too much bulk food, resulting in

too fat a mare, is as serious as too little food. For most mares, summer grass will keep them in good condition, but if the pasture is not too good or if the mare is a poor "doer" (one that does not develop well) then some oats and bran should be given to her. The protein content is particularly important. A mineral supplement is advisable from an early stage in the mare's pregnancy.

Winter Treatment

As fall (autumn) approaches, most mares need feeding with hay, hard feed and supplements, but the amount varies according to the type of mare and the pasture. Whatever the foodstuff, it must be good quality. The vital criterion of good health remains in the mare's appearance.

Winter necessitates, for most types, some form of shelter and an increase of feed. Hardier types are happy with a makeshift shelter in the field, but the more refined mares may need proper stabling at night.

The Last Stages of Pregnancy

As the foaling approaches, the foal's growth increases. In the last third of pregnancy, it increases three times in weight so the mare

will need help from extra feed to nourish herself and the fast-growing fetus, particularly when the grass is at its poorest. Protein is important for the foal's correct development and for the mare's milk production. Some dried milk can also be helpful.

As foaling time approaches, the diet is gradually changed. About 3 weeks from the date the foal is due, bulk food is gradually reduced to half of what the mare has previously been receiving. Oats are also reduced. To avoid the tendency for the mare to become constipated, give her plenty of grass, and a bran mash at least twice a week. Boiled linseed can be given with the mash. Mineral supplements are important at this stage.

Keep the environment of the mare as natural as possible, and encourage natural movement. She can be kept in work for up to 5 months after the start of the pregnancy, but this should pro-gressively involve less exertion and strain. Some people continue to give hardy types of mares light work for even longer, but it is advisable to let them run free in the fields to get their exercise. Movement is important up to the time of foaling, so if paddocks are waterlogged or icebound, allow the mare to wander around some enclosed area.

THE FOALING

It is important to make the foaling as natural as possible. The less human interference there is, the more relaxed the mare will remain. It will be better for the mare and foal, unless there are complications. Problems do not often occur and most foalings are uneventful, but it is advisable for someone to be present who is experienced in the foaling down of mares, especially if the mare is valuable or a refined type.

Preparation

As foaling time approaches, it's important to keep the mare under frequent observation. Because disturbances should be kept to a minimum, it is best to be able to observe the mare without going into the stable. Most studs have a peephole in the door or wall through which assistants can watch. The natural time for foaling is when everything is quiet, between about 11p.m. and 4a.m. Foaling native ponies left out in the field does not require nightly vigilance. The more refined the mare, the more human assistance she is likely to need. She should be housed in a stable where there is room to foal down and where it's easy to make frequent checks without disturbing her.

The foaling box for ponies should be at least 12feet (3·7m) square but for horses 12x16ft (3·7x4·8m) is acceptable. It should be bedded down deeply, with straw banked up along the sides and against the door for protection and to prevent drafts. Keep the temperature at about 59°F (15°C).

Cleanliness is very important, and the foal and mare are particu-

Above: View through a peephole into a foaling box.

larly liable to infections after birth. Before the mare is put into the box, it should be thoroughly disinfected, washed down and dried out. A previous foaling in the box can leave infectious material, and every precaution must be taken to ensure its removal. Assistants should also be completely clean before the actual foaling: they should wash their hands with carbolic soap and disinfectant in lukewarm water, and then dry them.

When preparing for the foaling, note the telephone number of your veterinarian. Collect the equipment that may be needed during foaling. This should include a pair of sterilized scissors, cotton or gauze, some antiseptic powder or lotion for the stump of the foal's cord, a bucket and a supply of warm water. Equipment needed for aftercare of the mare and the foal must also be ready for immediate use. This includes an enema syringe, liquid

Below: This mare produced her foal in the open, without aid.

paraffin, a baby's feeding bottle with a large nipple, petroleum jelly, disinfectant and the means to make a warm bran mash.

Indications of Foaling
The earliest indication the foaling is not far away is when the mare begins to "bag up". This is when the udder starts to grow stiffer, rounder and larger, due to enlargement of the mammary glands and the collection of milk. This milk has a very high level of protein, including globulin that helps protect the foal against disease and infection when it is born. Bagging up is not a reliable indication of foaling, because this enlargement of the udder can occur up to 2 weeks before the birth, and it is not unheard of for a mare to only "bag up" after birth.

Closer to the birth, usually 24 hours before but up to 10 days before, drops of honey-like secretion form at the end of the mare's teats. This occurrence is known as "waxing up."

Another sign is the "softening of the bones". Usually about 2 weeks before foaling, the pelvic ligaments start to soften. The muscles begin to relax to ease the passage for the foal. There are external signs of a gradual deepening of the vagina, and grooves appear on either side of the tail. The points of the hip become more prominent. Muscles around the anus and vagina also slacken, and as the time for the birth approaches, the lips of the vulva swell.

The mare's behavior also tends to change. She becomes more tense and antisocial and shows obvious signs of increasing discomfort as the time for foaling approaches.

Above: The deeply dropped belly of this mare suggests foaling may occur very soon.

Below: Shortly before birth, the teats exude drops of honeylike secretion; this is called "waxing-up".

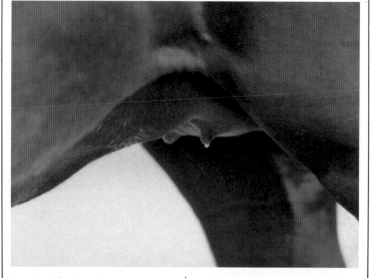

The First Contractions
Early contractions may not be noticed because they start by being light and infrequent. An indication foaling is about to commence is when the mare begins to show signs of pain. She may also sweat, paw the ground and look around at her flank at this early stage in the process.

The intensity of these actions varies. Some mares sweat profusely, others remain docile and unperturbed during this time. In some cases, the interval between contractions can be long, with the mare sweating, then cooling off again. It's more normal for the contractions to become gradually more frequent and intense, quickening from one every 5 or 10 minutes to one approximately every 30 seconds.

Usually it takes up to an hour from the first signs of pain and contractions to the appearance of the gray water bag and its rupture, called "the breaking of the waters." The allantoic fluid released is yellow brown and may gush through the vulva. Or it may be so small in quantity that there is only a trickle. It can even pass unnoticed.

Timetable
A timetable is only a guide, and the most important indication of a healthy foaling is that there is regular progress at all stages.

From the breaking of the waters to the birth of the foal usually takes less than an hour. For a mare that has had foals before, it is usually about 20 minutes. But maiden mares often take a little longer. In a smooth delivery, the yellow membrane of the amnion (also known as the caul) should appear about 5 minutes after the "breaking of waters". The foal should be delivered in 20 minutes, the cord broken within another 30 minutes, the foal suckling in 2 hours and the afterbirth (placenta) freed within 10 hours. If this timetable is not met, or if there is no progress, then veterinary assistance is advisable.

The Stages
Most mares lie down after the breaking of the waters. It is quite normal for a mare to change her position and even to get up and lie down again. But if it happens too frequently, this indicates she is having difficulties and the foal's position needs checking by an experienced person.

Once the foaling starts, the mare normally remains lying down. Usually only nervous mares, disturbed by humans, stand up. The contractions, which at this stage may be quite vigorous, are a healthy sign. A mare that is straining often indicates that the foal is incorrectly positioned, and then experienced help is needed.

Before checking the position of a foal, the hands of the experienced assistant and the anus of the mare must be washed with disinfectant and lubricated with paraffin. Then the assistant's hand slides into the birth passage, feels the foal and, if necessary, manipulates it into the correct position.

For a smooth delivery, one foreleg should slightly lead the other, with the foal in a diving position. The head should be straight and slightly behind the forelegs. If it is sideways or one or more of the forelegs are bent, skillful manipulation can correct this. If the hocks are ▶

visible or felt, it is a breech presentation, and this will require veterinary assistance by all but the most experienced breeders. The foaling is more difficult in the breech position because the broader quarters of the foal come first. Also, the cord is very easily broken in a breech birth. If this happens too early in the foaling, it can cause suffocation.

Although it's best to do as little as possible during foaling, there are occasions, such as when the mare is obviously exhausted and the periods between her straining are lengthening, when skillful assistance is needed to help the foal come through the birth canal. Before this is done, check the foal's position to ensure it is possible for the foal to get through the birth canal. Nature provides for pushing the foal through the birth passage but humans can only pull it through. Force should be exerted *only* as the mare strains and *never* when she stops. If excessive force is used, the foal's forelegs tend to damage its chest. It is only through experience that a person can learn when and where to assist the mare and foal, and how much help to give.

A common problem is when the foal's elbows stick behind the mare's pelvic brim. The head is another area that can get into the wrong position and cause problems. The broadest section of all is the shoulders and withers, so it is not surprising that they, too, can easily become stuck.

After delivery, the foal should be on its side in an arc, with its hind legs in the vagina. By this time the amnion should have broken but if it has not, it should be split by applying pressure between the foal's feet. If necessary, lift the foal's head out of the amniotic fluid. If the amnion is left intact, the foal can suffocate.

The Cord
It is best for the mare to remain lying down for a further half an hour. This gives time for her womb

Below: It is vital to check that the foal is in the normal position. A breech birth requires veterinary help.

and birth passage to contract. The foal's cord should break when the mare gets up or if the foal struggles away from her. The cord breaks naturally close to its belly and the stump can be dressed with antibiotic powder. The practice of cutting and tying the cord has been stopped because it was discovered if it is broken before the foal is breathing, the young animal does not receive all its circulatory blood.

In some cases, after breaking, the cord will bleed. This can usually be stopped by pinching it between the thumb and finger, or tape can be applied if necessary. On the rare occasion when a cord does not break naturally, it can be cut through with sterilized scissors, about 4 inches from the foal's belly. The stump is not tied, but it is dressed as described above.

The Afterbirth
The afterbirth (placenta) takes longer to be delivered. It is attached to the uterine walls during pregnancy, and it takes time to separate from it. Normally it does so about an hour after completion of the birth, but it can take longer. The afterbirth can be tied with twine so it hangs about the level of the hocks. When it falls off, check it out to see if it is complete and be sure no placenta is retained in the two arms of the uterus. A retention of placenta can cause serious infection.

The foal is born with a wet coat, soaked in amniotic fluid. If the weather is cold, or if the foal seems to be very weak, dry the coat to reduce heat loss and to stimulate breathing and movement. In most cases, this is unnecessary, and mare and foal can be left to themselves.

The Newborn Foal
A strong foal is on its feet and searching for milk within about half an hour of delivery. It is likely to be unbalanced and poorly coordinated at first, but it rapidly gains strength. If it has not suckled within 2 hours, or cannot stand without falling over within 3 hours, then there is a problem and veterinary advice is needed.

Some assistance can be given, but try not to frighten the newborn animal. Help it stand and direct it

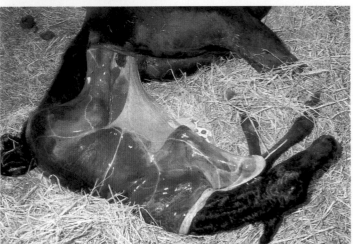

*The sequence of pictures on this page shows various stages in foaling.
Left: The mare is still standing as the water bag appears.
Right: The mare is now lying down; the front legs of the foal are visible. The front feet are clearly pointing down, so it is not a breech birth.
Far right: The foal has now broken through the water bag.
Below: Practically all of the foal's body has now emerged.
Below right: The foal is now completely free.
Below, far right: The foal is being rubbed down to stimulate its blood circulation and help dry its coat.
Bottom: At last—the wonderful moment of the first encounter between the mare and her foal.*

toward its mother's udder. If the mare is ticklish or maiden, it may be necessary to hold her while the foal learns to suck. Leave the mare alone as much as possible until she has licked the foal. Then she can be given bran mash with linseed.

The foal must pass meconium, which is a dark rubbery type of dung collected in the rectum, colon and cecum during its time in the womb. Foals often have a problem in passing meconium, particularly colts.

If the colt is standing with its tail up and straining 4 to 5 hours after birth, an enema is advisable. Use 1¾ to 3½ pints of lukewarm soapy water, and inject it into the rectum. But first the rectum must be cleared of any pellets by carefully inserting a gloved

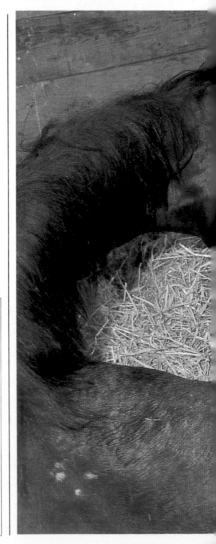

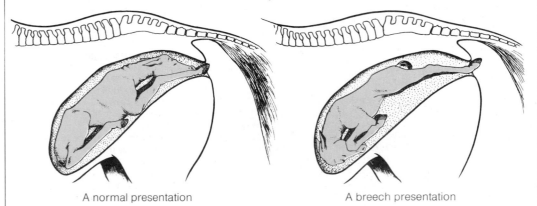

A normal presentation

A breech presentation

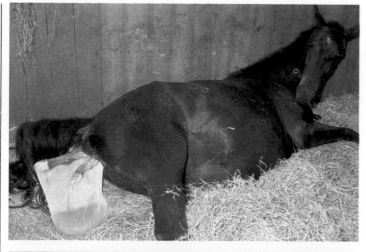
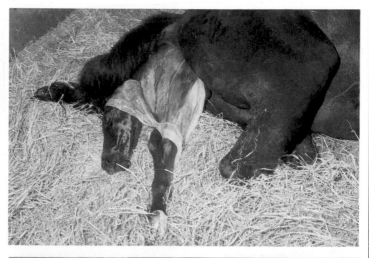

forefinger, lubricated with paraffin, into the anus. When giving a newborn foal an enema, use a rubber tube that is soft and has no sharp edges. As an alternative, liquid paraffin can be injected into the rectum. Only small quantities must be used. Be careful not to damage the foal. If this is ineffective, oil can be administered by mouth or through a stomach tube; in these cases, it is advisable to call a vet.

Dealing with Problems

Most foalings occur smoothly, but vigilance is necessary to make sure there are no serious problems. Close adherence to the timetable is important. If there are any delays, call an expert immediately. However straightforward it might appear, checking a foal's position and giving assistance during delivery should be done by an experienced person.

The most common problem during the birth is incorrect positioning of the foal. This is the most necessary point to check. After foaling it is important to look for weaknesses in the foal: any signs of a blockage or inability to behave normally.

Recording of events and their timing is a great help to a veterinarian if one has to be called in. Hopefully this will not be necessary, but if things start going wrong, speed is important. As long as the foaling progresses smoothly the mare, and when it is born, the foal, are best left to themselves.

Mare and Foal

For the first few days, keep the mare and foal (except those of hardy breeds) in the stable. The mare can be given boiled feed and mashes, and some fresh grass if it is available. This helps avoid constipation and encourage the flow of milk.

Watch the foal during these early days. The most common problem is a stoppage if there are any signs of straining and the tail going up, then the action described on the previous page is needed. If colic develops, or the foal has diarrhea with dark-colored manure, call the veterinarian. If the foal emits loose, yellow feces, the problem is not so serious, but the foal should be kept clean under the tail.

Depending on the weather and the strength of the foal, the mare and foal can be let out to graze for a few hours about 2 days after the birth. If they continue to do well and the weather remains mild, they can be left for longer each day, until they are eventually in the field all the time. Only very valuable, refined types need to be brought in at night when the foals are strong and the weather is good in the summer. Most stock is better off when allowed to remain in its natural environment.

The Importance of Play

When turned out into the field, the foal will almost immediately start skipping around and playing. It is wonderful to watch a youngster discovering the joys of being alive and being able to use its body to leap and gallop. After a few weeks, it will start to play with other foals if they are in the field. Play is believed to be important for a youngster's development, just as it is considered important for a stallion to play with other colts. It can appear quite rough, with plenty of rearing and biting, but it rarely results in any harm.

Feeding

During the first few days, a laxative type of feed may be advisable. When the mare and foal go out to grass, whether feed is necessary depends on the type of mare, the condition of the mare and foal and the quality of the grass. Thoroughbreds usually need oats or stud nuts, and from 5-15lb (2·3-6·8kg) can be given, together with an occasional addition of boiled linseed. The foal will gradually learn to eat oats by copying its mother and eating some of her ration. As the summer progresses and the grass becomes more scarce and less nourishing, hay may have to be provided. Mares that have been coming in at night should be given hay while they are in the stable.

Some mares may not produce sufficient feed for their offspring. Continual attempts by the foal to suck are a sign of inadequate milk production. If this occurs, give the mare more protein (clover,

Above: A mare and foal loose in an indoor school. In this type of place, they can exercise, even in winter.

alfalfa [lucerne], bran and linseed). If this doesn't help, call your veterinarian immediately.

Worming

Worms are a major hazard to youngstock and their dams. Worm infestation can cause colic and even death. Precautions to keep paddocks from becoming "horse sick" (infested with worms) are discussed on page 163. In addition, regularly worm all stock. Worm the mare 3 weeks to a month *before* foaling, then not again until she has been covered. The foal can be wormed at 8 weeks, then every month thereafter. The veterinarian will provide a special dosage appropriate for the foal.

Handling

Patient handling establishes respect and trust and will pay dividends in the future. Foals coming in at night can have daily handling sessions of 5 to 15 minutes. Those at grass can be left until they are weaned.

The basic concept in handling a foal is that it will stop struggling and resisting as soon as it realizes a human being is more powerful, that it can't get away and that there is no need to get away, because no harm is intended. In this way, it will learn that it can trust its handlers.

One of the first tasks is to fit a head collar. This is most easily accomplished in a stable. One person approaches the foal from the nearside, putting a left arm around the foal's chest and holding the tail at the root with the right arm. While the foal is being securely held, a second person puts on the head collar. If the foal is not weaned, a helper is needed to hold the mare.

The foal can be taught to lead by being pushed from behind — never pull it by the head collar. In the first few lessons, put a stable rubber around the foal's neck (this is soft and won't hurt) while holding the hindquarters with the other hand. This can be used to push the foal forward. The mare is led in front of the foal, which will encourage it to follow. Gradually, over a period of days, the pushing will become less necessary and the foal can be led more from the stable rubber. Eventually, as it relaxes, it can be led off the headcollar.

The other vital aspect of handling is getting the foal used to its feet being picked up. It's important to take care of the feet, and they should be regularly cleaned out

with a hoof pick. From about 2 months of age, regular trimming is advisable. If there are any deformities of the feet, corrections can often by made by the farrier. Success is more likely when the bone is still soft.

Weaning

Weaning is the separation of the foal from its mother. Do not do this until the 4th month, at the earliest. Thoroughbreds (except those that are weak or slow to develop) are usually weaned at 5 to 6 months, and other breeds at 6 months. If the mare is not in foal, weaning can be delayed until about 8 months, as long as the mare is keeping good condition.

Some breeders wean the offspring of mares in foal later than 6 months. The argument against this is that the foal is taking food from the fetus, but there is little veterinary evidence for this.

There are two main methods of weaning. The first is the more artificial, but it is safer and easier to manage, and is practiced at most studs. If the mare has been given grain (such as oats), this is cut down to reduce her milk production. Mares out at grass are brought in (at least at night) 7 to 10 days before weaning so the foal can learn to eat grain and hay. Feed mare and foal from separate containers.

Put them in a stable that is thickly bedded. For the last few days do not muck them out. The mare's smell ▶

Bottom left: First stages in teaching a foal to lead using a stable rubber around its neck and pushing, not pulling, it along.

Below: A foal being turned out for the first time. The mare is held so she will not gallop off until her youngster is used to the outdoors.

Above: A foal being handled when it is out in the field under the watchful eye of its mother.

Below: It is important for youngstock to play. Nibbling is usually considered a sign of friendship.

Right: Two yearlings gallop free. This will help to develop their athleticism and character.

▶ will remain in the box. The mare is led out quickly and taken far enough away to ensure that neither the mare nor the foal will hear each other's whinnies.

The foal is happier if left with other youngsters. It can then be turned out to grass with them after 2 or 3 days. This sudden separation is very stressful for the foal, and at this time it may lose weight and become particularly liable to picking up nervous habits, such as weaving, crib biting and walking the box.

The alternative, more-natural method is to turn a group of mares and foals out in a paddock and keep them together for several weeks so social bonds develop. To start weaning, two mares are taken out and their foals left. The youngsters don't usually become so upset because they have the herd to return to. After 2 or 3 days, two further mares are taken away; the process continues until only the foals remain. If the foals are stabled at night, the weaning is done when they are first turned out in the morning. In the evenings, pairs of weanlings are put in a stable together.

The mares must dry off, and their milk production must stop.

Above: A mare and foal being led in from the field to avoid the midday sun in Kentucky.

Less grain helps this. It is inadvisable to touch the udder, and the mares should only be milked if they are very full, because milking encourages further milk production.

Feeding

Diet is an important part of healthy growth. The first major growth period occurs directly after foaling. In the first month the foal's height increases by about 30%. The second growth period is from 6 to 9 months, when most foals are weaned. The third is after puberty. Good feed is vital to maximize growth and to ensure healthy development of the best possible individual.

The important factor is to keep the youngstock in good condition—not too thin or too fat. Overweight can have as serious an effect on bone development as undernourishment. Overfeeding leads to limb troubles (too much weight to carry), and underfeeding restricts growth, so it is important that a balance between the two is reached.

The amount of feed to give depends on the type of youngstock. Native ponies need very little, while Thoroughbreds need a good deal. Also important are the quality and quantity of the grass (in winter its nourishment value falls), the time spent in the stable and the future use of the youngstock. Those that need to mature quickly, such

as racehorses and show stock, should be given more grain.

The important factor, whatever the quantity given, is that the food is good quality. Particularly important is the hay, which if musty and dusty can easily cause wind problems with the lungs in the future.

Although the quantity of hard feed varies, a typical diet for a freshly weaned riding-horse foal would be 5lb (2·25kg) of crushed oats, and 1lb (0·5kg) bran. It is very important that youngstock eat sufficient calcium and phosphorus, so give supplements containing these. Small amounts of linseed (once or twice weekly), carrots, cod liver oil (daily in one feed) and sugar beet can be added.

Shelter

All but the hardy breeds need shelter in winter. This can be a shed with a wide opening to the field or a closed barn with a good bedding of straw. It's best to give youngstock a bigger area than a stable when they come in so they can be kept together and get some exercise. Any youngstock kept in a stable must be given regular opportunities to run free in a field or school. It is natural for them to want to gallop and play. Exercise is important for their mental and physical development.

Yearlings and two-year-olds

Much the same treatment is given to the youngstock as they grow up. In the spring, any stabled stock can be turned out. If the grass is rich when they are first allowed out, it's important to start with only a few hours of freedom and progressively extend the time, so they do not gorge themselves and develop colic. They should be turned out first by day, then all the time.

The feed given to the stock depends on their condition. Usually no hay or grain is necessary during late spring and early summer. Throughout their development, youngstock should be handled, regularly wormed and their feet trimmed. In the early months, colts and fillies can run together, but by 18 months, they should be separated.

Good feeding and handling establishes the basis for future training and work. The success of the youngstocks' life as adults depends greatly on their correct treatment, which should maximize healthy growth and establish a confident, respectful approach toward humans.

Breaking In

For most ponies and horses, work begins with the breaking in at 3 years old. Many racehorses are broken before they are 2 and some early maturing breeds begin their training at 2½ years, but these are exceptions. Leaving the youngstock long enough to become strong ensures the care and attention put into their breeding and upbringing yields the best possible results.

GUIDE TO INTERNATIONAL BREEDS

Each country has developed its own particular breeds of horses. Some, like the Arab and Thoroughbred, have become so international that they are found all over the world, but for the majority of breeds, the greatest numbers are still based in their country of origin.

This section lists all the breeds country by country, and aims to provide a clear, useful cross-reference to the descriptions of the breeds that appear in alphabetical order in the main section of the book, where they are divided into the three main groups of modern horses: ponies, work-horses and sports-horses. It also includes breeds that are rare or even extinct, and that were, therefore, not included in the main section.

The introductions to the breeds of each country give a concise and up-to-date outline of national horse-breeding activities. It is interesting to see how the different breeds have arisen according to the needs and character of each country's inhabitants, whether they favor spirited or docile horses, large breeds or small ones.

Algeria

Originally part of Barbary, together with Morocco and Libya, Algeria forms a major section of the homelands of the Barb. Horses used in this country are mainly of Arab and Barb descent.

Barb ▶91

Argentina

Although most famous for its Criollo horse and Polo Ponies, Thoroughbreds are produced in large numbers for the country's 400 racetracks.

Criollo ▶97
Falabella ▶27

Australia

There are no horses indigenous to Australia, so early settlers began importing them toward the end of the 18th century. The land in Australia and New Zealand proved conducive to rearing horses, and both countries became exporters of horses.

The first famous Australian horse was the Waler. Developed as a stock horse from Arab, Anglo-Arab and Thoroughbred stallions, it became very popular as a cavalry horse. "Country-bred" Walers were foundation stock for the Australian Stock Horse.

Australian Pony ▶14
Australian Stock Horse ▶90
Brumby ▶93
Waler ▶90

Austria

Austria is most famous as the country where the Lipizzaner was developed. Two other well-known and widespread native breeds are the Haflinger Pony and the Noriker Cold-Blood. Government-controlled studs also produce the Austrian Warm-Blood (based on European-Warm Blood imports), which is used in competition and leisure riding.

Austrian Warm-Blood
Haflinger ▶32
Lipizzaner ▶114-115
Noriker Pinzgauer ▶64

Belgium

Belgium is famous for its horses. Its Flemish horses date from Roman times. Today its cold-bloods, the Ardennes and Brabant, are known all over the world, but Belgium is developing a reputation for its new breed of sports horse.

Ardennes ▶52
Belgian Half-Blood ▶92
Brabant/Belgian ▶54-55

Brazil

With its 9 million horses, Brazil boasts one of the largest equine populations in the world. There are many imported breeds, but the native horse is the Crioulo, a smaller version of Argentina's Criollo.

Some Crioulo stock has been improved by crossbreeding. This includes the Mangalarga, a small riding horse developed at the beginning of the 19th century in the state of Minas Gerais. The important foundation stock was Altér Real and Andalusian stallions, put to Crioulo types. The result

was a strong, fast horse useful for ranch work. An unusual feature of the Mangalarga is its extra gait, the "march", which is a fast but comfortable rocking movement for the rider.

Another variation of the Crioulo is the Campolino, first bred in the late 19th century in Brazil by Señor Cassiano Campolino. It is an all-around type used for light draft work and riding.

The Campolino is heavier than the Mangalarga, with a deeper, broader body and shorter legs. The main foundation stock were the Criollo, Crioulo, Andalusian, Thoroughbred and Percheron.

Campolino
Crioulo
Mangalarga

Bulgaria

Horses are systematically bred at the Bulgarian State Studs controlled by the Ministry of Agriculture. During this century, three breeds have been developed

Left: Austria's most famous horses are the Lipizzaners, here seen performing a quadrille.
Below: Kladrubers from Czechoslovakia are famous as driving horses.

from local stock and Hungarian and Russian imports.

The Pleven is Bulgaria's version of the Anglo-Arab. The stock used was mainly Russian Anglo-Arabs and local Arab-type mares, with some Hungarian Arabs, Gidrans and Thoroughbreds. Established as a breed before World War II, the Pleven is a robust type of horse, with the beauty of an Arab, and is used on farms and in competitions. The Danubian is based on two Hungarian breeds, the Nonius and Gidran. It is a stocky horse used for draft work and riding.

The East Bulgarian is the most refined of the three new Bulgarian breeds. It was based on Thoroughbred, Arab, Anglo-Arab and English half-breds. It is very fast and has won the tough Pardubice steeplechase in Czechoslovakia.

Danubian
East Bulgarian
Pleven

Burma

Burma's ponies are closely related to those of northern India. The best known is the Burmese or Shan, which has been used by the hill tribes of the Shan states as a general work pony for a

long time. It is a larger version of the Manipur Pony from India. Both have Mongolian ancestors, but the Burmese has had more Arab added. It is very strong and compact.

Burmese/Shan

Canada

The number of horses in Canada is growing fast, but they are all imported breeds. After a few generations of breeding, some, such as the Canadian Quarter Horse and the Canadian Pacer gain the title "Canadian". The only native breed is the Sable Island Pony, developed on Sable Island off Nova Scotia.

Sable Island ▶43

China

Ponies have long been the work animals in China. The greatest concentration is in Mongolia, with its various native types of pony. In south China, Mongolian Ponies have been crossed with Arab and Thoroughbred imports to produce the faster China Pony, used for racing.

China Pony
Mongolian Pony ▶38
Przewalski's Horse/Asian Wild Horse/Mongolian Wild Horse ▶42

Czechoslovakia

Czechoslovakia has the oldest active stud in the world, at Kladruber, which has given its name to the native breed of warm-blood. There are also many other fine State studs. The breeds produced at these studs are mainly Arabs, Kladrubers and Lipizzaners.

Kladruber ▶113

Denmark

Although the numbers of its traditionally famous breeds, the Frederiksborg and Jutland, are declining, Denmark is gaining a great reputation for its native warm-blood, called the Danish Warm-Blood. Farmers are the main breeders, and there is little state aid for breeding.

Danish Warm Blood ▶98
Frederiksborg ▶101
Jutland ▶62
Knabstrup ▶114

Finland

Finland's native cold-blood still plays an important role in this heavily forested country, where it is used to pull logs. The riding horses, usually referred to as the Finnish Universals, are used for racing and sport and leisure riding. Their numbers are increasing.

Finnhorse Draft ▶58-59
Finnish Universal

France

For centuries, the state has played an important part in French horse-breeding. It has been responsible for the maintenance of stallion depots in the various regions. Horses are produced for racing, competitions, leisure riding, draft and meat (for human and animal consumption).

Several varieties of large French breeds are declining in numbers.

These include the Poitevine, Cob, Auxois and Ariègoise. The Poitevine is an unusual horse that is bred in the Poitou region of France. It was based on Dutch stock that was imported to help drain the marshes of La Vendée and Poitou. But since the 19th century it has been used mainly for crossing with asses to produce high-quality mules. In their heyday, mules had great substance and earned a worldwide reputation.

The Ariègoise is a work horse of ancient origins, dating back to the Romans and Julius Caesar. Although their numbers are small today, Ariègoises are still used for work, particularly in the mountains of the Pyrenees and the Alps.

Cobs are bred in Normandy: these are not true breeds and have no stud book. Their development started at the beginning of the 19th century, when a distinction was made between warm-bloods produced for riding and the Army, and those for work. Horses for work were called Cobs. Sometimes called Normandy Cobs, these horses are similar to the cobs of the British Isles.

The French Pony, a result of crossbreeding, has no stud book. Its increasing numbers and popularity as a children's riding pony make it likely it will have one in the future.

Anglo-Arab ▶88-89
Ardennes ▶52
Ariègoise
Basque/Pottock ▶16
Boulonnais ▶53
Breton ▶55
Camargue ▶94-95
Cob/Normandy Cob
Comtois ▶57
French Pony
French Trotter ▶102
Landais/Barthais ▶36
Percheron ▶66-67
Poitevine
Selle Français ▶132-133

German Democratic Republic (East Germany)

East Germany has not been as active as neighboring countries in breeding horses. Its two main breeds are offshoots of West German breeds. The Mecklenburg is based on the Hanoverian, and the East Friesian is based on the Oldenburg.

East Friesian ▶100
Mecklenburg ▶117

Federal Republic of Germany (West Germany)

In West Germany the breeds of sports-horses the country is most famous for are localized in the different regional States. An exception is the Trakehner, which is found nationwide, because it was a refugee breed from the east. The Federal Government promotes and finances regional breeding. Each State has its own breed, although the Pfalz-Saar and Rheinland-Nassau were amalgamated in 1977.

The brand mark given to a horse is determined by its birthplace, not the breeds of its parents. There is a considerable interchange of ▶

Above: Germany's best known breed is the Hanoverian and this jumper, Tigre, is a famous example.

▶ breeds — the Hanoverian is found in the pedigrees of most regional breeds.

Some lesser-known regional breeds not included in the main section of this book are the Bavarian, which is a more angular, longer-legged version of the Hanoverian. It has Westphalian, Trakehner and Thoroughbred blood. The Hessen, bred at the state stud of Dillenburg, is based on, and very similar to, its neighbor the Hanoverian. The Rhineland shares its state stud of Warendorf with the more-famous Westphalian, upon which it is based. The Rhineland Pfalz-Saar inhabits a region that was once part of France and has been influenced by French breeds.

Baden-Württemburg ▶90-91
Bavarian
Black Forest Chestnut, see South German Cold-Blood ▶71
Dülmen ▶25
Hanoverian ▶107
Hessen
Holstein ▶108-109
Oldenburg ▶123
Rhenish-German Cold-Blood ▶69
Rhineland
Rhineland-Pfalz-Saar
Schleswig Holstein ▶70
South German Cold-Blood ▶71
Trakehner/East Prussian ▶140
Westphalian ▶144

Greece
Once the home of classical riding, Greece now has only a few breeds of ponies.
Peneia ▶30
Pindos ▶30
Skyros ▶30

Hungary
Hungary has excellent soil and climate for breeding horses. It is famous for its horsemanship. Today, horses are bred at huge State stud farms. The major influences are the Arab, which has been used since the Turkish invasion, and the Thoroughbred.
Furioso ▶109
Gidran ▶109
Hungarian Half-bred ▶109
Kisber ▶109
Mezohegyes ▶109
Murakoz/Murakosi ▶63
Nonius ▶122
Shagya ▶133

Iceland
The climate in Iceland is not conducive to horse breeding, but ponies brought there centuries ago have prospered and developed into the breed known as the Icelandic Pony.
Icelandic Pony ▶34-35

India
Horses in India are mainly "country-breds," such as cross-breds of imported breeds (usually Arabs and Walers) and native stock. Typical of these are the Kathiawari and Marwari from

northwest India. Some believe they developed from a shipload of Arab horses that escaped and cross-bred with local ponies. The older native breeds of ponies are the Manipur, Spiti and Bhutia.

Bhutia ▶17
Kathiawari
Manipur ▶37
Marwari
Spiti ▶17

Indonesia

With its thousands of roadless islands and primitive economy, Indonesia has discovered ponies make a major contribution to the economy. The government supports the breeding of some breeds, in particular the Batak on the island of Sumatra. This breed has had a great deal of Arab blood added.

Breeds vary from island to island and are primitive types based on Mongolian or Tarpan stock or a mixture of them both. Probably the fastest Indonesian pony is the Sandalwood. Like the Batak, it has had infusions of Arab blood. It is used for racing, but riders are usually bareback and have bitless bridles. The Java is famous for pulling two-wheeled taxis, called *sados,* on the island after which it is named. The Timor is the smallest of the ponies. Because its home-lands are close to Australia, it has been exported there to act as foundation stock for the Australian Pony. The Bali is primitive in appearance, with its upright mane and dorsal stripe. The Sumba, another breed which is dun with a dorsal stripe, has become most famous as a dancer. It performs without saddle or bridle, with bells attached to its knees. A person on foot controls the pony as it moves to a tom-tom rhythm.

Bali
Batak
Java
Sandalwood
Sumba
Timor

Iran

Iran is the home of several ancient lines of horses. The Caspian Pony, the Persian Arab and the Turkoman come from the northern steppes. The Turkoman is dif-ferentiated into the Akhal-Teke and Iomud from Russia. The Iranian strain, known as the Tchenaran, has more substance and is more compact. Apart from these famous breeds, Iran also produced the Plateau Persian, which was an amalgamation of the Arablike strains known as the Fars, Basseri, Darashuri and Qashqai. The Pahlavan, which was a mixture of Plateau Persian with Arab and Thoroughbred, and the Jaf, a robust Arab-type horse, are also products of Iran.

These breeds were promoted by the Royal Horse Society, founded during the Shah's reign in 1971. But since the change in government, there has been little

Left: Hungarian horses are now best known as driving horses.

information about horse breeding.

Caspian ▶18-19
Jaf/Kurd
Persian Arab ▶77
Plateau Persian
Turkoman (see also Akhal-Teke and **Iomud,** under USSR) ▶140-141

Republic of Ireland (Eire)

Ireland is a country with a climate and soil conducive to horse breeding. The government-backed Irish Horse Board gives financial and administrative aid to horse breeders.

Connemara ▶20-21
Irish Draft ▶60-61
Irish Horse ▶110

Italy

About 400 years ago, Italy pro-duced her most famous horse, the Neapolitan. It came from Arab, Barb and Spanish stock. During the 16th and 17th centuries, the courts of Europe used the Neapolitan for High-School per-formances and as foundation stock for their own breeds. This superb breed is now extinct, and none of the present breeds have attained its stature, although most breeds are based on it.

Avelignese ▶14
Anglo-Arab Sardo ▶111
Calabrese ▶94
Italian Heavy Draft ▶61
Italian Saddle Horse ▶111

Below: The Irish horse Ballylusky ridden by Fiona Wentgis in the 1984 Olympics Three Day Event.

Maremmano ▶111
Murghese ▶120
Neapolitan
Salerno ▶111
Sanfrantellano ▶111
Siciliano ▶111

Japan

Japan is becoming more involved in horse breeding. It has imported many high-class Thoroughbreds and sports-horses. Its own breeds are ponies based on Mongolian stock. The best known of these is the Hokkaido, which is usually dun, with a dorsal stripe and dark points. Also native to Japan are the Kiso Pony, from the central part of the mainland, and the Wild Horse of southern Kyushu.

Hokkaido
Kiso
Kyushu

Mexico

Mexico's horses are based on Spanish and Portuguese stock, brought to the country in the 16th century, and on imported American breeds. The chief native breed is the Galiceño, a pony based on two Spanish and Portuguese ponies, the Garrano and Sorraia. The Galiceño is a fast, strong pony, with a running walk. It is used for draft and pack work and riding.

Galiceño

Morocco

Like Algeria, Morocco was once part of ancient Barbary, the home of the Barb.

Barb ▶91

Netherlands

The Netherlands is famous for its horses. The oldest existing breed is the Friesian, which dates back to Roman Times.

Dutch Draft ▶58
Dutch Warm-Blood ▶100
Friesian/Frisian ▶102-103
Gelderland ▶104
Groningen ▶105

New Zealand See under Australia.

Norway

Norway is the home of two im-portant old breeds, the Norwegian Fjord and Døle. Both have been utility animals for centuries. A modern breed version of the Døle is called the Døle Trotter. It was developed by introducing Thoroughbred blood to produce a faster horse to pull light vehicles and, later, to race.

Døle Gudbransdal ▶57
Døle Trotter ▶57
Norwegian Fjord ▶40-41

Peru

Peru was one of the main bases for the Spanish *Conquistadores* during the 16th century. Its most famous breed, the Peruvian Horse, was developed during that time. The local "criollo" was developed from Argentinian imports.

Peruvian Horse/Peruvian Paso ▶127

Poland

Poland has 42 major studs, which produce the largest horse popula-tion in Europe. There is a great ▶

▶range of breeds, from work ponies, based on the ancient Tarpan, to Thoroughbreds. A horse that falls between these categories is the Silesian, a breed intermediate between warm-blood and cold-blood. Its most important foundation stock is the Oldenburg, which it resembles, but Hanoverians, East Friesians, and Rhinelands have also been used.

Garvolin ▶68
Huçul/Hutsul ▶34
Konik ▶35
Kopczyk Podlaski ▶68
Lidzbark ▶68
Lowicz ▶68
Malapolski ▶117
Polish Arab ▶77
Polish Draft ▶68
Silesian
Sokolsky ▶68
Sztum ▶68
Tarpan ▶ 46
Wielkopolski ▶145

Portugal
The horses and ponies of Portugal have similar origins to those of Spain.
Altér Real ▶86-87
Garrano/Minho ▶29
Lusitano ▶116-117
Sorraia ▶45

Puerto Rico
Racing is popular in Puerto Rico, so the Thoroughbred is, economically speaking, the most important breed. The native breed is the Paso Fino.
Paso Fino ▶126

South Africa
All types of equestrian activities are becoming more popular in South Africa, with the consequent growth of horse numbers. The Thoroughbred is the most important breed, but many others are represented. The native breeds are the Basuto and Boerperd.
Basuto ▶17
Boer Pony/Boerperd ▶18

Spain
Horse breeding in Spain is on the increase, and it is promoted by the government, which runs regional studs. One of the rarest breeds, the Balearic Pony, is based in Majorca. It has primitive features and an upright mane and occurs in various shades of brown.
Andalusian ▶87
Balearic
Hispano ▶108

Sweden
The government supports horse breeding in Sweden and runs a National Stud at Flyinge.
Götland/Russ ▶29
North Swedish ▶65-66
Swedish Ardennes ▶52
Swedish Warm-Blood ▶135

Switzerland
Switzerland's national stud is at Avenches, where the emphasis is on breeding riding horses. Important breeds are the Swiss Warm-Blood and a dual-purpose Army and agricultural workhorse, the Freiberger (also called the

Franches Montagnes). The old Swiss breed of Einseidler, developed by monks at Einsiedl in the 11th century, has now been merged with the Swiss Warm-Blood.
Einsiedler
Freiberger/Franches Montagnes ▶60
Swiss Warm-Blood ▶136-136

Tibet
Various work ponies are found in Tibet. They are closely related to those from northern India.
Tibetan/Nanfan ▶47

Turkey
Turkish horses are famous, but they have been types rather than breeds. The Arabs, Turkomans and, more recently, Thoroughbreds are most important. With the establishment of the Republic of Turkey, efforts have been made by the government to improve the Arabs and Thoroughbreds and to upgrade local stock to establish the Karacabey. This is a purpose-bred riding and harness horse produced from Arab, Thoroughbred, Nonius and local stock.
Karacabey

United Kingdom
Britain has more breeds for its size than any other country in the world. Most of its ancient breeds are still flourishing, though some have become extinct.

The most influential of these was probably the Galloway, a term that has been used to describe a variety of ponies but more specifically refers to dark-colored ponies bred in the region of Galloway, Scotland. They were very fast and were Britain's original racehorses. They had an influence on many breeds, including the Fell, the Dales and even the Clydesdale,

Above: Portugal is well known for its breeds of High School horses, such as this Lusitano.

but became extinct by the end of the 19th century.

The Norfolk Trotter was the fast strong trotting horse of the 18th century. Although now extinct, it had a major influence on the Hackney and the Standardbred of the United States. The Norfolk Trotter started as a breed by crossing Thoroughbreds with native mares; famous progeny include Bellfounder, who was exported to the United States to become one of the strongest influences on the development of the Standardbred. Another name for the Norfolk Trotter was the "New English Road Horse."

A breed with a shorter history than the Norfolk Trotter was the Yorkshire Coach Horse. It was developed in the 19th century in an attempt to speed up the Cleveland Bay by crossing it with the Thoroughbred. With the advent of automobiles, the purebred Cleveland survived, but its offshoot, the Yorkshire Coach Horse, became extinct.
British Warm Blood ▶92-93
Cleveland Bay ▶96-97
Clydesdale ▶56
Dales ▶21-23
Dartmoor ▶24-25
Exmoor ▶26-27
Fell ▶28-29
Galloway
Hackney Pony ▶30-31
Hackney Horse ▶106-107
Highland ▶33
New Forest ▶39-40
Norfolk Trotter
Shetland ▶44-45
Shire ▶70-71
Suffolk ▶72-73
Thoroughbred ▶80-83

Right: The Appaloosa is a breed developed by the American Indians. Below: The USA's most numerous breed, the Quarter Horse.

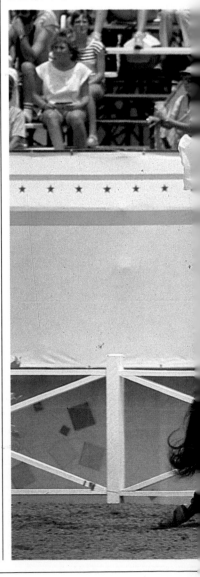

United States

The United States has no indigenous breeds. The wild horses that ran across its prairies emigrated or died out. For centuries, until the arrival of the Spanish and Portuguese, there were no horses. The early conquerors and settlers brought their horses, which led to the development of many new breeds.

Most breeds still exist today, but one important one became extinct—the Narragansett Pacer. It was named after Narragansett Bay, Rhode Island. This fast, riding horse was famous for its pacing gait. It probably developed from English and Spanish Amblers and the Indian ponies. Pacers were used for riding across the rough country and for racing. Although no longer in existence, this breed played an important part in the development of the American Saddlebred, the Tennessee Walker and the Standardbred.

USSR

Horse breeding in the Soviet Union is controlled by the Central Board of Horse Breeding of the Ministry of Agriculture, with affiliated bodies responsible for the Russian Federation, the Ukraine and Kazakhstan. All matters relating to selective breeding policies, equestrian husbandry, certain aspects of veterinary care and training at both practical and theoretical level come under the aegis of the All-Union Scientific Research Institute of Horse Breeding, which maintains a close working relationship with the State studs.

State studs, which date back to the 18th century when they existed alongside private breeding establishments, were reorganized in 1930 as part of the policy of collectivization. The 106 studs now spread over 14 Union Republics operate in conjunction with 780 stud centers on State and collective farms, 65 stud stables and 5 stud stations.

The first priority was to increase the number of horses used in agriculture and improve their quality. Although the traditional role of the heavy draft has been usurped by the tractor and the combine harvester, horse power is still more efficient and economical for peripheral farm work.

To keep pace with the rapid growth of the industries producing meat and *kumiss* (a drink of fermented horse milk) it has been recommended that the number of indigenous horses bred specifically for these markets, such as the Kazakh and the Bashkir, should be increased and improved.

The Central Government also recognized the need to improve further the quality of pedigree horses for the classical equestrian sports, racing and export. They wanted to provide larger numbers of suitable animals for the country's up-and-coming leisure activity of hacking and trail riding.

The native breeds
The many local breeds of horses distributed over the vast territory of the Soviet Union are normally classified as native steppe, native mountain and native northern forest types. But within these ecological groupings, there are numerous geographical subdivisions. Traditionally reared in herds as multipurpose saddle, pack and harness horses, many of these small indigenous breeds have been improved since the 1930s by the introduction of Thoroughbred, Don and Trotter blood. They also have been crossed with the Soviet Heavy Draft, a strong cold-blood developed in western Russia in the latter half of the 19th century mainly from Belgian heavy horses. This produces larger, heavier animals suitable for the meat trade. The breeds that are reared specifically for meat and *kumiss* exist in healthy numbers, but certain lesser-known breeds are in danger of becoming extinct and their survival is currently a matter of official concern.

Steppe breeds
The native steppe breeds, which include the Buryat, the Minusin and the Kazakh, are characteristically short legged, with long barrels and light, but dense, bone.

Like all Siberian breeds, the Buryat is a hardy animal, well-adapted to withstand the severe winters of its homeland. Buryats that have been improved with Thoroughbred, Don and Trotter blood are called Transbaikal and Amur horses.

The Minusin, from the Khakassk region of Siberia, comes from the ancient Khakassk breed. But its evolution, like the Buryat's, has been influenced by the Mongolian Horse.

The Kazakh, whose history goes back more than 2,000 years, evolved as a part of the life of the nomadic tribes who inhabited the vast area of present-day Kazakhstan. Two types are recognized within the breed—the Adaev, which as a result of cross-breeding possesses a more-pronounced riding-horse type of conformation, and the smaller, coarser Dzhabe, which is bred primarily for meat.

Mountain breeds
Horses have always played an important part in the life of the tribesman and nomads inhabiting the mountainous regions of the Altai, the Tien Shan, the Caucasus and the Carpathians. For work at high altitudes, the mountain breeds must possess strong hearts, lungs, muscles and tendons and flint-hard feet. To negotiate steep mountain paths cut in the rock, to cross narrow bridges over rushing torrents and to ford fast-flowing rivers, they must also be sure-footed, react quickly in moments of danger and have a temperament that can cope with hazardous situations.

The natural habitat of alpine and subalpine meadows, with excellent grazing most of the year, provides ideal conditions for herd rearing. There is a greater variety of mountain breeds than of the steppe and forest types. To this group belong the Altai, which for centuries has been bred in the Altai Mountains and has common origins with the Mongolian, the Huçul (Hutsul) and the breeds of Transcaucasia—the Tushin and the Megrel (now almost extinct), which are indigenous to the Georgian Republic, and the Deliboz and the Karabakh, both breeds of the light, riding-horse type native to Azerbaidzhan. The Karabakh no longer exists in its purebred form. Work to restore some of the

Above: The Latvian is one of the many breeds from the USSR.

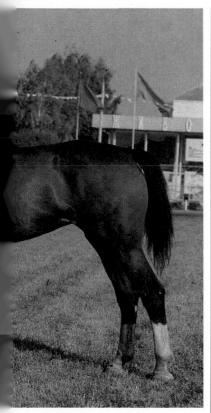

characteristics of the original breed is now being carried out at the Akdam Stud.

Northern forest breeds
The northern forest breeds are divided into an eastern group (the Yakut, the Narym and the Priob) and a western group (the Estonian, the Viatka, the Mezen, the Zhmud (Zemaituka), the Pechora, the Polessk, the Tavda and others). They are all uniquely adapted to the harsh climatic conditions of the northern regions of the country—subzero temperatures in winter and wet summers with swarms of mosquitoes. They possess considerable stamina, are able to exist on a minimum of food, have obedient and placid temperaments, do well in harness and show good paces at the walk and trot.

The northern forest breeds are small animals, with massive, long barrels, short legs and strong feet. A characteristic feature is the thickness of the coat, which grows to a length of 3-6 inches (7·5-15cm) in the coldest areas. The farther west they live, the larger their size and the more-pronounced their harness horse conformation. A number of western types, such as the Zhmud, Obva, Vyatka and Mezen, have been

Below: Quite a number of the older Russian breeds pull troikas.

improved by crossing with Estonian and Finnish horses.

Most forest breeds are named after the region to which they belong or a place or river wihin that region.

The Yakut comes from the Yakut Autonomous Republic, the Priob from around the River Ob, in the Khanty-Mansiisk region of Siberia, the Estonian from the Estonian Republic, the Pechora from around the River Pechora, in the Komi Autonomous Republic, the Mezen from around the River Mezen, in the Archangel region, the Tavda from around the River Tavda, in the Sverdlovsk region, the Polessk from the Belorussian Republic and the Zhmud from the Lithuanian Republic (it is sometimes referred to by its Lithuanian name Zemaituka).

New breeds
The policy of creating new breeds of horses is one that has been actively pursued in the Soviet Union since the 1920s.

In many cases, the formula of using three breeds of stallions with the foundation mares in various permutations at different stages of the breeding program has proved a successful one.

The Kushum, a breed developed primarily for meat and officially recognized in 1976, was evolved by crossing Kazakh mares with Thoroughbred half-bred Russian and Orlov Trotter stallions and at a later stage with Don stallions.

Kazakh mares crossed with Don, Strelets (an extinct breed from the 19th century based on the Arab) and Thoroughbred stallions were also the foundation stock of the multipurpose Kustanair horse, officially recognized as a breed in 1951.

The Lithuanian Heavy Horse is a strong, powerful horse that is used for draft work, for meat, and for crossing with other breeds to make them heavier and meatier. First recognized as a breed in 1963, it is the result of crosses between the Lithuanian Zhmud (or Zemaituka) and imported Swedish Ardennes.

The Latvian Riding Horse, still in the process of development, is based on Latvian mares of the lighter harness type crossed with Arab, Hanoverian and Thorough-bred stallions.

The Lithuanian Heavy Draft breed was registered in 1963 and has flourished since then. It was developed in Lithuania during the early 1900s mainly by crossing imported Swedish Ardennes with Zhmuds.

Local harness breeds
The Voronezh Harness Horse is based on the Bityug, a local breed from the Voronezh Province that lost its identity during the 19th century as a result of repeated crossings with English Heavy Draft Horses. In the 1930s, work began to re-establish the Bityug by mating local improved mares with the heavier type of Orlov Trotter. The desired type that was eventually

created became known as the Voronezh Harness Horse.

The Kuznets, the largest Siberian breed found in the Novosibirsk and Kemerovo Provinces, was evolved by crossing local breeds with Orlov Trotters, English Thoroughbred and English Heavy Draft Horses.

Venezuela
Like most South American countries, Venezuela developed a "criollo" from imported Iberian stock that was turned loose on its hot, dry plains. The Venezuelian version is known as the Llañero.

Yugoslavia
Yugoslavia has many State studs. The government promotes horse breeding because the animals are of great value in this predominantly agricultural country. Many farms are on steep hillsides, and it is difficult to mechanize. Most horses bred at these studs are imported breeds, but Yugoslavia has a native pony, the Bosnian, which is produced in very large numbers. The stud of Lipizza, the original home of the Lipizzaner, is also in Yugoslavia (it was in Austria when the breed was developed).

GLOSSARY AND POINTS OF THE HORSE

Aged is an older horse, usually over 10 years.

Ambler Old English word for a Pacer (see **Pacer**).

Ankle is an alternative term for the fetlock joint.

Back at the knee Foreleg that tends towards a concave shape when looked at from the side. Particularly obvious at the knee.

Barrel Term used to describe that part of the horse's body which is enclosed by the ribs.

Bone Measurement of circumference of the foreleg just below the knee. "Good bone" means the measurement is large.

Boxy Feet When viewed from the front, feet are narrow and not round in shape.

Cold Bloods Heavy draft breeds used in industry, agriculture and transportation.

Colic Equine pain in the stomach. A horse with colic shows signs of being in pain, tends to try and roll, and sweats.

Colt Male horse that has not been gelded (castrated), up to the age of 4 years.

Conformation The make and shape of a a horse. A horse with "good conformation" is stronger and more likely to stay sound than one with a weak conformation.

Country breds Horses or ponies that have been bred unselectively. They have no stud book, and their parents have usually been crossbred.

Cow hocks Hocks that turn inward at the point, like those of a cow.

Crossbreeding Breeding from a mare and stallion that are of different breeds.

Deep Horse is deep through the girth if the measurement is considerable from the withers to the elbow. Horse has "heartroom", especially if its chest is broad.

Dishing When forelegs do not move straight forward and back but swing to the side in an outward, circular movement.

Dorsal stripe Stripe found in primitive breeds that runs down the neck along the back to the top of the tail.

Ewe neck Top line of the neck, from the poll to the withers, is concave instead of convex or straight. It is also called an "upside-down neck."

Face markings These are shown on the page 201.

Face Front of the head; in outline it can be concave (dished), straight or convex.

Feather Long hair above, on and below the fetlock joints. It is usually found on Cold Bloods, rarely on Warm Bloods and never on Hot Bloods.

Filly Female horse or pony under the age of 4 years.

Foal Young horse or pony, male or female, up to the age of 12 months.

Forehand Front section of a horse—the forelegs, shoulder, neck and head. A horse is on its forehand when it is carrying a relatively high proportion of its weight with its forehand rather than hindquarters. This makes it less mobile and less able to spring

Points of the horse

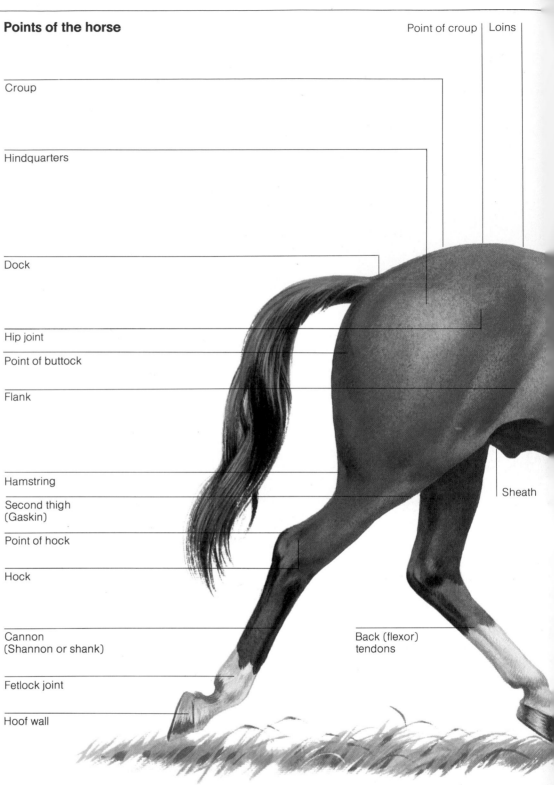

Point of croup | Loins

Croup

Hindquarters

Dock

Hip joint

Point of buttock

Flank

Hamstring

Second thigh (Gaskin)

Point of hock

Hock

Cannon (Shannon or shank)

Fetlock joint

Hoof wall

Sheath

Back (flexor) tendons

---

into the air.

Frog is a V-shaped area on the underside of the hoof. It consists of a horny substance that acts as a shock absorber.

Gait Also called **Pace.** Most breeds' gaits consist of the walk, trot, canter and gallop, but some special breeds have different or additional gaits, such as the five gaited Saddlebred and the Paso Fino.

Gaited horse One that is trained in artificial and natural gaits.

Gelding A castrated male horse.

Goose rump refers to a horse with hind quarters that slope very sharply from the point of croup to the tail. It is

a weak aspect of the conformation.

Hand Unit measurement (4in, 10.2cm) of the height of the horse. A horse is so many hands high, abbreviated "hh."

Heart room is used to describe a horse that is deep (q.v.) through the girth and broad through the chest so there is plenty of room for the heart and lungs. Such a horse usually has good stamina.

Height Taken from the highest part of the withers in a perpendicular line to the ground. It can be measured in hands or centimeters or inches.

High school horse One trained in Classical Riding and able to

perform classical or High-School airs, which are movements above the ground.

Hollow back Natural concave line of the horse is exaggerated and unnatural.

Hot Bloods Pure breeds, such as the Thoroughbred and the Arab.

Inbreeding Mating of brother and sister, sire (father) and daughter, son and dam (mother).

Limb markings illustrated on page 201.

Line breeding Mating of horses that have one or more common ancestors, but are some generations removed.

Lunging Method of exercising

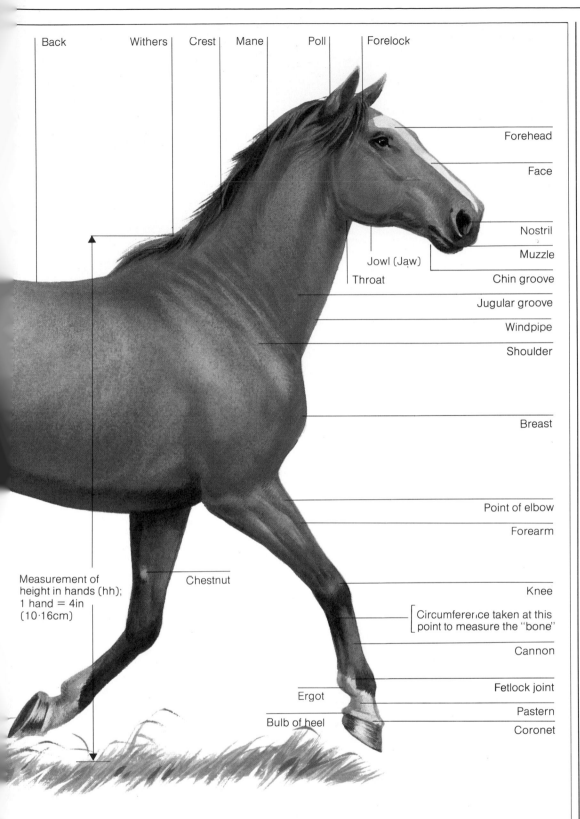

Back | Withers | Crest | Mane | Poll | Forelock

Forehead
Face
Nostril
Muzzle
Jowl (Jaw)
Throat
Chin groove
Jugular groove
Windpipe
Shoulder
Breast
Point of elbow
Forearm
Knee
Circumference taken at this point to measure the "bone"
Cannon
Fetlock joint
Pastern
Coronet
Ergot
Bulb of heel
Chestnut
Measurement of height in hands (hh); 1 hand = 4in (10·16cm)

moving rapidly, with short, equal intervals between each hoof beat, as in the American Saddlebred.

Roach back Conformation weakness; the back is convex.

Roman nose Describes a horse with a convex face.

Sloping shoulders The line of the shoulders runs obliquely from the withers to the point of the shoulders.

Straight shoulders Line of the shoulders is upright.

Sequence of gaits or paces For each gait, there is a correct sequence of footfalls. At the walk, four hoofbeats should be heard with equal intervals between them. They should fall in the order of right hind leg, right foreleg, left hindleg and left foreleg. At the trot, there are two hoofbeats, with legs moving in diagonal pairs separated by a moment of suspension. At the canter, there are three hoof beats followed by a moment of suspension. The canter can be on the left lead or right lead. On the left lead, the first hoofbeat is the right hind followed by the left hind and right foreleg together and finally the leading leg, the left foreleg. On the right lead, the left hind is first. In the gallop, four hoof beats are heard followed by a moment of suspension. On the left lead, the sequence is right hind leg, left hind leg, right foreleg, left foreleg. On the right lead, the left hindleg starts a similar sequence.

Sickle hocks Weak hocks that when viewed from the side are bent to form shapes similar to a sickle.

Stallion Also called a "stud" or "entire." It is an ungelded horse that should be capable of reproducing the species.

Standing square refers to a horse standing in balance with its legs lined up in pairs.

Tied-in is an expression used to describe the front legs of a horse whose circumference measured just below the knee is less than that measured a little lower and nearer to the fetlock joint.

Toad eye Mealy rim on both eyelids; it almost encircles the eye that is prominent. Found in the Exmoor Pony.

Wall eye Eye with a partial or total lack of pigment in the iris; it is pink or blue-white in appearance.

Warm Bloods Breeds that are not as pure and refined as the Hot Bloods or as large and slow as Cold Bloods. These breeds are used for riding, competitions and driving.

Worms Parasites harbored by horses. If present in large numbers, they can cause serious damage, such as colic, loss of condition and even death. There are many types of worms, but regular dosing of worm medicine and care of grassland usually prevents serious infestation.

Yearling Colt or filly that is over 1 year and under 2 years. For Thoroughbreds, the first birthday is taken as the 1st January.

Zebra marks Stripes on the limbs, neck, withers and/or hindquarters of horses.

a horse using a long rein (lunge rein) that is attached to a cavesson (a padded, tightly fitting form of halter) or to the bit of the bridle. The horse performs circles around the trainer, who stands in the center holding this rein.

Mare Female equine animal.

Mealy nose or muzzle Oatmeal color that runs up the muzzle. There are no white markings.

Near The left side or left limbs of a horse.

Odd colored Coat with patches of two or more different colors.

Off The right side or right limbs of a horse.

Oriental Name used to describe breeds from the Orient, including the Arab and breeds based on the Arab.

Over at the knee When the foreleg viewed from the side is convex in shape, particularly at the knee.

Outcrossing Use of outside blood in breeding.

Pacer Horse that trots using its legs in lateral pairs, such as near foreleg and near hindleg together. The normal trot uses diagonal pairs, such as near foreleg and off hindleg together. A pacer once was known as an **Ambler.**

Pace Another term for **Gait**; also a variation of the two time gait (trot) when the horse's legs move in lateral pairs.

Parrot mouth When the upper jaw overhangs the lower jaw so there is no true contact between the upper and lower incisor teeth. In bad cases, grazing is difficult, and the horse often has digestive problems. It is also called an "undershot" mouth.

Pigeon toes Toes that turn inward.

Points Term used to describe colors; refers to the mane, tail and lower limbs.

Prepotent When the sire or dam tends to pass on his or her characteristics to their progeny.

Rack Four beat gait with each foot

199

COLORS AND MARKINGS

COLORS

There are many colors; if there is any doubt as to which color a horse is, the muzzle and eyelids are examined and are used as the deciding factors. The most common colors are black, brown, bay, chestnut and gray, although the gray is not a color but a failure of the pigment cells in the hair roots to produce color.

Bay
This is a brown color with shades ranging from red and yellow to very close to brown. Points are black.

Black
The coat, limbs, mane and tail are black; any markings are white.

Blue roan
There are various shades of roan; the blue roan has a basic color of black or brown and a sprinkling of white.

Brown
Dark brown or nearly black, with brown-to-black points.

Chestnut
Also called *sorrel,* this is a ginger, yellow or red color to the coat. The mane and tail are the same color as the coat or lighter.

Claybank
A reddish-yellow dun color with a slightly darker mane and tail.

Cream
Cream-colored hairs on an unpigmented skin. The eyes often have a pink appearance.

Dapple gray
The white and black hairs of a gray horse are not uniform, and in this case darker circles form dapples which are separated by lighter areas.

Dun
The more common variation of the dun is the *yellow dun,* usually referred to simply as *dun.* The hairs are yellow on a black skin. Points are normally black, and there may be a dorsal stripe and zebra markings on the limbs.

Flea-bitten gray
This is a gray in which the coat is flecked with hairs of a darker color.

Gray
Hairs are white and black on a black skin. There are many shades, from light to dark gray, and variations, such as the *Flea-bitten* and *dapple grays.*

Liver chestnut
This is the darkest shade of chestnut.

Palomino
Various shades of gold, with a flaxen or white mane and tail.

Piebald
This is one variation of the *pinto* or *calico.* The large, irregular patches are black and white.

Skewbald
Large patches in the coat are white and any color but black; usually brown.

Above: An Appaloosa mare and foal. This breed has a white coat with various patterns of spots. It is not the only breed of spotted horse; others include the Knabstrup (see page 114) and the Pinzgauer, a line within the breed of Noriker (see page 64).

Strawberry roan
This variation of roan (an admixture of white hairs with another color) is white and chestnut, which gives a pink-red appearance to the coat.

Bay

Black

Chestnut (Sorrel)

Claybank (Red roan/Red dun)

Blue roan

Brown

Cream

Dapple gray

MARKINGS

Markings are areas of white on the head, body and limbs. The other type of marking used for identification is a whorl, which is a pattern formed by hairs around a small central spot.

On the head

Star is white on the forehead.
Stripe is a narrow white mark down the face.
Blaze is a broad white mark down the face, usually extending from the eyes to the muzzle.
White face is a white forehead, eyes, nose and parts of the muzzle.
Snip is a small area of white around the nostrils.
Wall eye is white or blue-white coloring in the eye.

On the legs

Stocking is white on the leg from coronet to knee or hock.
Sock is white covering the fetlock and part of the cannon bone. Other markings on the leg are described by the area they cover.

Star

Stripe

Blaze

White face
(Bald face)

Snip

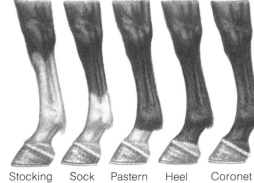

Stocking   Sock   Pastern   Heel   Coronet

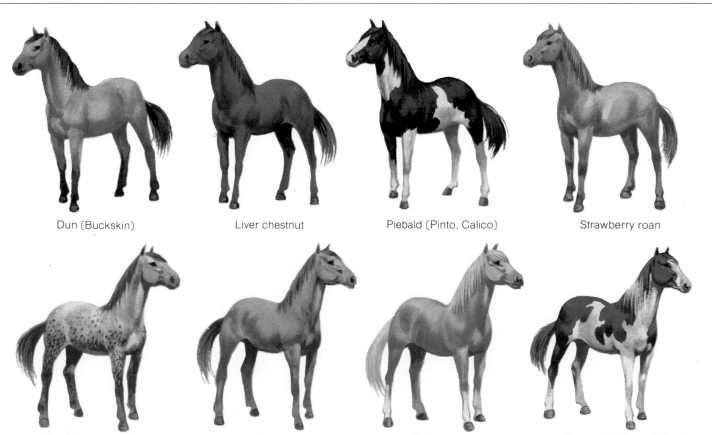

Dun (Buckskin)

Liver chestnut

Piebald (Pinto, Calico)

Strawberry roan

Flea-bitten gray

Gray

Palomino

Skewbald (Pinto, Calico)

PICTURE CREDITS

Photographs
Photographs are credited by page number and by their position on the page, as follows: T (Top); C (Centre); B (Bottom); BL (Bottom Left); FL (Far Left), etc.
Robin Adshead: 37(B), 47(T).
Animal Photography: Sally Anne Thompson, 19, 23, 25(B), 29(T), 29(B), 30, 34(T), 34(B), 35, 37(T), 40(T), 40-41, 47(B), 49(T), 49(B), 55(T), 55(B), 56, 57(T), 57(B), 58, 59, 60, 62, 63(T), 63(B), 64(T), 64(B), 65, 69, 71(B), 72(T), 73(T), 73(B), 76, 79(T), 81, 84, 85(T), 89, 94(B), 95, 99(T), 101(T), 101(C), 101(B), 103, 105(T), 105(B), 107(T), 107(B), 112(T), 112(B), 112-113, 113(T), 114(T), 122(T), 122(B), 123(T), 124, 128, 130(T), 133(B), 138, 139(T), 139(B), 140, 142, 144, 156(T), 156(B), 196-7(B), 200; Zofia Raczkowska, 145(B); R Willbie, 8-9, 71(T), 100(B), 123(B), 135(B), 148(T).
Ardea: Jean-Paul Ferrero, 14(B), 16,

16-17, 87(T), 93(B), 164-165(T), 168(T), 170(B), 176(T), 180(B); Clem Haagner, 97(T).
Vivienne Burdon: 36
Bruce Coleman: Mark Boulton, 8(C); Jane Burton, 46; Eric Crichton, 6(T), 8(B); World Wildlife Fund/F. P. Jansen, 8(T).
Kit Houghton Photography: Endpapers, 9, 10(T), 10(B), 10-11, 11(T), 12, 12-13, 14(T), 15, 18(B), 20, 21(T), 21(B), 22, 22-3, 24, 25(TL), 25(TR), 26, 27(T), 28, 31(T), 31(B), 33(T), 33(B), 39(T), 39(B), 41(B), 42, 44(T), 44(B), 45(T), 45(B), 50, 50-51, 52, 53(T), 53(B), 61(T), 61(C), 61(B), 66(B), 66-7, 67(T), 67(B), 72(B), 74(B), 74-5, 77, 78(T), 78(B), 79(B), 80, 82(B), 82-3, 83(B), 85(B), 86(T), 86(B), 87(B), 90(T), 91(T), 91(B), 92, 93(T), 94(T), 96, 97(B), 98, 99(B), 100(T), 102(T), 102(B), 106(T), 106(B), 108-9, 109(T), 110(T), 111, 114(B), 115, 116(T), 116(B), 116-7, 118(T), 118(B), 119, 120, 121, 125,

126(T), 126(B), 127(T), 127 (B), 129(T), 129(B), 131(T), 131(B), 132-3, 133(T), 133(T), 134(T), 134(B), 135(T), 136(T), 137(T), 137(B), 141, 143(T), 143(B), 145(T), 146-7, 148(B), 149(T), 149(B), 150, 150-1, 151(T), 152-3, 154(B),154-5, 157, 158(B), 158-9, 159(T), 159(B), 160(T), 160(B), 161(T), 161(B), 162(B), 162-3, 163(T), 163(B), 164(T), 164(C), 164-5(B), 165(B), 166(T), 166(B), 167(T), 168(B), 169(T), 169(B), 170(T), 170-1, 171, 172 (BL), 172(BR), 172-3, 173(T), 173(B), 174(B), 174-5, 175(T), 176(B), 176-7, 177(B), 178(T), 178(B), 179, 180(T), 181(T), 181(B), 182(T), 182(C), 182-3, 183(TL), 183(TR), 183(CL), 183(CR), 184(B), 184-5, 185(B), 186(B), 186-7, 187(T), 187(B), 190(T), 190-1, 192(T), 192(B), 193, 194(T), 194-5, 195(T), Back Jkt.
Nova Scotia, Canada, Department of Tourism: 43(T).

Senckenberg Museum, Frankfurt, Dr. Jens Franzen: 6(C).
Victoria Settipassi: 38.
Vision International: Robert Maier, 68; Elisabeth Weiland, Contents page, 7, 17(T), 90(B), 104-5, 108, 110(B), 117(T), 146(B), 188-9, 196-7(B).

Artwork
All artwork is by John Francis, except for that of Leg Markings, page 201(C), which is by Eric Tenney. Copyright of all artwork is the property of Salamander Books Ltd.

EDITOR'S ACKNOWLEDGEMENTS
I would like to thank Vickie Walters and Suzanne Willcock for help with picture research; Louise Egerton and Beverley le Blanc for copy-editing and proofreading, and Isobel McLean for preparing the index.

Jonathan Elphick

Above: Mares and foals, Kladruby Stud, Czechoslovakia.